BLOOD CLOT

In Combat with the Patrols Platoon, 3 Para, Afghanistan 2006

Jake Scott

BLOOD CLOT

In Combat with the Patrols Platoon, 3 Para, Afghanistan 2006

Jake Scott

Helion & Company Ltd

Helion & Company Limited
26 Willow Road
Solihull
West Midlands
B91 1UE
England
Tel. 0121 705 3393
Fax 0121 711 4075
Email: publishing@helion.co.uk
Website: www.helion.co.uk

Published by Helion & Company 2008

Designed and typeset by Farr out Publications, Wokingham, Berkshire
Cover designed by Bookcraft Limited, Stroud, Gloucestershire
Printed in the UK by the MPG Books Group

ISBN 978-1-906033-31-6

British Library Cataloguing-in-Publication Data.
A catalogue record for this book is available from the British Library.

For details of other military history titles published by Helion & Company Limited contact the above address, or visit our website: http://www.helion.co.uk.

We always welcome receiving book proposals from prospective authors.

I dedicate this book to the members of the Parachute Regiment, past and present, especially those who laid down their lives during actions in Afghanistan. We will remember them!

Contents

List of Illustrations

Colour section 1

Colour section 2

Colour section 3

List of Maps

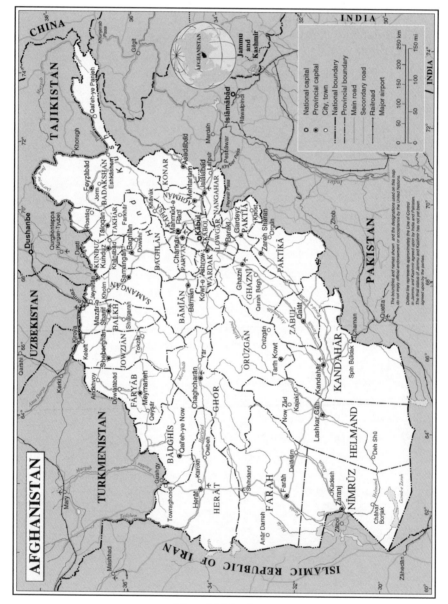

Map of Afghanistan

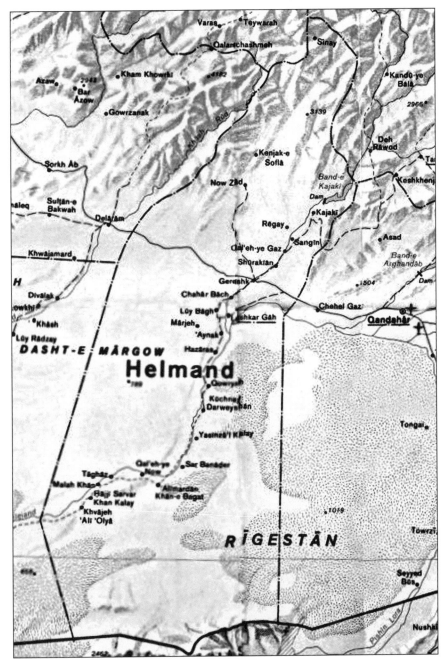

Map of Helmand Province

Acronyms and Abbreviations

.50 Cal	50 Calibre heavy machine gun
9-liner	US medical request form sent over the radio for CAS-E-VAC
AK47	Russian made 7.62mm Kalashnikov rifle
ANA	Afghan national army
ANP	Afghan national police
AO	Area of operation
Bayonets	Fighting men
berm and hesco	Sand berm (piled up sand) and pre-packed wire mesh frames full of sand (large sand bags)
Blood clot	Parachute Regiment
C-130	Hercules C-130 troop-carrying transport aircraft used also for dropping paratroopers
cadre	selection process
CAP	Company Aid Post
CAS-E-VAC	Casualty evacuation
CH47	Chinook troop-carrying helicopter
Circuit	Close protection
CO	Commanding officer (Lieutenant Colonel in command of a Battalion)
Comms	Any sort of communication, mainly by radio
CP	Close protection (also known as 'the Circuit')
CPO	Close protection officer
CQB	Close-quarter battle
CSM	Company sergeant major
CTR	Close target recce
Cud's	Countryside, desert, anywhere out in the wild
DF	area normally pre-recorded for distance fire (mostly for the use of indirect fire)
DFC	Safety checks and rigging before parachuting
Dicker	Term given to people deliberately watching our movements and passing on information to the Taliban
Dish-dash	Arab full-length clothing
DZ	Drop zone (parachute)
E+E	Escape and evasion.
ECM	Electronic warfare counter-measures
EFP	Explosive formed projectile (Higher level of IED using copper which can penetrate all levels of armour)
ERV	Emergency rendezvous
Eyes on	Expression given to getting an eye on a target or enemy location

FAC	Forward air controller
Face-to-face	An expression given when commanders meet during operations on the ground to discuss matters they don't want sending over the radio
Fast ball	An event that occurs quickly with little or no planning
Fat Albert	Hercules C-130 troop-carrying transport aircraft used also for dropping paratroopers
FFD	First field dressing
FIBUA	Fighting in built up areas
FOB	Forward operating base
FOO	Forward observation officer
FRV	Final rendezvous
FUP	Forming-up point
GPMG	7.62mm General Purpose Machine Gun
GPS	Global positioning system
GSX-R	Suzuki superbike
Gun	Term given to the GPMG and .50 cal
Harbour	area in which to conduct admin
HCR	Household Cavalry Regiment
HE	High explosive
Head Shed	Battle group, Battalion, Company or platoon officer's SNCO in charge
H-Hour	The time an operation (assault) will take place
HLS	Helicopter landing site
Humvee	US armoured vehicle
IED	Improvised explosive device
IR	Infra-red
IRF	Immediate response force
IRT	Immediate response team
IRT	Immediate reaction team
ISO	Metal container for shipping of supplies
JAM	*Jaish al Mahdi* (Shi'ite armed faction)
JDAM	Joint direct attack munitions
JOC	Joint operations centre
KIA	Killed in action
LAV	Eight-wheeled light armoured vehicle
LEWT	Light electronic warfare team
Licked	Expression given when physically and mentally drained
Long	A personal weapon (SA80, M4, M16)
LZ	Landing zone (helicopters)
Maroon machine	Parachute Regiment
MFC	Mortar fire controller
MIA	Missing in action
Minimi	5.56mm belt-fed machine gun
MSR	Main supply route

MT	Mobile transport, drivers
ND	Negligent discharge
NTM	Notice to move
NVG	Night vision goggles
OC	Officer commanding (Major in command of a Company)
OMLT	Operational mentoring liaison team
oner	whole platoon
On the ground	expression once we moved from our base location
OP	Observation post
Op	Operation
Op Telic	Operational name given to operations in Iraq by British forces
ORBAT	Order of battle (a patrol/section/platoon/company/battalion set-up dictating what soldiers go where)
P4	Plastic explosives
P4 (Casualties)	term used when a soldier is dead. Now changed to T1 (no vital signs shown)
P-Coy	Pegasus company. Name given for the hard selection course to proceed onto parachute training and join airborne forces
PF	Pathfinders
Pinz	Pinzgauer 4 x 4
PRR	Personal role radio
PSC	Private security companies
QBO	Quick battle orders
QRF	Quick reaction force
quick clot	medicine used for stopping major blood loss from arteries
R & R	Rest and recreation
RAP	regimental aid post
Recce	Reconnaissance of an area
'The Reg'	Parachute Regiment
RHA	Royal Horse Artillery
RIP	Relief in place
RMP	Royal Military Police
RP	Red phosphorus
RPG	Rocket-propelled grenade
RPK	Russian-made 7.62mm machine gun similar to the GPMG
RSM	Regimental Sergeant Major
RTU	Returned to unit
RV	Rendezvous
secured fils	A FIL chip inserted into radios to stop non-friendly forces listening into communications by making the radio indecipherable
Shemagh	Arab head scarf
Short	A 9mm pistol or side-arm
Shura	Meeting of locals
sit-rep	Situation report on what is going on on the ground

SNCO	senior non commissioned officer
SOP	Standard operational procedures
SUSA	Sight unit that fits to .50 cal heavy machine gun. Similar to SUSAT (sight unit, small arms, trilux) on the SA80
T1	term used when a soldier is dead (no vital signs shown), previously known as P4
TAB	Tactical advance to battle
TI	Thermal imaging
TIC	Team in contact
UAV	Unmanned aerial vehicles
UGL	Under-slung grenade launcher
VBIED	Vehicle-borne IED
VP	Vulnerable point (bridge, cross roads, entrance to town etc.) on the ground
Wadi	Dried up river bed
WMIK	Weapons mounted installation kit
Yank SF	US special forces

Publisher's note

As Jake Scott writes in his personal note, operational security and respect for the privacy of members of the armed forces and their families has led to some names being changed, as well as other information being slightly altered to protect identities. Likewise, the identity of a number of the soldiers within the photographic sections has been disguised to protect their identity. We ask for the reader's understanding with regard to these procedures.

Inquests have yet to be held for some of the deaths about which the author comments. As the author notes, he has made every effort to report the facts as known to him, as accurately and as truthfully as possible. Any insult or injury to such individuals or their families quoted within the book is unintentional, and the publishers would be pleased to amend inaccuracies in later editions.

Mick, the author's father, deserves our thanks for helping with the initial contacts. Jake took up the challenge of recording his personal experiences, and at all times proved enthusiastic, helpful and had a great 'can do' attitude. We would also like to thank Paula Edwards at the Ministry Of Defence for her assistance with preparing the manuscript for publication.

The views expressed within this book are solely those of the author, and do not necessarily reflect or correspond with those of the publishers, the Ministry Of Defence, British Army, or Parachute Regiment. This is one soldier's very personal view of the war against the Taliban.

Author's note and acknowledgements

The following reports and accounts in this book are as accurate and as truthful as possible although many personal identities, place names, dates and even parts of operations have been changed for security reasons, and some have been completely removed. I have given my accounts, judgment and my opinions in many places of this book. I have tried to give the view from a soldier's point of view, as a member of the Patrols Platoon, operating frequently on our own with little coverage about our many incidents. Any hurt to any family or friends of the deceased or injured is unintentional and for this I apologise in advance.

I would like to thank my dad, without him that none of this would have been possible. Also, Duncan Rogers and the rest of the staff at Helion, the MoD, especially Paula Edwards, all the lads in 3 Para (especially the lads in Patrols who I worked and fought alongside), my family for all their help and support, including my dad Mick and and my loving wife, Ali, who has stood by me throughout this.

Jake Scott

Prologue

I was born in 1981 in Sunderland General Hospital. I had a good upbringing, enjoying a close relationship with my immediate family, and still do to this day, although due to hard work I didn't see much of my dad in the early days. He was working a further two jobs in addition to his full-time job as a firefighter, coming in from nightshift and then driving buses all over the country and Europe before parking up at the depot and going back to work, or onto another of his part-time jobs. My dad was someone I had always looked up to. He is a fiery character, something which often rubbed off on me, and a jack of all trades with a wealth of knowledge and advice that I always turn to when in trouble. My mom was a full-time dinner lady and worked in a clothes store on Saturdays, before becoming a cook for special needs children. She was the nicest person you could ever meet, she would go well out of the way to help anyone out or listen to their problems. She rarely had a bad word to say about anybody, and maybe was sometimes too nice for her own good. I realise later that the reason my dad worked all the hours he did, and that my mother worked six days a week was so that my brother and I could have the best in life. They grafted all they could so they could afford new things for us. My father and mother got together at a young age and never looked back, rare for a relationship in these times. My brother Chris is three years older than me, although I normally get mistaken for the older brother. Chris is definitely more of a homing pigeon who likes to be around the family and home. Whenever I was on leave I knew where to find him. On the other hand, I needed to get out into the world; hanging around Sunderland at a younger age wasn't that exciting for me. My brother moved to and from a lot of jobs, always trying to better himself. When younger, we would fight like cat and dog but as we grew up we became drinking buddies, more friends than brothers. I always looked out for him, and often would find myself rolling around the floor with someone who had taken the piss or caused a problem for him.

As young as I can remember I had always been army mad. My uncle served over 35 years in the Royal Signals, and used to pass down posters, books and old army clothing to me. As I grew older I heard about the Paras, a small elite group of men that jumped out of planes. I began to read books and talked to my dad who now served in the fire service with some ex-Paras. I found out that these were the elite of the British army, renowned for being better and tougher than the rest of the British forces; everywhere I looked it was 'Para' this and 'Para' that. Their reputation in battle and on home ground always preceded them. Everyone had heard of these paratroopers or Paras. They stood out from the crowds with their maroon berets and silver winged badge. I also like the fact that they have a separate course to the rest of the army, a longer, harder physical and mentally demanding course that was a pass or fail event known as P-Company. They were first into any situation that would arise around the world, and I fancied some of that.

Founded in 1942 Winston Churchill needed an extraordinary breed of men. The Paras were born and sent into operations deep into enemy territory with little or no support. Their most well-known operation was at the height of World War II, Operation Market Garden. On 17 September 1944, 10,000 paratroopers jumped into Holland to seize a crossing point over the Rhine River. It remains the largest airborne operation in history. British Paras jumped in to take the furthest bridge deep into German-controlled territory, later joked of as a 'bridge too far' - maybe you have seen the film of that name? They were to hold the bridge in a small town called Arnhem for 48 hours until Field Marshal Montgomery arrived with his armoured reinforcements. Unfortunately, the reinforcements never arrived and only 2500 men from the original 10,000 made it to safety; the rest were either killed or captured holding the bridge for an amazing eight days. After this, the Paras received a nickname and a lot of respect from their enemy, the Germans. The Red Devils were born. From then on the Paras were always sent into action first and proved themselves in the Second World War, Cyprus, Radfan, Borneo, Aden, the Suez Canal, the Falklands, Sierra Leone, Kosovo, Iraq, and of course Afghanistan. After the bloody battles for the Falklands, the Prime Minister of the time, Margaret Thatcher, commented on her paratroopers "Paras should be sealed behind a wall of hardened glass and only broken in extreme emergencies."

I left home at 17 years of age in 1998, my journey to join the toughest regiment all, the Paras. I began training at an early age, for me school wasn't important and I would often bunk off to get away from it. I knew what I wanted to be. When I left school I worked at the local brewery as a dray man until I was old enough to join up. I would wake up at 4:30 a.m., and run 8 miles before pedalling down to the brewery to start a full day's work. Being a dray man was good, and it had some good perks to go with it - moving from pub to pub delivering beer, and 90% of the time getting a beer back in return. After six or seven deliveries I was normally well oiled. To end most days I would finish off with the lads in the *Lazy Pig*, a local pub across the road, ending up absolutely pissed and pushing my bike home or getting a taxi, having some tea, rolling into bed and starting the whole process the next day.

After leaving the comfort of home the training was intense and hard going. I didn't expect anything else and I soon passed P-Company and my jumps course, gaining my maroon beret and wings, which was the proudest time of my young life. I was sent to join the 3rd Battalion the Parachute Regiment. From there I deployed to operational theatres such as Northern Ireland and Iraq, although none were as challenging as Afghanistan in 2006. It was the highlight of my career, and I was in the best possible position. I was at the top of my game, a full corporal in the Patrols platoon, the most experienced soldiers in the best regiment of the Armed Forces. I was so proud to be fighting alongside these fellow airborne warriors, the renowned 'blood clot'. I think Brigadier Ed Butler, commander of the UK Task Force Helmand in 2006 got it right when he gave a speech:

My six months as Commander of British Forces Afghanistan, in 2006, was the most challenging and risk intensive command tour I have undertaken in my career. Over six bloody and ferocious months in Helmand Province the 3 Para battlegroup was involved in over 500 contacts, with half a million rounds of small arms and over 13,000 artillery and mortar rounds being fired. It saw the blooding of the Apache attack helicopter and the joint helicopter force flying over 100 CASEVAC (casualty evacuation) missions to extract some 170 casualties with sadly 33 KIA (killed in action). Contacts could last for 6-8 hours, with paratroopers fighting in 50°C and carrying 70lb of fighting equipment on their backs. Young men quickly matured beyond their years, battle hardened by an intensity not witnessed since the Korean War. Some would spend weeks fighting and sleeping in their body armour and helmets, after snatching no more than a few minutes rest between enemy attacks, and drinking water the temperature of a decent brew. Phenomenal stuff.

Hundreds of Taliban were killed and injured, but not once was I in any doubt that the battle group was in danger of being defeated. By the end of the summer the Taliban had been tactically beaten, deciding to take on the members of 16 Air Assault Brigade in a conventional and attritional fight. In my judgment the Taliban seriously underestimated the professionalism, raw courage and self belief of the Airborne soldier, the current wearers of the maroon beret more than live up to the reputation of their forefathers.

The cost of this 'break-in' battle into southern Afghanistan was high in blood and treasure, and we will never forget those brave men who paid the ultimate sacrifice, including Corporal Brian Budd VC and Corporal Mark Wright GC, daring all to win all. All their names, along with the towns of Now Zad, Musa Qaleh, Sangin and Gereshk will remain firmly listed in regimental history. And rightly so.

People often asked me what Afghanistan is all about and whether it is worth it. To me delivering success in that country is essential for a variety of strategic reasons. The Brigade deployed in April 2006 to make a difference to the ordinary Afghan. Not only did the brave men and women make a difference, but they also laid some really solid foundations for the other Government Departments, the Royal Marines and subsequent follow-on forces to build upon. Although there is still plenty to do in Afghanistan across all lines of operation, the Airborne Community, serving and retired, can be hugely proud of the Brigade's achievements. I for one am.

I salute the courage and endeavours of all those who I was privileged to lead across the UK Task Force, 16 Air Assault Brigade and especially those in the 3 Para Battle Group.

In 2006 we Paras were sent there to do a job, we don't ask the reasons why, we just get on with it. If you ask any Para who was there he'll tell you the same, he will also tell you that in the thick of battle we don't fight for Queen and Country, we fight for our mates.

I left the Paras in the early months of 2007 for personal reasons and find myself back in the Middle East (Iraq) as bodyguard in the close protection role. In 2006 we went looking for a fight, now my job is to avoid one and protect my clients.

This is my account of what happened to me and the men around me. I was asked to give my account and don't wish to step on other people's toes. I was asked to tell, from a soldier's point of view, what happened in Afghanistan in 2006 from my perspective, not anybody else's. I have not mentioned a lot of what went on for the simple reason that I was not involved in such incidents. I've also tried to not give too much information about the deaths of fellow comrades and friends for the simple reason of not digging up the past and upsetting their families and loved ones. This goes out to all the lads who were there, those who were injured and the lads who died fighting.

Next time you see a soldier on the TV or in the street, whether Iraq, Afghanistan or some other faraway and dangerous country, just think of what he has been through, being sent by his country and its people to defend and protect his people (YOU). Whether you believe in what they're doing or not, soldiers may not believe it either, however we still have to do it. All we ask for is the support of our own people back here in the UK.

Chapter 1

Contact

I woke with the early morning sun; my head was pounding due to dehydration from the long patrol the previous day from Bastion camp to this small remote town to the north, known as Now Zad. I sat upright on my roll mat that had kept me off the ground and had been my bed for the night in between my two WMIK Land Rovers. I washed away the sleep and grit from my eyes as I woke from my few hours of much needed sleep. I checked my watch. It was 06:15hrs and the sun was already showing its face. I looked on as the local Afghan police, dressed in a mixture of blue uniforms and civilian dish-dash clothing, sat 20 metres away on a carpeted area surrounded by desert wasteland in the confines of the fort eating their breakfast of local Arab bread which they later offered us, and was a change from B and C menu rat-packs we had been on. From my knowledge they seemed happy that the British had come here to help; what lay beyond the gates was a different story.

The platoon was up and beginning to cut around as the sun rose higher in the sky. Each of the lads had their little jobs to do and would carry them out every morning, the drivers sorting and first parading the vehicles, the gunner removing the night sights for day optics and oiling the .50 Cal that sat on top of our WMIK Land Rovers, my signaller Tommo checking his communication equipment while I met up with the other commanders to discuss the mission ahead. All of the above were priority, and our life savers. I made my way over to my boss's wagon at the rear of the fort, a brew in hand. The other two commanders, Ray and Steve, were already waiting at the front of the WMIK. Ray was a tall skinny guy with brown hair and an unbelievably big nose, hence he received the nickname 'Jew boy' from the lads. He was a full screw (Cpl) like me and had spent a lot of time in the reconnaissance (Patrols) platoon. Steve was a small bloke of around 5ft 10 inches and was our C/Sgt in charge of all admin and re-supplies for the platoon, and also the 2i/c (second in command) of our band of merry men.

'Alright lads, you all get a good head down?' the boss opened with as he interrupted our small gathering. Our boss was Swanny, a captain and well respected officer. He had been a private soldier in the REME before becoming an officer in the Paras and got the nickname 'Spanner' by the blokes due to his previous job.

'Just a quick warning order; orders are in 15 minutes in that building there.' He pointed to a white building at the rear of the fort that looked like a small classroom.

'We will leave here at 10:00hrs. Ray, I want you to plan a route and lead us in to this area', pointing to a track junction on the map.

'Take a Freddy, boss', I said. You never use fingers.

'Yeah, especially with Tough's sausage fingers' Steve jumped in. The boss gave me a little glare. He had been up a lot earlier than us sorting and planning the mission; it was obviously too early for piss-takes but it was still fair point. This wasn't a common error for him to make, but like I said, it was early. A finger can cover a whole grid square on the map and that's why it was never used whereas a blade of grass can pin-point the exact position that we needed to be.

'Our Patrols are to hold this area here', he continued, using his pencil to cover the area on the map.

'H-Hour will be around 12:10hrs on this target here.' Again he pointed to an area on the map. 'OK? A Company will be conducting a Search Op arriving by helicopter. Any questions so far?'. None of us spoke a word as I continued to sip my morning coffee.

'OK then, get the guys ready' he said as he about-turned and headed off to the main building in the middle of the fort grounds. I gave Ray a little nod; it was either me or him who led when we moved as a platoon, and I had led the patrol up here yesterday so it looked like it was his turn. The boss's call sign would normally sit behind one of the lead teams and Steve's would bring up the rear. I walked back to my team with a clutch on my mug like a lion on its kill.

'Gather round, lads!' I shouted as I parked my arse on the front of my WMIK.

'OK, fellas, orders in 15 mins in that building. The sketch is we are going to move from here to this position as a oner.' I pointed to the area the boss had previously told me. 'From there we will be breaking down into our teams and cover the west of the target area which is here, while A Company conduct a search.' I pointed to a small group of buildings on the map. 'This is all I have to go on at the moment, lads.'

'Mega, another day of sitting round', Tommo said sarcastically.

'Yeah, when are we gonna get a decent task?' Lee continued. By this they meant confrontation with the Taliban.

'I know, fellas, but it's still an important role here, this place could be crawling with Taliban so we need to hold it and prevent anyone getting into A Company's position and ambushing them. Let's just get in there and get this done', I answered in a half snap. The blokes did not seem convinced. As Patrols platoon, the eyes and ears of 3 Para and the Battle group, we were expecting to be conducting reconnaissance missions on targets and the setting of conditions for an attack or strike op on possible Taliban strongholds. I understood that the boys weren't happy with some of these tasks, especially the convoy protection which was starting to look more and more likely for us. I wasn't exactly jumping with joy on this one either, and I was just as eager to get my hands dirty as the rest of them.

'OK, if there's no questions then finish off the weapons and wagons and make sure your shit is squared, and get yourselves in there in 10 mins', and with that I began to sort my own personal kit before the brief.

The first thing we all did was prep our weapons before we sorted ourselves or anything else, just in case. For me this was the 'gun'. The gun (GPMG) was my primary weapon while moving and patrolling on vehicles, mounted to the front left of the WMIK on a swing arm. A 7.62 belt-fed weapon with a rate of fire of 1000 rounds per minute, it was an amazing piece of kit nicknamed 'the widow-maker' for an obvious reason. It was an area weapon spreading its rounds into a beating zone capable of taking down troops in the open up to a range of 1800m if mounted, and even further in the right hands. Anything in its way would go down. At close range it would tear you apart, literally. I loved this weapon and was glad to be on the trigger again. I brushed the dust that had collected during the night with my paintbrush and off the ammo and the inside and outside of the gun's body and working parts before giving the barrel a quick pull through and applying more oil. I cocked it several times to ensure it was fully lubricated and working correctly. The last thing anyone needed was a stoppage on this effective piece of kit; it's like losing your right arm. Then I re-oiled my long (SA80) that I had on the front of the dash and bonnet for quick use in close quarters. My long was my dismounted weapon. I had previously put a pistol grip on the front to make it more steady and ideal for CQB situations and then of course I had a short (pistol) which was my sidearm and went everywhere with me.

After that I placed out my map on the bonnet and got a better look at some of the areas in detail while brushing my teeth and arranging my chest rig. My chest rig held the bare minimum. From my furthest left pouch it carried a red phosphorus grenade followed by four magazine pouches capable of holding two 30-round mags (although for desert use we only loaded 28 rounds) each on Velcro quick release, then a HE grenade on the furthest right pouch. There was a small map pocket that sat behind the mag pouches that held a small head torch, a small pencil maglight torch, a lighter, an Asherman chest seal (used for gunshot wounds to the lungs and chest cavity), my Silva compass and a sachet of quick clot. Two FFDs were taped to the chest rig harness along with a torque and my PRR system so they were easily accessible along with a karabiner.

I would then wrap around a bandolier that had been tailored to hold five extra 30-round magazines, thanks to a lad called Cheesey who had been my gunner before being removed to work in the stores, but who had managed to get himself out with us on this mission as an extra gunner. Some people have many different ways of loading their magazines. My team loaded their rounds the same as me: three normal ball 5.56mm at the bottom followed by three tracer 5.56mm; this way you had an indicator that you were nearly out of rounds when your tracer starts flying down range, because you never count your rounds when it goes for real. Plus there were too many important things to be thinking about, and unlike in the movies, we don't have never-ending magazines. The rest was made up of normal 5.56mm ball until the top. Again I put three tracer 5.56mm together with two 5.56mm ball sitting on top to finish my magazine.

In the army there is a sequence on reaction to effective enemy fire: the first being the double tap in the direction of the enemy, which would use the two normal 5.56mm ball rounds at the top of your mag. The drill that followed was dash, down, crawl, observe, muzzle clearance and then fire. As a commander – or anybody who could locate the enemy – the best way to bring any of your members onto the target was called 'watch my strike' (a term I have witnessed many times down town on the piss before unleashing on Hats or some gobby civvy) unloading tracer rounds into the target area and therefore clearly identifying the enemy position to your muckers around you. It worked not only for identifying targets but making you aware in the heat of the moment that you would soon be out of rounds and prepare you for a mag change.

The outskirts of the town were crisscrossed with tracks but with no previous recces we had no idea what these were like. Our main aim would be to travel cross-country which is fine outside of populated areas but an absolute no-go here or in any built-up area. We had found this out a couple of weeks earlier conducting small Patrols from Bastion camp to Gereshk (FOB Price) A small outstation hosted by US forces before PF, A Company with elements of D Company, Patrols, snipers and signals had took over on the west of the town. We had found that the ground around all buildings and farmland was a nightmare. Ploughed fields made any movement slow and unpleasant with deep irrigation ditches all around making some routes impossible to cross, with high walls and orchard fields all of which were not marked on our maps. I could see some of this being a problem as we moved as a oner to our first position. Speaking to Ray, we agreed that it would be better to split the Patrols in half: four vehicles moving south then up northeast, and the other four or five east as originally planned. Not only would this give us a decoy but it would also be safer. Swanny ruled this out just in case something big did come off and I could understand him from a safety point of view; we would have more firepower as one convoy.

The orders were given by a Gurkha officer; he was in charge of the police station fort here in Now Zad since taking over B Company 3 Para. The fort itself was a two-storey mud-walled building with rooftop access overlooking the town from its location on the southern edge of the town. The building was surrounded by high walls with four sangar positions on each corner that had been reinforced with sandbags and manned by Gurkha soldiers that had relieved B Company 3 Para a few days previous. As most officers do, he waffled on about loads of crap before getting to the important facts and details of the mission itself.

It became clear that it was a search and arrest operation east of Now Zad town. The target was a known Taliban leader reported to be in a group of buildings approx 7k east of here. Patrols were to move in with our WMIKs and hold and seal the western edge of the target while the Gurkhas who were based at the fort would venture north, then drop south and cover the eastern side of the target, thereby providing a 360-degree cordon to prevent any enemy forces coming in and out. A Company 3 Para had been tasked to conduct the search, flying in by two Chinook helicopters on H-Hour to search the target and the surrounding area. I looked back at my team; their expressions said it all. My team had been assigned to A Company when we first deployed to Afghan acting as a fighting section on an advance party while patrolling a town called Gereshk. It seemed now that some tasty jobs had come up and we had missed out. Or so we thought. As the Lieutenant-Colonel waffled on about - shall I say - less important parts of the mission I began to study the map and the air photo that I had just been given that was sitting on my lap, paying particular attention to the target building and to where us Patrols would be.

As we wrapped the orders up, our boss held us commanders back to put a little more meat on the bones for our task, giving us more indication where he wanted our teams so if anything did go wrong we knew where each would be located. Ray showed us where he would lead the full convoy, our FRV at spot blue 7 before we broke down into our individual teams to cover specific areas. Looking at an aerial photo it didn't seem too bad. There were lots of greenery and tracks with a few outhouses but it looked crossable; but without a 3D image we were going in blind and had no time to recce any of the surrounding areas. I was starting to feel like this could go tits up before we even started as two hours isn't too long when you need to get in and be in place in an unfamiliar area.

The Gurkhas had further to travel, heading north to box round the target out of sight before moving south into position, so they would leave the fort first, ten minutes before us leaving only a skeleton crew stagging on in the fort.

I called over my team and briefed them up a final time, giving them all the details I had on the mission and to quickly brush over a few actions on in case the shit hit the fan as well as the ERV which would first be the FRV then the fort unless we were directed otherwise.

As always in Patrols the banter began flying round as we waited impatiently in the sun for the off; there was always a good atmosphere between us. Just before we left we took a quick picture on my camera of our call sign 21D, all of us posing at the front of our vehicles, tops off and tatts out. Little did any of us know that minutes after this photo was taken we would be fighting for our lives.

Patrols were a ten-vehicle convoy consisting of seven WMIKs and two Pinzgauer 4×4s. Our WMIKs were open-top 4×4 Land Rover Defenders with a weapons platform on the back (the name WMIK means Weapons Mounted Installation Kit). Excellent vehicles for long range reconnaissance over hard terrain like this. Each patrol consisted of six men and two WMIK Land Rovers. Each WMIK was fitted with a GPMG on the front left controlled by the commander, and a .50 Cal on the rear operated by the gunner, as well as our own personal weapons and grenades and not to mention two 84mm SAW anti-armour rockets in the back of the vehicles. The .50 Cal was a scary weapon, well, if you were on the receiving end anyway. Its rate of fire was slower than the GPMG but it could hit targets up to a mile away. The force was unbelievable and it could cut through men like a knife through warm butter. The two vehicles were split into Charlie and Delta, Charlie being the primary and Delta the secondary and support WMIK. This was known as a Patrol, each Patrol was six men strong. I commanded the Charlie vehicle and Johnny the Delta. Johnny was my 2i/c and also the team medic; if anything happened to me he would take over the team. Lee was my driver; he was from Leeds and a good mate, new to the Patrols from machine gun platoon, an asset when it came to problems with the heavy weapons and a brilliant driver to say the least even though he did think he was still driving his Impreza back home sometimes. Tommo was my gunner and my primary radio operator for the team, a young lad with blonde hair and a dedicated paratrooper through and through.

He was disliked by a lot of the Head Shed and other company soldiers due to the fact that on the piss he was often a social hand grenade and was constantly dropping himself in the shit while under the influence. However, when it came to being a paratrooper he was a hard working, fit and reliable soldier. He reminded me of myself when I first joined the Paras. My 2i/c, Johnny, was a very good mate of mine who I had known for years. An outspoken and funny character he always had me in stitches. He had brown hair and a horse-shaped head, although this was a sore point to talk about. I had previously asked him to be my 2i/c when I moved back to the platoon as a Patrol commander; a reliable bloke I could trust and let get on with tasks without having to watch over him. His driver was Brett, a laid back South African lad; in fact if he had been any more laid back he would have been horizontal. Another good driver to have on our team, he definitely earned his money saving our skins later in the tour. The Delta gunner was a little lad called Luke, a young guy from Bristol who had recently moved over from a rifle company and hadn't spent that much time in the battalion. Luke was a good lad. However, for a new boy he didn't know when to keep his mouth shut in front of the boss and the platoon 2i/c Steve K. Steve hated Luke for it and the feeling was mutual, much to our amusement.

The WMIKs were our transport, our weapons platform and our homes. We moved, ate, slept and fought from these Land Rovers. We inherited the name 'gypsies' from the American and Canadian troops due to our appearance. We wore ripped and faded T-shirts, shorts or stained desert trousers, shemaghs or baseball caps and Oakley sunglasses. Our Land Rovers were loaded with kit, enough to last the mission, however long it would be. All our kit and equipment were located on and around the vehicle for practical and tactical use. The floor and sides of the inside of the vehicle were lined with boxes and boxes of 7.62 and .50 Cal ammunition, our bergens were strapped to the outside for quick access as well as our 24 hour grab bags which were within arm's reach. Radios were stashed behind my seat and were looked after by Tommo but used by me. There were other bits of equipment hanging off almost everywhere, like spare tyres, jerry cans and tank tracks. To a bystander I could understand that it looked like a bundle of shit on wheels but believe me it was all there for a reason. The US and Canadian troops could not believe that us, the pride of the British army, were still racing round the desert like we were sixty years ago in northern Africa, but hey, it worked. Not only did they think we were gypsies but also insane! The US went everywhere in mass numbers, their vehicles were all eight-wheeled LAVs with 30mm cannons encased in armour and here was us, open-topped Land Rovers with only our body armour, helmet, if we wore it, and some ballistic matting for protection.

I remember talking to a Canadian officer on this while harboured up amongst their convoy for a night in the desert, he too thought we were mad. But as I explained to him and many others who question this, our Land Rovers could get in and out of most areas without being spotted unlike the big US LAVs that were seen miles off. We were small and relatively quiet, light and fast; it provided better cross-country capability and the reason why we would stay off the main routes where others would fall foul and pay the price with roadside bombs. We had better arcs of fire and a 360 view while moving. We could lie low in wadi beds and in mountain gullies. We also had the option of debussing very quickly if need be.

'You happy Johnny?' I said as I adjusted my body armour and chest rig.

'Yeah mate, let's get this done', he said, smiling.

'Well let's just hope we have somewhere to come back to, if the Taliban knew that this place is getting held by only a skeleton crew then we could find ourselves fighting back in here.' Johnny gave out one of his big roaring laughs, something he was renowned for; he wasn't the quietest of blokes.

'Aye, we fucking could be', he said. I was joking with Johnny but I was also fully serious. It would be an ideal time for the Taliban to take the fort; then we would have a major problem on our hands. Just like what had happened at the fort complex in the town of Mazar-i-Sharif in 2001 when the Taliban held the fort where they were imprisoned for some three of four days against coalition forces.

We mounted the vehicles, and I began giving a radio check. I had comms with my team on PRR and also the other commanders on a separate radio net.

'OK lads, load and make ready' I shouted above the sound of the engine. This was just for the two guns as our personal weapons were kept ready at all times and if we had been out in the desert then the guns too. I opened the top cover on the gimpy and fed the belt of 7.62 across it, making sure it was in place. I slammed it shut and cocked the gun. Tommo give me the thumbs up, the .50 was ready. Johnny gave me a thumbs up too.

'OK boss, 21D are ready to go', I called over the net.

'OK, wait one, Scotty' he replied. We waited for the Gurkhas to get clear before moving.

As the boredom crept in waiting for the off the slaggings started and were beginning to get thrown around from wagon to wagon and team to team; there was very little time that it didn't and everyone including the boss was a target.

'Do you know where you're going, Ray?' an unknown voice came over the radio.

'Nah, he can't, his map's upside down', another jumped in.

'It's because he can't see it past that nose of his', Lee called up.

'OK lads, knock it off', Steve snapped.

'Yeah cheers Steve' the voice reappeared, a sarcastic tone in it, as there were two types of cheers that we used. 'Cheers' as in thanks very much, and 'cheers' like in 'yeah fucking cheers for that'. This was definitely the latter. This was another reason why we were so close compared to the rifle companies; we tried to treat everyone equally and like grown ups, rank didn't really matter to be honest, always letting them speak up. Myself and the other commanders always let the blokes give us their opinions and knowledge on the missions, plus if you did tell them to wind it you would just get told to get fucked anyway unless it was during a mission.

My map was strapped to my right leg along with my GPS with some buggy cord. I already plotted the waypoints in and had my first checkpoint up on the screen. The FRV was some 3ks away east of the town.

'When you're ready, Ray', the boss called, breaking the banter. The local Afghan police opened the steel gate that looked on the main street of Now Zad and we began to move out and into the unknown.

The main street was busy with the local Afghan people dressed in coloured dish-dashes and turbans, mostly males and children who were all intrigued by the new presence here. The last time these people had seen foreign soldiers in and around their town of Now Zad was many years ago. The Russians would often move through and set up camp in and around the area and as you can imagine these invaders weren't well liked; I hoped they would see us as friends trying to rid them of the Taliban rather than foe.

Ray led the convoy of WMIKs north through town towards purple 11. Ray's wagon lead the order of march and Gaz his 2i/c behind, then the boss's WMIK followed closely by the two Pinz 4×4s as they didn't have much weaponry on board. The Pinzes were holding the interpreter, some intelligence guys, an RAF captain who was our FAC, some engineers, medics as well a couple of members of the MT which drove these vehicles. My WMIK was five back in the convoy followed by Johnny with Steve's team holding the rear. We kept the spacing to around 40–50 metres between vehicles through the busy street.

Our tactical spacing depended on the environment; here in busy areas we could afford to bunch slightly and back up other call signs. The use of blocking techniques to cut off traffic and the teams bounding to secure pieces of ground at a time were also used in these congested areas, plus we still had the sangar position from the fort overlooking our move through the main part of town. We had used this bounding technique the day before when we entered Now Zad from the south. Each team would bound up and take fire positions covering the route in and potential threat locations; once in place another team would then drive through and bound up further, most of the time to prominent junctions, corners, areas of possible threat and so on, until we had reached our safe haven, a slow but safe means of clearing our route.

The sun was starting to get hotter as my team moved through the street. Ray had already broke track and was heading east to another spot on the map. We took the right and moved from a tarmac road to a dirt track: our route took us through the back roads of town. It was pretty tight going as we pushed through. I had already ordered my gunner Tommo to lock down the big .50 Cal, as it was rendered useless in these narrow streets, and have his Minimi out while me and Lee had our shorts drawn. I don't think the Afghans expected us to move through their small back streets but to follow out the Gurkha patrol on the tarmac road to the north 15 mins before us. It certainly looked that way as we pushed the vehicles through.

The buildings were run down shanties of mud walls and a mix of tin and thatched roofs all of which were flat. So far I had found that the conditions of living in Afghanistan were far poorer than that of Iraq, as a whole anyway. My eyes were scanning everywhere as we used the element of surprise to pass through unscathed. You feel very exposed on vehicles as you become a big target and can't cover all your arcs which you can on foot. I remember escorting a large number of Challenger 2 tanks into Basra during the invasion in 2003 for this very reason. Although we were the first troops in and secured Basra centre on foot for the tanks, they got all the media and credit. Without us paratroopers on the ground they couldn't do it as they were large targets. One thing here did remind me of Iraq, the streets were litted with shit. It's just one of those things in some areas of the Middle East: they just seem to dump all their unwanted crap straight out into the street or if they are feeling energetic then in a nearby field.

Within minutes we had moved into more open ground but we began to incur problems. We had now moved into farmland that surrounded the settlement with buildings and town behind us. Tracks on the map weren't there and we soon realised we had problems trying to push through onto our target due to large irrigation ditches, buildings and high walls. H-Hour was closing and we had to push though and get into position before the helicopters arrived with A Company, otherwise they had no protection to their flanks. This was easier said than done and we soon realised we weren't the only ones struggling. The Gurkha call sign were also coming across similar obstacles. Their route north out was open ground and they had made good ground but as they moved south towards the target the farmland had slowed them up just like us. Our convoy began to slow as Ray up front tried his best to find routes through in toward the objective. I began to feel very uncomfortable and I wasn't the only one.

'Scotty we got locals watching from the rooftop behind us', Tommo called.

'OK mate keep eyes on them. Johnny watch Toughs in the next field on our left mate.'

'Roger that, Scotty got a visual on them', Johnny replied. It was very frustrating for Ray at the front; I knew exactly how he was feeling. He had the whole convoy behind him; one mistake in the route could result in all of us having to turn around like something out of a Dad's Army episode. It would also make us more vulnerable to attack as we were very limited on where we could move. To make matters worse he had the boss on his case and very little time before H-Hour which was supposed to be 12:10hrs.

After crossing a ploughed field we found ourselves on a track running north to south. This is what we wanted and would take us south to our central FRV where the boss would position himself before the rest of us break down to our own areas. The move was slow; our vehicles were channelled down a single track no wider than 10ft. We were pushed up against a high wall running along the left side of the track, low enough for the gunners to see over in parts. Tommo tried to scan over the wall but due to the trees that were over the wall the view was very limited. On our right we had a large irrigation ditch, far too deep to cross, then another high mud wall. We seemed to be moving through a maze of orchard fields that were divided by high walls.

We were now very enclosed, bunched and vulnerable; being caught in an ambush here could have devastating effects. Ray told us that there was a slight opening up ahead and a gate leading to one of a couple of farm buildings through an orchard field. I looked down and checked my GPS.

'300m from the RV', I told Lee.

'Yeah got that Scotty.'

'You OK up there mate?' I shouted over to Tommo behind me as he scanned over the walls.

'Yeah, sorted, but I can't see much, mate', he replied. I turned back round just as a whooshing sound broke the silence of this so far peaceful morning. For a split second my mind tried to distinguish what that sound was, that was until the 7.62mm ammunition from AK47 began to erupt in front of us. The crack and thump from the rounds was deafening as the lead wagons reacted and began firing back with GPMG and .50.

'Fucking hell! We are getting engaged!' Lee shouted. No shit, tell me something I don't know, I thought.

'Boss this is Ray, we are taking incoming on our left flank!' Ray screamed into the radio. I jumped on my seat to try and look over the wall.

'Tommo get eyes on over that wall, they could be trying to flank us!' I yelled. Two guys came running back and jumped onto the rear Pinz in front of us. It was a medic and Intelligence guys that had been attached to us and were in the front Pinz behind the boss and Ray's WMIKs. They had obviously found themselves too close to the contact area and wanted out; unfortunately little did they know they would be driving through the contact in a few seconds.

Ray's voice broke out over the radio. 'I got enemy troops in the gateway, boss. I have to push through.'

'Yeah OK, move', Swanny replied. 'All call signs, we need to push through the contact, move now, move now!' he screamed. The Pinz in front of me began to move forward. As I said before we were in a much channelled route and it was near impossible to go back. The only choice was to drive through the contact area, all guns blazing and hope that we got to the other side in one piece.

That drive through the contact area lay ahead of us, but how had I ended up in Afghanistan in the first place?

Chapter 2

Ready for Anything

In the House of Commons on 26 January 2006, the UK Defence Secretary released a statement about the conditions of Afghanistan. The same day the Ministry of Defence made it clear that operations would soon start in the Helmand province of southern Afghanistan and described the commitment of British troops to that region. The building of the new camp, Bastion, would provide a base location for British forces while serving in the south.

Reveille was at 04:00hrs on Monday morning; Hugh from Snipers woke to hear me smashing around next door. He came to find me in bed fully clothed after just getting in from a hard session. I and a few of the boys had decided to go out and get some Sunday scoff and do a bit of last minute shopping before the battalion deployed to Oman early the next day. From the years of experience I should have realised that it wouldn't end at just a scoff. Several hours and pubs later I found myself with some of the blokes in Chicago Nightclub in Colchester, off my face, typical Para Reg style.

I woke to find myself in someone's house down the road from camp and after a quick persuasion grabbed a lift back to camp. I was in a shit state.

'Fucking hell, Scotty we are off in 20 mins', Hugh said, shaking me from my drunken coma. With the help from my mate I got dressed and made a feeble excuse of a shave taking half my face off in the process. He handed me a brew to try and sort me out. I had done the same for him many times before.

Johnny came up to my room. 'Sober bloke!' he laughed.

'Yeah, can you square the guys, mate; I don't fancy playing today' I replied.

'No shit!' he laughed. 'Yeah, no bother' and he left me and Hugh to finish packing my day sack that I would be taking on the flight. I tried to keep as low as possible on the parade square and the bus move to South Cerney then RAF Brize Norton. This lasted about 60 seconds before the blokes spotted the fact I was in shit state and still pissed and ripped into me, but looking round I was glad to see I wasn't the only one who had had a rough night.

We arrived at South Cerney just after first light. South Cerney was an RAF station that was used for prepping kit and equipment before moving it by air and also pre-parachute checks. This was one thing that always made the blokes snap; we would all get our kit searched here and then be processed before being put back on the buses for another 40min drive to Brize Norton. It was worse than travelling out of Heathrow on holiday, I can tell you. It wasn't long before we were aboard a civilian 747 bound for Muscat, Oman.

One of the only memories I have of this journey was as the young air stewardess gave the safety demonstration for the life jacket and the use of the tube to blow into if you had to manually inflate it in water, with much cheering from the couple of hundred blokes sitting watching her.

The point of this overseas exercise was to get the battalion ready for desert operations. The exercise or build-up training was to last just over three weeks in which time we were tested in our abilities to carry out what we were getting sent to Afghanistan to do, offensive operations. In simple terms, war fighting, definitely not peacekeeping duties, that's for sure. The battalion was located out in the desert: a makeshift camp for exercising troops hidden away by surrounding features. A small group of air-conditioned tents were built up around four hardened buildings which acted as the scoff house, officers and stores/armoury.

With little time we had a lot to do. The rifle companies worked more on section, platoon and company attacks which are their main purpose as well as all the stuff involved in their pre- and post-attacks. Patrols had to cover all the rifle company stuff in case we were used as a reserve platoon as well as our own patrol tactics and reconnaissance skills.

We began with team movement and SOPs training. Moving into overwatch positions and the setting up of observation posts (OPs) in the desert environment as well as calling in Apaches' and indirect fire. Within a week our foot (de-bus) skills and SOPs were spot on so we began to move onto the vehicle drills (operating, fighting and observing targets from the WMIKs) as well as live firing contact drills and attacks on foot and from vehicles. The grand finale was a live firing company attack in the baking sun followed directly by a company night live firing attack. It was hard going on the blokes with only two weeks' acclimatisation and several members fell foul to heatstroke, which wasn't surprising.

Things were going really well through the attack and with Patrols being in reserve we were used last, my team moving forward to take the last of the enemy bunkers of the range. The last position on the day attack ended in an argument when due to the lack of men I sent Dewi, a Patrols tom (private soldier), to take a position while I moved on to cover his exposed flank. Normally I (or the commander) would follow him up. The Royal Irish officer decided to follow me while Dewi continued to clear a bunker by throwing a grenade into the position I had ordered him to take, making a huge explosion and sending fragmentation all over including between the lads closing up and exposed. The one-pip South African officer went mad as no one was aware that the grenade was about to go off and blamed me and Dewi for being unsafe. It came close to blows at the de-brief which happened a few minutes later. Myself and the others were not happy about this crow of an officer gobbing off: definitely a bad idea with a lot of hot, sweaty and angry paratroopers with live rounds up the spout around him. I tried to calm myself and explained that it was his job to co-ordinate the safety of the range, not ours. It wasn't long before he realised this and his arse soon dropped out but apart from that it went well.

Also the rifle companies had a final exercise, to find and attack possible Taliban training camps. Some of the HQ would set up two mock camps; A Company were to locate and attack one and B Company the other camp under the cover of darkness. Patrols had the job of working against them, to find and observe A and B Company, gather intelligence and make everyone aware of their actions. My team and Ray's were tasked with A Company who were operating in the eastern area, the boss's and Steve team B Company. Ray had the WMIKs and tried to push south to get eyes on A Company while they patrolled north to find the target. My team was on foot. After a map study I needed to gain some serious high ground in order to have any chance in locating the Company in the pitch black. Unlike Ray we were on foot, slow, and only a 6-man team; we wouldn't last long against 70 blokes if we were spotted or confronted. Our job was to locate them but without being detected ourselves.

We left our camp for the surrounding desert. Ray dropped us in a wadi bed before disappearing into the night. The weather was a lot cooler as I directed the lead scout Dewi through the wadi and up onto the features. The climb was hard especially due to the loose rocky ground and that it was night, but within a few hours we reached a plateau under a small peak 50m higher. I set up a base station on the plateau using the peak as cover and then set an OP on the top. The peak was steep, over 45 degrees, it was hands and knees job and I didn't realise how small the summit was till I was sitting on top of it. We struggled to get the three of us who would observe on there, two watching while the other slept. The view through our night optics was good considering there wasn't much ambient light off the moon. It wasn't long before we located the camp A Company were trying to find: a small light and fire giving away its position. We watched through our night and TI optics for any signs of movement around the dark and surrounding features, knowing full well that A Company recce patrols would be venturing in at some stage. I knew that to gain intelligence and find areas in which to attack from they would have to try and obtain a 360-degree recce of the camp.

Early into the morning lying freezing our bollocks off Tommo woke me.

'Scotty, I think I see them.' I struggled to sort my head from the half sleep I had received.

'What you got?' I asked.

'Looks like a small recce party of around four blokes', Tommo said. Through the night aids he brought me onto the figures.

'Got ya' I said to myself. The small team was moving around the northern side of the camp. I radioed to the lads below on the plateau to send the sit-rep forward onto our OC. The base station had all the Comms equipment as it was easier to control and conceal.

'Shit, I lost them, mate,' Tommo cursed, 'they moved into that area but that's it, I can't see them anymore.'

'OK, just keep scanning' I told him. It wasn't long before I put the blokes back on routine to get some sleep, one bloke from each party awake and watching the area while the remainder slept.

During this time I have no idea how none of us fell off the feature, we balanced ourselves on the tip of the rockface while we slept, we often woke thinking we were on the brink of falling, and we were. As I woke and took over from Tommo I realised there was movement below us.

'You see that Tommo?' thinking it was my tired eyes playing tricks.

'Yeah I see them.' There was a wadi bed directly below us. With more scanning I could see their extreme right and left flank, I could even see all their commanders gathering in the centre with a very small light only visible through night viewing aids to discuses what their plans were. It was a FUP location and they were using the wadi to conceal themselves and as a start line from which they would attack the enemy encampment. I sent the message down and plotted the grids of their far left, right and centre groups for indirect artillery as well as a location forward and behind and further up and down the wadi in case they tried escaping from the incoming rounds.

After the confirmation I gave the order to pack up and bug out, our job here was done, and we began moving off the mountain under darkness. If daylight broke we would be stuck up on the mountain. Easier said than done, and all of us had some sort of fall during this steep descent. Later at a debrief, A Company had no idea of our presence however they had slipped through Ray's rolling OP screen further south. Neither Ray's team or A Company had seen one another.

It was a lesson for both sides and in reality could have been a big problem. It showed how easily a force could slip through our OP screen even though it was only one team, usually there were more, and also how easily they could have been targeted by artillery from an OP location run by ourselves. But it did show how good both groups worked – it was very difficult to locate them.

It had been a busy year for the battalion over the last twelve months. There was a lot going on with the battalion on airborne exercises, live firing and courses. I had been away from 3 Para on and off while on courses over the last eighteen months finishing off on the Patrol Commanders' Reconnaissance course in Warminster. I finished in the back end of November to catch the last of the Patrols cadre that we run ever year. It's a cadre run by the boss and NCOs of the platoon designed to teach, train and test all the new blokes from other companies who had been put forward or volunteered for the Patrols platoon. It's a hard few weeks, covering all aspects of reconnaissance from OPs, searches, CTR contact drills, hill fitness, navigation, tactical moving, medical training, communications (use of radios), setting up of FUP and start lines and the setting of conditions for rifle company attacks. Those selected will be brought on board to join the Patrols. Due to the weather being freezing like the course I had just finished it had made the cadre harder than Gary Glitter in PC World but the lads had done well, we had gained some strong lads from the cadre.

After finishing the cadre and a small spell at Colchester for a few piss-ups the platoon found iself at Castlemartin ranges on the south-west coast. We now had the opportunity to put all the foot and vehicle drills into practice using live rounds and then continually beast it to make us slick. It was the first time a lot of the blokes had used the big .50 Cal on and off the WMIKs and the first time we had worked in the new teams and as a platoon. The .50 is the heaviest of the British army machine guns. Its ability to engage targets from long distances would prove very effective in the open plains of Afghanistan. To man pack the .50 Browning is at least a four-man job. We had the ability to carry these weapons on top of the WMIKs; the only disadvantages were that it made the WMIK top heavy and easy to roll if it wasn't positioned right, and secondly the noise was deafening for the commander and driver who sit forward and beneath of it. I remember one day on the ranges my earplugs got blown out due to the noise and I was left with a ringing in my ears for about six hours. The ranges were excellent and I and the platoon managed to get our first confirmed kill while on one of these. My team drove down the range waiting for the targets to pop up, these instigated the range representing an enemy ambush or coming across enemy troops. Due to the nature of our business our drills are simple while out on patrol unless told otherwise: return fire with as much firepower and aggression as possible and getting the hell out of there, whether on foot or vehicles as fast as we could. We were too small a force to hang around scrapping, plus we were normally well in front of our lines out on a limb. As our weapons – the commander's GPMGs and the gunners' .50 – began firing on the targets a group of deer ran straight through our arc of fire. Let's just say we weren't totally avoiding them and the local range wardens lived on deer for the next few weeks. It was definitely good 'moving target' practice.

We conducted and rehearsed our drills in lots of different scenarios and the platoon went through more ammo than I had ever seen through all my years in the Paras. Our contact drills were shit hot to say the least, and the platoon had gelled massively. It wasn't long before we found ourselves on Christmas leave but like many others my mind kept thinking of what lay ahead.

Myself, Hugh, Matt and Ratty had many a chat in the evenings on the Sniper/Patrols floor over a brew about what we thought would happen in Afghan and the incident reports that came in every couple of days. A couple really stuck in my head. One was of a Canadian officer who went to an elder's house to hold a *shura* and with protection around him got an axe in the head when he took off his helmet. The other was an ambush of several ANP members in which they tortured them and booby trapped their bodies. We had read up on books from the Afghan/Russian conflict and I knew from them it would not be pushover. Unlike Iraq, these were hardened warriors; most of which were ex-Mujihadeen that had fought for generations against foreign invaders, one being the British many years ago. The Russians had also been fought and chased out after their invasion in the 70s and 80s. This was not as easy as what some people may have thought. As well as the incident reports about the death rate of the local ANP and Canadian troops, I read up on how they dealt with the captured Russian soldiers. Brutality was their main way and a favourite of these was cutting the Achilles heel off the soldier's feet, opening up his abdomen and leaving him in the baking sun on the rocks for the wild dogs.

After leave the battalion and Battle group had to go though the usual pre-deployment briefs and mini exercises. One of these briefs really struck home for me. Emlyn Hughes was our man in the Int (Intelligence) cell; he really knew his stuff. The Taliban had already forwarded a message to us before even deploying. In 1880 the British were defeated in a major battle in Afghanistan (Maiwand). It started the withdrawal of the British Empire from that area. The Taliban's message was that we would suffer the same fate as our great-grandfathers back in 1880 and our bodies buried next to them. For me this had just got personal.

The training kicked off and started with the normal Op Telic or Northern Ireland scenarios that were mandatory for all deploying troops. It finished with a large exercise moving from Colchester to Thetford to Salisbury Plain and up into Otterburn. Most of the exercise was directed more towards the big cheeses, using the troops as pawns on a chessboard. A lot of it was the usual sketch of hurry up and wait. For Patrols it was more of the latter. We used the vehicles to lead a mobile task force into Salisbury Plain training area, surrounding the FIBUA village Copehill Down. We held this for three days before B Company parachuted in and seized the village. The lads and I were beginning to worry that all this sitting around stagging on could be our major role over in the Middle East and it wasn't till the final part of the exercise did we find Patrols been used for their main role.

Arriving at Wattisham airfield on a cold rainy night we set our camp cots out in the rubber hanger that was used as the parachute refreshing training and DFC before taking part in airborne exercises or jump training. It was called the rubber hanger as it was just that: large scaffolding that was wrapped in a rubber sheet. Just as we had settled we were given a warning order for a full set of orders on mission taking place in Otterburn. Within minutes we found ourselves seated to receive orders. I didn't know what to expect and the lads started slagging off the ideas of what was yet to come as we sat stinking from the previous few weeks living out in the Cud's. Me, Johnny, Ray and Gaz joked of the possible mission ahead.

'Probably want us to go up there and dig their trenches for them', Gaz said. He was referring to the rifle company boys who would catch us up once we got into position.

'Yeah, have their scoff and brews ready for them as they come in, won't be doing fuck all else' Johnny continued. The OC began as we finished off our piss-takes.

'Ok, Patrols, I want you to insert by helicopter to an area no less than 15 to 20ks from the target location.' The target was a disused airstrip. Only long enough for helicopters and possible harriers. 'I want you to tab in, meet with an informer at a bridge location, he has some good intelligence for us and then move on and set up an OP screen around the target and report back the situation and the whereabouts of enemy forces if any are in the vicinity' he continued. 'I'm sending some attachments with Patrols.' He began reeling off names that were to join our recce group. It was a mix of signals, engineers and FOOs from 7 RHA. 'OK then your pick-up is at 10:00 tomorrow so I suggest you get yourselves sorted and get some good head down' he said. 'Captain Swan, I'll leave you to it' and he marched off out of the hanger. Swanny thinned the blokes out while he started his mission brief. We stripped the vehicles of kit and the drivers handed them over to the MT who would take them back to Colchester and the remainder cleaned their weapons. The boss's brief was quick and to the point, most of it had been covered before with the OC. I got the job of picking a decent HLS and leading the Patrols into the target location so while the lads got their heads down for some quality sleep I remained up and planned and plotted a route in. It was working out at some 30ks (about 18 to 20 miles). After working with crap hats before, I was hoping this bunch were up for this mission. It was going to be a long hard insertion.

The next morning we knelt next to our bergens on the wet grass of the airfield waiting for the two Chinooks to come and pick us up. The morning had been busy with collecting rations, radios and batteries, ammunition, OP digging and camouflage equipment before breaking it all down and into our kit that we would slog over the gruelling insertion tab (Tactical Advance to Battle) ahead. It was cold with a slight drizzle. I laughed at how this weather was prepping the boys for operations in Afghanistan.

The Chinooks approached and span round above us no higher than 30ft. The down draft is very powerful from a Chinook, it can easily knock you over if you are carrying heavy kit on your back. Once they had landed we got the thumbs up from the loadie to board. We had to get as comfortable as possible as this was going to be a long old flight from the airbase in East Anglia to the Scottish border area of Otterburn. With earplugs in I was soon asleep, only waking during the two refuelling and piss stops along the way. However, this was broken as I got a nudge off one of the lads next to me. I gave him a hacky look for waking me from my enjoyable sleep. He nodded out the back tailgate which we were close to. The Chinook's ramp was down and we could see the other helicopter following us, a blanket of snow-coloured fog was laid out over the land making it impossible to see through. It was a brilliant sight. A report came down from the pilot that the weather conditions were very poor, a freezing fog had cast over the whole of the area. I could read the expressions on the boys' faces; they believed it was going to be sacked. Many a parachute jump was cancelled due to the weather. The RAF didn't like getting cold or wet but there was no way they would abort now after this long a flight to get here. I was right; there was a gap in the freezing fog just off the HLS, a convenience that we could have done without.

The two big helicopters touched down and we ran off into the ankle-high heather. The two Chinooks began to power up again and lifted off and slowly disappeared out of sight as we covered our arcs. The weather was fucking freezing even by a northern standard. I had to get this patrol, which altogether was now around 40 strong, up and moving fast. In the Paras we have what we call cold starts. Any time we move from position to position in a tactical environment we would remove our entire warm clothing first no matter how cold it was. As you begin to tab or patrol your body generates heat due to the amount of kit and equipment we have to carry. At first you're freezing your bollocks off and wish you had kept your warm kit on but you soon realise that it would be a bad move if you had, and if we were ambushed during the insertion there is just no way you can E+E with your warm clothing on.

I set my bearing and checked my map; we had to follow some tracks through the woods before meeting the agent at the bridge some 6 or 7ks from here. I gave the order to get the kit on and start moving. I was second man in the patrol, the normal position for the navigator and commander with only a lead scout up ahead of me. Daylight was fading fast and I wanted to make the most of the light.

We began tabbing off through the woods but by the time we reached the bridge it was completely dark. We changed our day optics to night time optics just out of view of the bridge and I lead my team forward as an advanced recce party. We could see the agent in his car, engine running to keep him warm. I called the rest of the patrol up. The commanders closed in and got an update from our new friend while my Patrol pushed forward to give us protection. He got quite a shock when I tapped on his window and he saw me peering in, my faced covered in cam cream, he hadn't seen any of us coming.

It was pitch black and slightly foggy with no ambient light or moon. I had to change some of the route as it looked as if the ground was more to our advantage. I took the patrol out of the wood leaving the agent behind and over the open hilly ground. Our pace was fast going and it began to take its toll on some of the guys. I had to slow the pace and put in more water stops although this was also a problem. Due to the weather conditions our water bottles had frozen. We had covered some good distance, but there was still more to go. Most of us were carrying around 90lb plus of equipment on our backs and it was beginning to show. After the recce commander's and other courses I had done over the last few months my tabbing fitness was excellent, however I couldn't drag everyone else around. I needed to get the blokes to our OP screen and set up for the rest of the night so they could eat and rest, although for tactical reasons we can't eat hot food at night due to exposing flame, smoke and steam. At every stop I would walk up and down the line of kneeling and sitting silhouettes to make sure they were all OK.

Some exhausting hours later I pushed the blokes on their final leg, up a large hill to the FRV. We arrived and most of the blokes dropped down exhausted but it wasn't over yet. From the FRV we had to split down into our Patrols and move to our OP area. The boss and Steve with the FOO, signals and engineers stayed at the FRV. My team had to move to an area a further 4–5ks away, not far but after a long slog can feel a hell of a lot longer. The OP site I had chosen was a tree line on the forward edge of a slope just next to a fast-flowing river that ran past the edge of the wood, good for covering our noise while we made the OP in the dark tree line. On approach we had to look for a crossing point over the river. After some 15mins I found one. The river narrowed down close enough to jump. We all threw our bergens across and then jumped the gap in darkness one at a time. We all made it over but Brett was the last to jump, we watched as his silhouette took a run up and leaped. He misjudged the river and didn't make it. His poor effort cost him to get soaked up to his knees in freezing water, his boots and socks were now totally soaked. The rest of us fell to the floor pissing ourselves laughing at Brett's fate. It was the last thing anybody needed after that and in these shitty conditions too. We moved to the tree line and Brett sorted his feet out as the rest of us built the OP. We had been on the move well over 14hrs and the boys were feeling the strain.

The next day we settled into routine and watched the target area, our doss bags covered in a light sheet of ice. It was all quiet and as other forces moved into the south, east and west of us, so we collapsed our OP screen and moved into a small copse just off the landing strip giving the blokes maximum chance to admin themselves and scoff up after our tasty insertion. The rest of the battalion arrived three days later by bus as the freezing fog refused to lift and cancelled the C-130 drop-offs.

The last few days of the exercise finished with us Patrols leading the companies into a holding position and conducting arty target (artillery spotting). This was one of the jobs for us while in Ops. The lads firing the 105mm artillery guns can't see their fall of shot so we would have to call in and adjust their fire for them from covert positions, plus this enabled us to use heavy weapons to smash our targets without giving away our position. The battalion had proved again their worth during these exercises and now we waited for the real thing.

Chapter 3

Bastion Dust Cloud

The plan was for 3 Para Battle group to deploy in April 2006 with an advance party of some 150 troops, 80 of them fighting troops. The remainder of the Battle group would follow and be in place by late May and finish the tour in October 2006. The aim of this Battle group was to help the Afghan Government and people to ensure there was no interference by Taliban forces as they slowly built the security to their region. Once they had the security and stability then development and reconstruction could get underway. This province was Helmand, an area to the south that ran from the borders of Pakistan up along the Helmand River that ran through it and up to the north. Helmand was a flatter region compared to the mountainous areas of Kabul to the north but had the biggest infiltration of Taliban and drug smuggling from the neighbouring country of Pakistan. The province was under almost complete Taliban control in some of these areas and the Canadian forces were having a hard time. This is something I knew: that the Taliban would not give up without a fight. The UK Defence Secretary John Reid had to send in a hard fighting British task force. Like the Falklands campaign, Kosovo, Sierra Leone and Iraq there was only one force capable of breaking in, patrolling and fighting if necessary. He was sending in the Paras.

I got the train down from my home town of Sunderland; I had sold my Audi and tied up as many loose ends as possible before deploying the next day. I didn't want to spend a penny while I worked overseas. Like everyone else I had said goodbye to my family and friends and sat in silence as the train rumbled down the tracks. My mind kept jumping back and forth between my family and friends and the tour.Once I stepped into the 3 Para lines it all faded away as I gathered round my other family who were all sitting round on the Patrols and Sniper floors shooting the shit about what they had been up to on leave, mostly the shagging and drinking side, or the lack of it in some cases. There was a volume of anticipation and excitement on the floor. Two patrols, mine and Bernie's (although Benny was standing in as commander as Bernie was on compassionate) and a couple of sniper teams were first to deploy with A Company group who were moving out as an advance party. We said our goodbyes to the lads who weren't deploying till later on in the tour.

On the early morning of 15 April we dropped our bergens and grips that were full of our military and civilian or personal kit onto the trucks, collected our weapons from the armoury and boarded the coaches and repeated the journey to Brize-Norton via South Cerney. Boredom is a big part of military life and this was no exception. There is always a lot of hanging around, waiting and queuing. We Paras have to keep ourselves amused in times like this and so the fun and games soon began.

We sat in the waiting lounge drinking brews like it was going out of fashion and looking for ways to stitch up anybody who would give us a reason while we waited to move. Lads off to take a dump in the outside portaloos would find themselves getting shaken around just as they reached the critical stage or being locked in. Blokes who fell asleep would often wake to find a piece of kit missing or their bootlaces tied together, something childish and stupid but guaranteed to get a snap from some. If it was none of the above then it was the usual piss-takes and insults being dished to one another. These little childish games were just a way of passing the time, it was just a good job there wasn't any beer around, that's when things really start going wrong. I remembered back to the day before we were about to leave the Falklands after doing a four-month tour down there. After a good skinful one of the lads thought it would be funny to shit in the bags of one of our pay clerks who was travelling with us. He didn't find it till well over 24hrs later during a stop over in Ascension Island. Not exactly a nice surprise.

A Company was commanded by Major Will Pike, a man who was disliked at first when he had come back to 3 Para but who gained more and more trust and respect from the fighting troops as time went on. By the end of Afghanistan it was the total opposite, he was liked and respected by all who worked under him. His dad was the CO of 3 Para during the Falklands conflict of 1982, Lieutenant Colonel Hew Pike, a renowned CO who commanded his men through the hard conflict and bloodiest battle for the Islands, the battle of Mount Longdon. I suppose he had something to prove and live up to his father's history.

My team was assigned to 1 Platoon, commanded by a young officer called Lieutenant Hugo Farmer. He was in his mid-twenties, thinly shaped with brown hair. Unlike most officers he would use the experience of his platoon Sgt and NCOs and listen to their years of experience and advice before carrying out any task. They were all outstanding soldiers and good friends of mine. The platoon sausage (Sgt) as we called it was big Dan Jarvie, a big Scot who was respected through the ranks of the battalion. Dan was like a rock, unbelievably strong, physically and mentally. Hugo Farmer could not ask for a better Platoon Sgt and section commanders who were Prig Poll and Charlie Curnow (Bry Budd joined later in the tour) – although if Hugo Farmer did I'm sure he would have been fish hooked till he thought otherwise (Dan's party piece). I was happy to come on board and offer my Patrol's knowledge to the A Company lads and be used as a fighting section for the first part of the tour. I had deep feelings for A Company: this was the company I had joined when I passed P-Company, gained my wings and came to the 3rd Battalion. I had spent some of my best years in the Paras in this unit. Four and a half years I had spent before moving on, something at the time that I did not want to do. It was always renowned as being one of the better companies in the 3rd Battalion.

In the sunny afternoon of 15 April the advance party settled down for the flight over via Dubai, something the Head Shed had kept quiet about. We soon realised why. We arrived in Dubai after around six hours of travelling not to mention the travelling from Colchester at 04:30 that morning. We were told we weren't allowed to leave the aircraft and move around the airport without civilian clothing. We couldn't even go out for a tab. This went down about as good as a fart in a space suit. Most of us couldn't get civilians in our day sack anyway because of the amount of optics and serial itemed kit that we were not allowed to put into bergens or grips that were in the hold. Also we also had no reason to bring civilian clothes with us – but it still would have been nice to have been told about this. So we all sat and dished out sly comments at the senior NCOs and officers as they left with smart civilians obtained from their half-filled day sacks. I couldn't believe that we were off yet again to sort some mess out in a faraway country yet we couldn't leave the aircraft in case we offended someone. After a piss-taking two and half hours we were ready to fly the next leg, a further six to seven hours to Kabul airport in north Afghanistan.

The sun was shining as the aircrew told us of our descent. I looked out of the windows to see the mountains below with their peaks still covered in snow. The order came over to place on body armour and helmets. I and many of the other blokes just burst out laughing. 'As if this is going to save us if we get knocked out the sky', I said at nobody in particular. We landed in Kabul and I got my first impressions of Afghanistan. The northern part anyway. From the airport we could not see much, just the outskirts of the city that sat on the lower plains of the mountains that surrounded the airport from almost all angles. The sun was strong but there was still a chill in the air. I imagined it could get very cold around here; these mountains were the southern edge of the Himalayas. For the next few hours we sat around the hangers getting briefed by some jobsworth's corporal who liked the sound of his own voice and looked like he was on a power trip after being promoted from brew bitch to arrival brief manager (holiday rep), something his mother and father must be so proud about. We had to wait for a C-130 to take us down to Bastion. Due to the amount of airframes in Afghan at that time the RAF had to do shuttle runs to get the whole advance party down there as there were only around two C-130 in theatre. Most of Patrols got the last flight in; there was no hurry to get down there just to sit around waiting again.

Obviously Paratroopers are at home with the C-130 as this aircraft is normally the one we jump out of, so as soon as we boarded we snuggled into the seats, earplugs (or in my case my ipod) in and we fell fast asleep. The Hercules had this effect on most of us due to its rocking motion as it warmed the engines on the pan before taxiing out and taking off.

In the Paras this was our means of travel and getting from A to B. Other soldiers use armoured tin cans or coaches and 4-ton Bedford trucks to get to an exercise or operation. The Reg used the fat Albert, the C-130 Hercules or helicopters to get us in and it's an amazing experience jumping from one, totally different to civilian parachuting or sky diving. Military parachuting is equivalent to eight hour work or stress. There is a lot that goes into it, not a case of turning up and jumping out which a lot of people think. We often leave our barracks on an early morning; it usually took us four hours by coach to get to RAF Lyneham via South Cerney of course where we weighed our containers and ourselves. Due to health and safety rules that came out around 2000, you can only jump with a maximum weight of 350lb all up, as the cables that you hook your static line parachute onto inside the aircraft can only take so much weight. If we were lucky we would get a breakfast before DFC, placing on our parachutes and having our safety checks, last minute briefs and boarding the aircraft. After taking off the pilots and crew would conduct their own training with a few hours of low level flying, not something that bothered me, I quite enjoyed it, but some of the guys would curse the pilots and end up being sick all over everyone else. Forty minutes out from the DZ we would have to stand and fit all our equipment to our legs, get checked again then move into the door ready for the exit. Forty minutes is a long time to stand up with around 100lb plus hanging off your waist and a further 35lb main parachute and 15lb reserve, no matter who you are. With two lines of paratroopers on each side we were extremely crammed. It was hot, tight, stinking now of sick and hard to keep upright due to the weight. At this stage most of us wanted to get out of the door anyway.

The C-130 would slow to around 140mph or stalling point. The two-minute warning would come and go, followed by the red light and the blokes screaming 'RED ON!' to make sure everyone was aware we were about to jump. After a long two or three seconds the light below would turn green. That was it, we were going, struggling with all the kit on to get to the para door and make a clean exit, stepping out into thin air at around 140mph. Over 100 paratroopers would go out the port and starboard para doors in a matter of seconds and litter the sky with parachutes and leave the C-130 empty. The slipstream would throw you around the sky before your canopy deployed above your head, and that was just the start of your worries. Blokes would collide with one another: you can find yourself in another parachutist's rigging lines and entangled in their chutes. Other Paras fly under you causing you to have an air steal and drop 40–50ft before finding fresh air re-opening your chute; hopefully you're not too close to the ground as that means falling with all your kit 50ft towards the ground like a lead balloon. These were just some of the fun and games we would have before dispatching our kit on a rope 15ft below us and hitting the ground at around 20mph. It was even better at night! The para descent is just a means of getting in. Once on the ground the real graft started: another reason why the Paras are pushed to the limits and have to do a separate selection course known as P-Company as part of our training. Five days of gruelling tests see if you have the mental and physical robustness to continue when your body wants to throw in the towel. The reason for this is simple. Once you leave that aircraft you're on your own.

After about an hour I woke with the 10 min-out warning order. As with jumping and helicopter flights, they usually break the last part of the flight down: 30 mins, or with jumping 40 mins out, then 10 mins, followed by 2 mins, 1 min, then either RED ON, GREEN GO or the landing of the aircraft.

We hit the ground hard. Bastion was still in the process of getting built and the runway was still a desert strip at this point. The Herc eventually slowed and came to a halt, the tailgate lowered and let in the bright sun and hot wind. I walked off the aircraft with the Arctic Monkeys playing in my ears. The C-130 killed its engines as I gathered next to the other Patrol and Sniper lads.

'So this is it is it?' I said looking round at the empty desert surrounding us.

'Nah, they must've dropped us in the wrong place, I can't see any camp here', someone said. He was right. I knew that Bastion hadn't been finished but from what I could see it hadn't been started.

We located our bergens and grips and threw them on a 4-ton Bedford that took us into camp – or lack of. I looked around at the makeshift camp and wasn't too impressed. Our CO had told us that the accommodation was ready for the advance party but not the full battalion; I wondered if it was ready for a section never mind a full company plus attachments of HQ, support and Patrols. Jumping off the 4-tonner we were grabbed by Dan Jarvie and some HQ blokes who had been here a few days earlier.

'We gotta stay in 12×12s at the moment, Scotty. It's just temporary' Dan said. The 12×12s are the standard British army old green tents dating back from the Boer War, or so you would think. They allocated the blokes to the tents which were in a line side by side. The first was for the Company HQ, then the next 1 Platoon, the third 2 Platoon and the last one an overspill tent. I stood and watched as the blokes grabbed an issued camp bed and moved into their new accommodation. All apart from mine and Benny's teams (Patrols) who were still standing there sweating in the hot sun. They had known how many blokes were coming in yet there weren't enough tents. This was resolved when I had a 12×12 tent, still wrapped, thrown at my feet. We had been on the go now for some 48 hours plus, and this was taking the piss. When you jump into an exercise or operation you're going in with what you have and expect to rough it out. But here we expected to move into a camp from which we would operate over the next six months. We all had bergens and grips with personal kit including laptops, cameras, ipods and suchlike, something to make our stay that little bit better. So now we began erecting the tent in the baking sun.

I could tell that the blokes were licked already, I was too. They had put down a gravel surface before erecting the tents to reduce the sand inside but it still got everywhere. This also made it almost impossible to hammer in the pegs without the proper equipment and due to an arrival brief we had to do the best we could using other rocks to hammer in the pegs. Half way through the brief by the OC the wind began to pick up and I watched as our tent on the end of the row blew away with a lot of our kit attached to it, flying off down the camp in a mix of cloud and dust. Well fucking mega, welcome to Afghanistan, I thought.

So for the next few weeks we made these tents our homes. For the time being we had no lighting, air-conditioning or electricity but we had all been in a lot worse conditions and made as best we could. It certainly wasn't the Ritz and no matter how much we complained we never got upgraded to five star, all inclusive. It would be the last time I book Helmand Costa del Bastion, I can tell you. We were given times to wash and shave at, in an area that had already been built in another part of camp. Due to the lack of supplies and resources we had to keep this to a minimum. The chefs began cooking scoff from ration packs, the only food they had at this time, and we occupied ourselves with useful lessons such as basic greetings in Arabic (Pashtu) as two toms, Webley (Snake eyes) and Dave had done a basic Arabic course before deployment. There were medical lessons by the battalion doc, SOP training and test firing our personal weapons. We even built our own multi-gym using storage cages and scaffolding poles to keep ourselves ticking over.

As the camp was still being built there was a lot of digging and construction going on making it almost impossible to run due to the very fine sand that had been dug up and laid on the surface; this gave off an enormous very fine dust cloud that got everywhere and prevented you from breathing properly and seeing even a metre or so every time a vehicle drove by or the wind picked up.

After a couple of weeks we got a warning order to gather around the OC tent that night for a possible move to FOB Price, a little camp outside a town called Gereshk 27ks east of Bastion. Later that night I stood with the rest of the Patrols and A Company around the OC's tent in complete darkness with only our head torches to see what we had to write.

'OK then, I have been in touch with the CO back in the UK and he wants A Company plus attachments to move to Gereshk and begin routine patrols and the taking over of the camp until relieved by other forces.' He paused to let this sink in. 'At present US troops are holding the encampment with the Pathfinder platoon. We will fly up by CH47 Chinooks and take on the guard and protection of the camp. Once this is established then we will begin to look at operations into the town of Gereshk itself.' Again he stopped and looked around the large number of head torches around him.

'At this moment we have no real intelligence picture of what's going on in the town as yet as nobody has been in. OC Pathfinders will be giving me a brief on what they have done so far on arrival.' He finished off with some timings for the move and heli and then we all headed off to prep our kit for getting out of this shithole.

I felt some small amount of excitement in my stomach. I was also happy about getting out of this place and geting on with some proper soldiering. It's what we were here to do.

Gereshk is a town I had never heard of. There was still a lack in mapping but I managed to get my hands on one and have a look at this unknown place. Straight away I pinged it for being a major piece of ground for the Battle group to hold and defend; it would become a major area that would always need Coalition presence as long as we operated in the south. On the east of the town it had a bridge that crossed the Helmand River. This was the only crossing point in around 70ks north and south of the town. Without having control or security this could cause a lot of problems for patrols and re-supplies heading north and east to Sangin, Musa Qaleh, Baghran, Lashkar Gah and Kandahar and then back again.

There was an MSR running east to west through the centre of Gereshk and over the bridge known as Route 5 and called the A1 by UK forces. It was one of the only long-distance tarmac roads in the south but with my experiences of Iraq would soon draw lots of attention and turn into a prime location for IEDs if used by convoys and military vehicles.

On 20 April we found ourselves flying out of Bastion and east to FOB Price. We left all our grips and personal kit behind and took only essential and operational equipment with us. We touched down at the rear of the small camp and after the usual briefs and camp orientation settled down and sorted our kit. We were due to start the takeover as soon as possible.

There were two main areas of the camp, a new and an old part. The new was an area now full of the new British air-conditioned tents located at the front of the camp and the old, full of old brick buildings cased in small compounds to the rear next to the generators and helicopter pad which PF and the Yank SF were in. The whole camp was surrounded by large berm and hesco walls. In the centre was a large OP tower some 40ft high giving a 360-degree arc and good views of the surrounding desert and tribal outstations. The US military had paid the local tribes around the camp for a total of four outposts 1k around the FOB to protect it, and guess what, it worked. At one point when the Yanks had first set up here they refused the tribes their offer for protection. This resulted in constant attacks, not by the Taliban but by the local tribes in the area. Once they began to pay them it all stopped and FOB Price once again fell silent. One thing to understand about the Middle East is that money talks. It was the same in Iraq; one tribe would protect an area but another would move in and hit one of our CP teams indicating how much damage they could inflict unless we began paying them for the local protection. This was the way it worked and they were playing with lives, our lives. The tribes had fought the Taliban for years but would easily turn on friendly forces, i.e. us, unless they were getting a backhander in return.

The A Company group soon got into routine. A normal rifle company is split down into four groups: HQ with the OC, CSM and C/Sgt, etc, then three fighting platoons. The platoons were then split down again into four: a platoon HQ (a commander, a lieutenant normally, platoon Sgt, radio operator etc.) and then three fighting sections all of which should be eight men strong, although due to the lack of manning this wasn't always the case. My patrol only operated in a team of six for stealth and had to get two members of the rifle company to join us. Each section or patrol was commanded by the full screws or Jedis as they were known with an L/Cpl as their 2i/c and six toms. The full screws had the most important job in the platoon, company and battalion. This is often forgotten by the Head Shed especially back in camp but on operations it's a different story. The officers give the main order and conduct their plan and pass it down but without the screws on the ground leading and controlling the fighting men nothing will get done and obviously without the blokes (toms), then no battle will ever get won. As my Patrol mixed and adapted into 1 Platoon's orbit I looked around some of Charlie and Prig's sections. In 2006 the battalion had some very young paratroopers. The average age of the toms in the rifle companies was around 19 or 20 years of age although after this tour most would gain a lot more years on their lives. Young or old I knew these boys had good screws: Charlie and Prig with big Dan as their platoon Sgt. They had been trained well and I was pleased to be alongside these men as we entered a new theatre of this early tour: our first mission, our first patrol of Afghan.

Chapter 4

Wheels are Down

Within a week of being in FOB Price we got the green light to patrol the town of Gereshk. Before then we had rotated Platoons 1, 2 and the remainder of the Patrols platoon who had now come to join us, from guard, QRF and the rest.

This would be the first time British forces had moved into and patrolled any main town here in south Afghanistan, Helmand province. PF had patrolled the local area for several weeks and had even moved further afield but 1 Platoon 3 Para would be the first into the town centre.

A couple of days before the mission, PF gave us an update on what had been going on in the area, plus a brief on a contact they had further north a few weeks ago. PF had deployed ahead of the Battle group in March 2006. They had been operating from FOB Price and had pushed north to a town called Now Zad, a town I would hear more and more of. PF had patrolled and pushed to the south of the town during one of these night patrols. At the south of Now Zad there was a small hill. The Afghan National Police had set up a position on top of the feature unknown to the Pathfinder platoon. As they moved up conducting their CTR the ANP opened up. Due to the ANP not knowing British forces were in the area and PF the same for the ANP a fire fight broke out. PF operated on WMIKs as we did, they like us had a lot of firepower on board. Talking to a mate of mine later in Gereshk, he explained what had happened. They fired a burst of automatic fire in front of the wagons.

'As another burst opened up, so did we', he said. As with all recce forces you're out there on a limb, operating well in front of the main Battle group. Any contact with the enemy needs to be hard and fast using all the firepower and assets you have to get yourselves out of that situation and asking questions later.

'Our rear WMIKs were spaced out and firing while the front vehicles began pulling back, tracer rounds were firing everywhere and lighting up the night sky as both groups believed that they were being engaged by the Taliban.' As the PF patrol quickly bounded back exchanging fire, one of the WMIKs hit the side of a small wadi, steep enough for the wagon to roll.

'We now had three lads down and didn't know if they were OK', he said. 'Another vehicle pushed up just as the three soldiers got out of the now overturned WMIK. They continued their extraction drill with their three injured team mates. It was really confusing at night', he continued, 'especially when that WMIK rolled. PF moved out of the contact and went into silence drills and watched the upside-down WMIK left out in the darkness. Normally we blow the vehicles or burn them out to prevent enemy forces from getting their hands on any important equipment but PF hadn't done this. The ANP could not see any movement through the night and believed the mobile force had withdrawn.

The ANP moved from their hilltop and pushed forward. It wasn't long before they found the WMIK Land Rover overturned. PF knew they could not let this equipment fall into enemy hands. As they watched the enemy moving around their vehicle through their night and TI optics, PF began opening up with the .50 and GPMGs but before that sent a Milan anti-tank missile straight into the WMIK now surrounded by darkened figures.'

For the remainder of the night PF stayed in an overwatch position till first light. It wasn't till the light came up that both groups realised what had gone on. PF were invited up to meet the ANP who did not seem too upset about the previous night's engagement. PF had inflicted a lot of damage and injury; they had killed a few ANP and a further four were injured during the contact with only three minor injuries from the rolled WMIK. Several weeks later it had emerged from a local that the ANP position at the top of the feature had been under the influence of the Taliban. From now on we weren't taking any chances.

PF had another incident only days later on their next patrol. During a recce south of a area called Sangin one of their WMIKs hit a land mine. All three lads were injured with the rear gunner losing his leg. We now had the first casualties of this tour.

The mission was going ahead for the next day; between then and now the lads moved into battle prep. Dan grabbed the 2i/cs and went to collect more ammunition. We were taking in as much as we could carry. Tommo went off to sort the radios out making sure we had our secured filters fitted (making all information passed to and from our teams secure from anyone listening in) and the rest of us cracked on with personal admin before the OC's orders later that night.

Johnny came back with the extra ammo and 24 hours' worth of emergency rations that each man would carry. Every man with a long was carrying twelve 28-round magazines with a further 10 mags in bandoliers on our backs as well as belts of either 200 or 400 rounds for the Minimi and GPMG. Two HE grenades, one red phosphorus and one smokescreen per rifleman. It was an 'in and out' op so we would deploy in fighting order: belt kit which held mainly ammo and water and a day sack holding radios, ECM, medical equipment and extra ammunition. Everything else we began to bin to keep the weight to a minimum, there was no room for luxuries. After swapping kit round, adding extras bits and pieces and binning other non-essential kit we eventually agreed on what was carried by whom and how much of it was to be carried. As well as the 5.56mm ammunition we agreed that each man would carry two full water bottles on his belt kit and a 2ltr camel pack in the day sack with a hose attachment so we can drink on the move. The weather was now averaging 45 degrees. We hadn't fully acclimatised and without enough water we would be taking on heat casualties without firing a single round.

Tommo was carrying the HF radio so he couldn't carry anything else. He also had the Minimi: a fuck-up by myself but I didn't have much choice. He was the best signaller I had and he couldn't take on another weapon as it wouldn't be zeroed in to him. Little Luke took the other Minimi and another lad called

Tommo attached from A Company was bringing up the rear with the GPMG. Paras are one of the only units who still carry the GPMG in the light (foot) role as most have adapted to the 5.56 Minimi. I don't think you can replace a weapon like the GPMG. If it kicked off we would need that hard stopping power of 7.62mm. The downfall however was more weight; 7.62mm ammo weighs a lot. A box of 200 rounds is around 7kg and the gun is 10.9kg too. We were tabbing in with 800 rounds of 7.62mm between six of us as well as a further 800 5.56mm links apiece for the two Minimi. The other two Patrols, Tommo and Brett, carried the radio and ECM and spare batteries. Johnny was the team medic, he had received extra training and courses and carried the team med pack – again heavy and bulky kit. Every man carried a personal medical kit with two FFDs, tourniquet and quick clot and two morphine injections, hopefully this was enough to conduct self aid till Johnny or one of the medical team back in HQ could reach us. The weight was slowly growing and I was a bit worried about the blokes.

'OK, lads, I want as much ammo as possible on the body or in your belt kit. The remainder on the top of your day sack', I said. 'If the shit hits the fan then dump your day sacks and HF radios'. We have all got our personal radios and I have the 349, a small team radio on my belt kit. I and a further three other members were taking NVG night viewing aids just in case things went wrong and we began reenacting *Black Hawk Down*. The others were carrying improvised stretchers made from our own ponchos as we hadn't been issued any so our ponchos would have to do.

I moved to the cookhouse where the orders would be posted with my team and the 1 Platoon boys. It was packed; it seemed that every man and his dog wanted in on this first Op; the CO and even RSM had flown in. Major Pike started off his orders and the breakdown of the groups. 1 Platoon would be the main effort moving ahead with the CO's rover group following up behind. The rover group was the CO himself, the RSM, provo staff, signallers and FOOs, then there were our own medics, the doc and sniper detachments that were also coming in with us. The OC began breaking down the plan into stages. Two Chinooks would drop us in to the HLS which was in the south of the town: an open disused market area around 100–150 metres square. Once the helis were down we had to move fast and set up a perimeter around the HLS. The OC wanted my team to move at best speed up to the canal where there were two bridges. These had to be secured fast before the remaining force could move up. The first objective was to go to the local heath clinic. The doc was going to have a look round and see if we could help or bring in supplies next time we ventured in as this was just a quick recce and meet and greet. The rest of the patrol was just a general orientation, showing a presence and getting a feel for the atmosphere. My team was to operate on the right-hand flank on the east of the town. Prig's team was on the left and Charlie's team plus Lt Farmer and Dan would move through the centre with the CO's rover group to the rear. We were to move through the centre of town and out to the north. Once we had put some ground from us and the town then we would tab it back to camp as the helis had other jobs to do unless we needed them for CAS-E-VAC. It was the OC's ball game; the CO was just part of the patrol.

I woke early with the boys and we made a bee-line for the scoff house; we shovelled as much scoff down our throats as we could. It was going to be a long day and we wouldn't be eating again till around 10–12 hours later, plus a lot of us from experience would eat as much as we could. In environments like these we never knew when our next meal would be. If things went wrong it could be a long time. I went back in to see the boss, Dan, Prig and Charlie. Again we went through what we were going to do, who was where and the areas throughout the patrol where we would RV at to speak face to face. Also the ERVs which are normally done on the ground but we put in two initial ones just in case. The helis were due in at 09:15hrs.

I went back to the tent and my team and dropped a few water bottles down my neck. It was an SOP that everyone had a FFD and tourniquet attached to their kit, and personal med kit clearly marked up. We all checked each other so if one of us went down then your mate next to you knew where your morphine and medical equipment was. A golden rule within the army is that you never use your own medical kit to treat others, you always use theirs unless absolutely necessary: 10 minutes later you might need your own.

'OK lads, action's on', I said. I began going over our team's SOPs once again, so I was completely happy that everyone knew what to do if something went wrong – actions on heli drop off, the bridge, halts, build up of crowds, heat casualties, ambush and contact with the Taliban.

'OK lads, let's get kitted up and get down the heli pad', I said. Dressed in our desert combat trousers and shirts we placed on the issued body armour, a ballistic material with two Kevlar plates at the front and back of the body armour. The blokes had a mixture of webbing, in the form of a belt kit which was standard but we upgraded it with extra pouches and quick release clips and Velcro on the magazine pouches making magazine changes a lot quicker. Some of the blokes used chest rigs and assault vests as it was sometimes easier while patrolling or on vehicles, but for foot ops I preferred my belt kit. As I said this was full of water and ammo, a little scoff, med equipment and some command kit for myself. I hung one of the bandoliers around my body and then put on my day sack and helmet. I looked at Johnny, he started laughing and then we all did.

'Fuck me, this is ridiculous', he said, 'We are gonna be in shit state if we get into a contact', Luke followed.

'Carried more than this in Iraq when we moved into Basra though', I said.

'Yeah fuck me that was even worse', Johnny replied laughing.

'OK lads, this is "man's kit" [hard work], keep an eye out and look after each other out there. It's going to be hot day and a hard slog.'

We had tried to break the weight down as much as possible but the gunners were carrying the heaviest kit especially Tommo who also carried the Bowman HF radio as my signaller, but he was fit and I knew he had no problems carrying it. In all we were carrying roughly 65–70lbs of bombs, bullets and water each at the very least. We all forced down a couple of extra bottles of water as the two Chinooks came in and settled on the heli pad. We ran on and sat in our order of march: my team closest to the tail ramp so we could get off quick to secure the

HLS. The two big Chinooks powered up and began to take off. Most of us were in our own thoughts as the helicopter chucked itself around the sky, a quiet only broken by the odd piss-take or slagging that helped relax us. Numerous things entered my head but mainly it was the mission ahead of us.

I watched past the tail gunner and out through the lowered ramp at the desert wasteland below us; we crossed over farmland and started flying over the outskirts of the town as the pilots banked and turned this big airframe from side to side.

'Two minutes', the loadie signalled using his fingers in the noisy environment. Everyone passed on the message and began moving around, undoing their seat belts and positioning themselves so they could get up and move quicker when the wheels touched on. I squeezed my weapon that was facing down between my legs and checked that the safety catch was still on. The RAF get very anal about soldiers having weapons made ready on board their precious aircraft and always told us to only make ready as you leave the aircraft. Fuck that, my lads were made ready before we even got on; the last you need is to be pissing around cocking your weapons when you're running off and taking incoming.

'One minute' was shouted around. A slight mix of nerves and excitement filled our bodies. I felt the Chinook strain as it began to slow into a hover, angling itself towards the HLS.

I patted Jim T. on the shoulder, 'You good?'

'Yeah Scotty' he replied.

'There should be a building straight in front of us, head for that and cover the left-hand edge, if not then push out a good bound and go firm', I shouted.

'Yeah no dramas' Jim answered back. I saw the tops of the buildings as we got ready for the landing about 30ft off the deck, then it was all just a whirlwind of dust. With a thud the Chinook touched down.

'Wheels are down' came over the radio. The loadie didn't even have time to signal, we were off down the ramp and running through the thick dust.

My heart was racing as we sprinted off the back of the heli and into the cloud of chucked-up sand. Jim disappeared and I followed. A second later I saw the one-storey building to my front. Jim had already moved to the left-hand edge and I slammed into the wall behind him. Crouching down I looked back to watch as the remainder of my team emerged at full speed through the cloud and filed in behind me along the wall. The gunners took positions looking into the town. Within seconds the two Chinooks took off and disappeared out of sight. We were in.

Johnny moved over to where I was kneeling. I checked my GPS, map and compass. We were no more than 500m from the bridge.

OK, everyone ready', I called. I got the thumbs up from the lads.

'Scotty when you are ready mate move out', the boss called over the radio.

'Yeah roger that, we are moving now', I replied. I pointed to where I wanted Jim to head for and we broke cover from the shelter of the wall and headed to a road 100m to our front. The local Afghans were now crowding in the area we were heading for, coming out to see what was going on. We had certainly taken the town's occupants by surprise.

'OK boss that's my team on the road and heading north towards the objective', I said.

'Roger that, we are following', he replied. I moved in staggered file, four men on the right and four men on the left of the road. The street was full of garages side by side looking back onto the road. They had been converted into shops selling everything from meats, bread and fruits to handmade rugs. Moving through the local people at first was tense on both us and the Afghans; it was narrow, no more than 15m across. Most of them moved to one side to let us go by but almost everyone stopped and watched. Unless they had been around when the USSR invasion happened this could be the first time they had seen 'white eyes' before; they were wondering who these strange foreign soldiers were. Me and Jim were the first into this virgin territory.

My eyes were everywhere, watching for any sudden movements up ahead, tops of buildings and side streets. I continued to drip feed the rest of the patrol behind me on what was going on and coming up ahead of us.

'Scotty I have eyes on target', Jim called over the PRR (personal radios).

'Roger that'. I had been pacing the ground since we left the HLS and knew it was just ahead although I could not see it yet. Charlie called over the net telling me that his primary team would hold the away bank, the side in which we were moving to. My team was to hold what we call the home bank; the bridge over the canal was only around 30m long. It parallels another crossing point 100m to our left. These two bridges were definitely VPs (vulnerable points) but not with IEDs. We had moved in too quick for that and it would be stupid for them to blow up one of their only crossing points. The most dangerous area for a bridge for example would be 50–100m either side as you get channelled into the crossing, especially with vehicles. My main concern would be a sniper or a multi-weapons shoot from the areas left and right of the bridge. But it was busy which is always a good sign that it won't kick off – although this is never 100 per cent.

We moved into position on the bank. We could see a lot to the exposed left and right flanks. After the bridge you had more buildings which were the centre of Gereshk itself, mainly 2–3 storey buildings then a mix of wasteland and thick greenery off to our right. My four blokes covered the right-hand side of the bridge and Johnny the left.

'OK Charlie, the bridge is secure.'

'Roger, Scotty, I'm moving over now mate.' The main section, Charlie, Dan and the boss moved over the bridge followed by the COs rover group and then Prig and his section. Once I got the go that they had pushed further north I ordered my team to move over the bridge.

'OK fellas let's move. Once you get close hard target across to the other side', I called up. 'Hard target' was an expression used in Northern Ireland, in areas such as these when you're exposed to possible sniper or ambush areas. You run as fast as possible to get to your next bit of cover zig-zagging as you go. Once over the bridge my team had spread itself out along both sides of the bank now facing south. The Doc, CO and OC began meeting the locals in the health centre.

'Lads get yourselves comfortable and keep your eyes on the green belt', I briefed everyone. I was moving up and down the banking from one bloke to the next, it was really hot now, the sweat dripping down our faces. The locals were being more cocky too, a few of them riding up on bikes and taking photos and video footage of us on mobile phones. This was pissing me off; it was obvious that these men were looking for reactions, skills, weapons and the general condition of the blokes. Talk about a close target recce, they couldn't get any closer and we had no idea if they were possible Taliban. I began to get them away from the blokes. Kids were starting to come closer too. This I didn't mind; they were fucking annoying but the more they were around the less chance we had of being engaged, if the Taliban had any consideration for their own kind.

There was a small building next to me opposite the row of shops overlooking the canal. I didn't want the locals seeing that I was the commander by pulling out maps and my GPS so I moved round the back of this small building and did a quick map study and planned on where to move next. I didn't really notice the smell, it all stank of rubbish and burning but there were a lot more flies buzzing around my face, more than usual. I sorted my route and turned around. I had been kneeling next to a huge pile of human excrement. I say pile, it was more like King Kong had been up here, they must have been using this place for a while. I now realised why there was so many flies flying round, jumping off the shit and onto my face and lips. Mega, I thought, just what I need.

I got the order to get ready to move, it was sweltering and to be honest I wanted to get moving. Charlie's team was still in the main street; we would push through them, then patrol the right side of the town, giving the primary team more room to operate and for us to secure the right flank. Moving into the centre of town was even busier with the standard Middle Eastern Toyota pick-up that every Afghan with a bit of dollar had driving around, that or the many of the local mopeds that sped up and down.

My team had its own little groupies following us now, the local kids. I was more than happy to have these around me. We pushed east and out of the congested area. It seemed that everything was orientated around the main few streets, which was mainly made up of shops. There was a street a couple of blocks up, it hand railed some open ground which sat on the right behind a wall. Moving into this area we began to feel very strange. It was too quiet, there wasn't a soul about apart from the few kids following. To the left were some old buildings and to the right an old broken wall with wasteland and trees behind. It seemed like a good place to ambush us with little or no collateral damage.

'Scotty, it's Luke, we have a pick-up truck speeding towards us on our 6'. Half my team was now in the start of this quiet street running north–south whereas the other half hadn't moved round the corner and were still in the other street we had come from. I turned round but due to the wall could not see round the corner. Johnny had just moved round into sight, he also turned to see what was going on behind him. Just then Johnny moved his weapon into the aim as the other lads who could see what was going on did the same. There was shouting from Johnny and Afghan voices and I expected to hear the sound of firing any second. I ran back to the corner just as the situation seemed to calm itself. Luke, Johnny and Tommo were close to opening up; a pick-up truck had come racing up behind us with a heavy weapon on the back. It turned out that they were the local ANP, although it was hard to identify them properly as some had uniforms and others didn't and could have easily been thought of as Taliban. Most seemed quite friendly as we tried to make pleasantries in my poor Pashtu but they did seem a little on edge, almost nervous, all of us picked up on this. The commander of this group began to ask where we were going. I just pointed down the road which was about as much information I was going to give him.

'Yes, yes, good', he said and began pointing, Go, go. His troops behind him moved the children away in the opposite direction shouting and threatening them with sticks.

'Come with us', I gestured.

'No, no, you go, please you go', he said this time, a little more nervous as he looked over my shoulder down the road. I turned round to look, there was a weird feeling about this, it was still, an eerie still.

'Right, let's move it!', I shouted.

'Fuck going down there, Scotty', Johnny said, 'looks fucking dodgy this. Let's push back into the other street.'

'Yeah I know this looks dodgy, a possible "come on" [set up], let's get away from this', I agreed. I grabbed a quick photo with some of the ANP so I could show our intelligence blokes back in camp and also the fact that one of these men had the longest face I had ever come across, before directing my team through a different route.

The rest of the patrol seemed to be going without incident apart from when I lost all communications with the other call signs later in the patrol. By this time I had to halt the patrol in a dirty back street. I studied the map; it wasn't a major drama as I knew the route the primary team was taking but we need Comms in case we came under contact and had to inform the others of what was going on and our location for support.

'Try again', I repeated to Tommo who was now kneeling next to his radio set.

'Nah, still nothing', he said. I was kneeling next to Johnny checking our position and looking over the map with the rest of the blokes providing us protection.

'Better put it to full power then', I said to Tommo with an evil grin on my face. The Bowman HF radio can give out a large amount of energy on full power, with the fact that it is not properly earthed due to us man-packing; it can give a very nasty electric shock and burn to go with it, another reason I had my own signaller and didn't like to do it myself. Tommo looked at me, his face said it all: a mixture of annoyance and apprehension. I looked up to check the route ahead through the small channelled side streets and heard the yelp from Tommo behind me.

'Twat!' he called out, 'fucking message sent'.

'Ha, roger that mate, prepare to move', I said, still laughing at Tommo rubbing his ear.

There were definitely mixed feelings in the town. I had noticed that the people as a whole were a lot more stand-offish, compared to the people of Iraq. I found that these were a proud set of people; they didn't want handouts, but to work for it. My view of this place and Iraq were totally different. In Iraq the people want anything you had to offer and some things that weren't. We would hand out water to the people and kids; they would take a few sips then chuck it away. Here they weren't interested, they had got along just fine before us and they would after we had gone.

The patrol headed further north and it began to get quieter, a few kids and the odd local walking past but that was it. We had been on the ground a number of hours now and I made sure the blokes were taking on plenty of water. It seems simple when you're in a hot country to drink a lot of water but when you have things on your mind and a threat over your head you can easily not take on enough.

My boss wanted to get the commanders in for a brief or a face-to-face as it was called. He sent me an RV where to meet and I navigated the patrol through the tight and narrow streets towards it. At the north of the town just off the centre was a large fort overlooking Gereshk. I'm no historian but it had been there many years and the buildings around it probably just as long. These buildings we were now moving through seemed very primitive and surrounded by 6–8ft foot sand-coloured walls with doorways every 10–20m or so. Either side of the road there would be narrow drainage channels taking used water, piss and excrement away. It was an easy place to get disorientated as it all looked the same, a maze. I kept the blokes in a street just off the RV and moved forward to see the boss.

The RV was in a cross junction; my team held the right, Prig the left, Charlie's the front and members of the rover group the rear. Although we hardly ever saw the other teams it was important to know exactly where they are.

'Scotty, all good?' the boss asked on my approach towards him.

'Yeah, sorted', I replied. I nodded at the commanders gathered around the boss. 'Fellas'.

'Scotty, how you doing son?' Dan replied. 'Your blokes OK? Enough water and that?'

'Yeah, we'll manage mate.'

'OK, I reckon things were all good in the town and we are going to start making our way back to the FOB', the boss said. 'This will be the primary route that we'll take. Scotty, Prig, you two just keep doing your thing but be careful not to push out too much. If they are going to hit us my estimate would be around the old disused buildings on the outskirts and as we move out into the open.' We all nodded with acknowledgment. 'See you back at the FOB, lads' the boss finished with.

I moved back to the team and began moving north some 600m right of the main call sign. The outskirts of Gereshk was a maze of large compound walls; they did not seem to have much in them, I could only think that they were used for farm use at one point but they didn't have anything growing in them, they looked abandoned and disused, an ideal location for ambushing us with limited collateral damage and injury to fellow Afghan people. We kept our eyes peeled as we ventured out into the open plains to the north.

The QRF had come down with vehicles to support our move out. I stopped my team along the shade and protection of a walled compound right on the outskirts of town. The QRF – mostly the Patrols and machine guns guys – came forward and handed us some cold water from the back of their vehicles. Gaz and Dale, two lance jacks from Patrols, dished out some slaggings commenting on the fact that we looked ball bagged. There weren't far from the truth. We had been on the go some six hours, a long time with 70lbs worth of kit on your back and 45+ degree temperatures especially while still trying to acclimatize. As the primary team began to push to the west back to the FOB my team had to up the pace and move further out to the north as we were on the right side of this big pivot that was now swinging west. We moved past the main A1 road and continued on course over the open desert. The sun was at its strongest and the blokes including myself were feeling it. They was nothing around us now but desert wasteland and the FOB to our front in the distance that didn't seem to get any closer. I started think of the Carry On film *Carry On Follow That Camel* when they are tabbing across the desert. It was heads down and arses up as we tabbed it back to camp.

Thirty minutes after returning from patrol we had a hot debrief, an open parliament about what anyone had seen or heard while out on the ground. Mostly the commanders gave their feelings and I told of the nervousness of the ANP call sign that tried to push us down a certain route east of the town. The general feel from the town was that they had no interest of supporting the Taliban; however there were Taliban members in the town and they had a large influence on these citizens. One of the interpreters had even seen a truck full of Taliban moving through the primary team as they patrolled –the problem being they all looked the same and no weapons were seen. The Taliban take the views of the locals one of two ways, they were either with them or against them, there is no in between. As we found out later on in the tour, any local or village elder seen to be talking to us would pay the ultimate price. They would be killed. I did however have a large view on how things would turn out later. Talking that night with Dan, Prig, Charlie and the boss and Johnny we talked how the things had gone. Our first op had gone really well, the boys had grafted and the commander's movement and tactical SOP were spot on. However I mentioned that the more we moved into and patrolled this quiet area the more we would turn and piss off the local people. It did have an influence of Taliban but we would start to turn the locals against us constantly moving through their small towns in our large, heavily armed vehicles and with an aggressive look. I was proved right only weeks after our first patrol.

A typical airborne exercise undertaken before deploying
anywhere around the world. (©DPL)

Paras boarding a Chinook during a pre-op exercise. (©DPL)

Patrols take a break during a patrol down the back streets of Gereshk.
Note the narrow maze of streets.

Me next to a weapon-free zone sign. I don't think so!

The boss's wagon setting off on to another mission with Chalkie, Swanny and Dave on the gun. The other patrols can be seen to the rear.

The view through my sights of one of the other Patrols deep in Taliban country, June 2006.

My team in the Now Zad fort minutes before being ambushed and spending six hours fighting for our lives, 4 June 2006.

Ray's team pushing south along the channel track after our first contact. The open area to the front was where we were ambushed for the second time. Now Zad, 4 June 2006.

Dale moving towards the ruin during the contact in Now Zad in early June. Note the fire and smoke from tracer fire, plus the two gunners running around the ruins.

Me and Johnny having a face to face in a bit of cover after the first contact in Now Zad.

Some of Patrols near the ruin at Now Zad moments
before coming under contact from the wall.

Patrols under contact at Mutay, at rear left of the ruin facing east. The author is
firing over the bonnet in the centre, with Tommo running to man the .50 cal.

The magazines that took two Taliban 7.62 mm rounds. Bash holds the magazine that took two 7.62 mm rounds, saving his life.

Prig letting a young Afghan boy try his helmet on in the orchard field to the south of Sangin platoon house after the Op to get in and hold Sangin, June 2006.

ANA soldier ready for CAS-E-VAC after being shot
in the arm and leg, Sangin, June 2006.

Gaping hole in the FGS tower at Sangin platoon house that
killed Jabron Hashmi, Peter Thorpe and an interpreter.

Chapter 5

Sangin, IED and Bullshit

Days later 1 Platoon found itself back in Bastion on a five-day rotation of IRF. For five days at a time a platoon would be assigned to one of two Chinooks that we had in Bastion. If anything went wrong on the ground this IRF would respond to protect the medical team that would aid the engaged call sign and casualties, if any, on the ground. Our platoon was split down into two sections, one on immediate notice to move for the IRF at any one time and the other on one hour's notice to move – which was really rest. Giving that section time to wash and chill and air their feet.

It was at this point that I realised that the some of the Head Shed of the battalion were not taking this operational deployment seriously. The HQ elements were based at Bastion permanently. There was a main Ops room a couple of hundred metres from the 3 Para accommodation that was being built. This was known as the JOC, (joint operations centre) nicknamed The Joke by us 'other ranks' after some of the shit that began oozing out of it at irregular intervals. Me and a lot of the blokes believed at one stage that it was a secret opium den or glue sniffing party in the evenings, because at this point things were running smoothly and without incident in the south, so, as always the fuck-about started.

Patrols, A company and attachments of Support and HQ had been on the ground some four weeks now. The Bastion camp wasn't even built and water was a problem. Most of us hadn't been able to wash any of our kit yet, and with patrols of the town starting up plus everything else this was becoming a problem. We were issued three sets of desert combats but operating in these conditions we had been through the lot and it was stinking, not only that but lads soon started suffering with prickly heat and rashes. We could only wash at certain times of day in Bastion which meant if you were on IRF at these times you missed out, which most of us did. WO1 Bishop was RSM of 3 Para at the time although his nickname was 'Bang Bang Bish' for the amount of NDs he had during his time in the army, a man who, in my opinion and those of many of my other mates, should not have been the RSM especially at this critical time, and he began stamping his authority here in Bastion.

Simple things were going wrong and annoying us rather than just letting us settle in and get on with our job here. Other ranks, that is us, weren't allowed to cut around in our proud, maroon regimental T-shirts, giving our bodies time off from our sweat-stained shirts, and also it wasn't right and didn't show a good image in front of other units. Soldiers had to be cleanly shaven every day with sideburns at a correct level, bearing in mind that we didn't even have enough water to wash our combats and operational clothes and sometimes drink with. As nothing seemed to be happening just yet, members on IRF were now the general dogsbodies for Bish. The lads found ourselves stagging on The Joke; setting up the cookhouse before meals and cleaning afterwards; cleaning toilets, showers and the accommodation including the SNCO and Officers' tents and filling sandbags for the Joke's sangars. It was a joke and myself and the other fellas were snapping. Not only had Bish now extended that reaction time of the IRF from Immediate NTM to around 15–20 minutes NTM, but it also meant that the blokes deploying on the ground if an incident had occurred were now fatigued, dehydrated and generally licked before they even got suited up and boarded the Chinook. One last thing had really pissed me off and the blokes; even though we cleaned the SNCO and Officers' shithouses we weren't allowed to use them. We

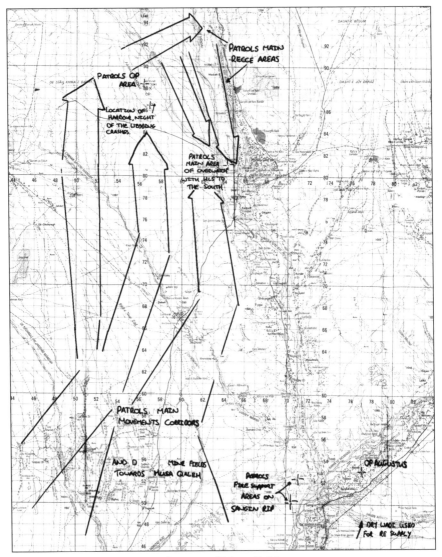

Sangin and Musa Qaleh

had to venture around 500m or even more across camp in search for one; this obviously caused problems with the reaction of the IRF but also a nightmare for the blokes who were coming down with the shits which we all had at some point. It's the last thing anyone needed when you're shitting through an eye of a needle to run around for a shithouse. It seemed that the RSM in particular was treating this like a typical Northern Ireland tour; and abusing the job of the IRF in particular as no one else was around. It would take a big incident to give these people a wake up call. That would not be long.

Days later we were back in Gereshk, finishing the IRF without much drama. I was just happy to be back away from the Head Shed, it was getting me down. Far too much bullshit for me. As part of 1 Platoon we again went through the rotation of guard, QRF and patrols (patrolling local areas and Gereshk town). We conducted a few patrols in and around the town but without incident, but threat warnings were beginning to come in.

Standing outside on a moonless night, 1 Platoon and Patrols were all ready kitted up for a patrol. The mission was to be dropped off silently by vehicles and move into the north-west of the town and gather intelligence on the night routine if any. Again we had a lot of kit to carry but without the baking sun on our backs it would be a little easier. Four out of the eight of my team were wearing NVGs. The boss wanted my team to lead and recce forward; as Patrols do most of their operating by night this wasn't a problem. I took my team to one side and in the pitch darkness went over the contact and CAS-E-VAC drills with my boys so it was fresh in everyone's mind just as the boss returned from an update. The Op had been sacked; apparently a large group of Taliban forces were waiting for us and another group closing in on the FOB for a possible ambush of the vehicles on our route out or on the camp itself.

'Let's get out there, then', one of the lads said in the darkness. All of us were itching to take the fight to them. The boss issued some QBOs and our job now was to get on the ground around the FOB itself and locate anything moving in. Already kitted up I gave my QBOs to the blokes and we headed off silently into the night on foot.

Using hand signals and whispers in each others' ears when halted to pass information, as it is amazing how noise travels through the night, we cracked on into the night. Even with NGVs it's hard to see in the desert if there isn't much ambient light. Our NVGs were pretty good, it was an optic that went over one eye on a helmet bracket or face mask. The face mask made you look a bit like Buffalo Bill in *Silence of the Lambs*, something my mate Joe D. had demonstrated on junior Brecon, getting caught by the instructors with a set of NGV on, his trousers round his ankles and his dick between his legs saying, 'I'm Buffalo Bill, you want to fuck me?' Classic! The downside is that it didn't give you 3D image like a double optic would. The NVG used ambient light from the moon and stars as well as lighting from towns and villages miles and miles away. Without these it struggled to light up the area in its green glow. At the time we only had one piece of TI equipment per team too; as the Patrols platoon, the 'eyes and ears' as we were known, we relied on this a lot to identify enemy positions and movement.

We still used the old Lion sight, good in its day but very outdated and bulky to carry and operate, but it was the best we had. There was a new Viper sight out that was an excellent piece of kit, however I hadn't seen it in Afghan yet.

My team had the area of ground from 12 o'clock through to 4 o'clock to cover while Charlie and Prig covered the others making a full perimeter around the camp. Our teams tried to cover as much as possible but with over 2ks between teams this would be difficult without the right equipment. I needed to find some good high ground so I could look over my area but without silhouetting my team at the same time —easier said than done in this quite flat and open ground.

After further map studies and directing of the patrol I found a suitable but not fantastic area to position ourselves: just in front of a small wadi which would act as my escape route if things went wrong. What I was worried about was the local tribe protection that were around the FOB; we were around 800m from one of those tower positions and a track that ran north-west to another compound and tower around 1.5ks to my left. If these mistook us for Taliban then we would be in a blue on blue (friendly fire) situation. I didn't trust these anyway and they could easily be allowing Taliban through and passing on information to them. We had previously agreed that any blue on blue situation, if we were taking close incoming and it was more than one burst or warning shot, we would have to return fire and go into our SOP and contact drills. We weren't going to sit there and take casualties or worse KIAs even if they were on our side. PF had almost lost blokes before in one of these situations – we didn't plan on doing so, and we still weren't 100 per cent happy that these were on our side. As I mentioned, one day they are, the next they may not be. We patrolled from position to position for another few hours; every couple of hundred metres we would get down and listen for possible moment in the pitch black but there was nothing, and before daybreak we patrolled silently back in to camp and to our beds.

In the time we were in Gereshk we only had one incident: 2 platoon were on the outskirts of the town to the north, near the abandoned compounds. They had been dropped off by the QRF and had patrolled some of the town. As they RV with the QRF vehicles on the north-west which were taking them back to camp, two large bursts of heavy machine gun fire pasted between the vehicles from the direction of the disused compounds. Instinctively 2 Platoon returned fire at the direction of the gunfire but failing to identify a firing point ceased fire and pulled back to the FOB. It was at this point I knew things in Afghan were going to turn noisy. Over the last few weeks of patrolling I believed that they had been watching us carefully – how we moved, our drill and skills on the ground and if we were setting patterns. Now they had set a shoot and scoot to watch our reaction drills under fire. They, like us, were trying to gain as much intelligence as they could on their new enemy.

The last few days up in Gereshk we were on constant standby, we thought we could well be getting sent up to FOB Robinson to help out our US partners in the Sangin valley: the last few nights they had been under constant attack. FOB Robinson was just outside of the town of Sangin. It sat on the south east of the town some 7ks away from the centre and the Taliban had been attacking the camp under the cover of darkness almost every night in the last week. Every night between 19:00 and 03:00hrs we got the call to stand to. The lights would go on and it would be a tornado of mayhem until things calmed down again and the mission canned. All our kit was good to go so it would only take minutes to get sorted and head down to the heli pad and get a G2 update on the situation. However the first of these crash outs was a bit of a flap for all concerned. Most of the GPMG ammo had been boxed and stored away as there wasn't much of it in Gereshk, so that needed to be collected, broken down and dished out to the gunners; radios had been swapped between teams and had to be found, maps were still in short supply and commanders searched to get correct mapping. This was a lesson learnt. My lads in our tent would put the CD player on as a priority every time we called crashed out. Normally *Bad Moon Rising*. I thought this was quite appropriate and it chilled us out a bit, so it became the Patrols song any time we got crashed out. Unfortunately the Chinooks never took off and for Patrols and A Company Sangin would have to wait.

News came in that C Company had arrived in theatre, and they were heading straight to FOB Price and taking over the A Company group. We would be heading back to Bastion. It was also time for my team to leave A Company and go back to Patrols platoon. Our WMIKS had turned up and Patrols platoon could now become a proper platoon again and begin mounting route recces north of Bastion. The C Company boys turned up and were keen to get all the intelligence on the town and surrounding areas.

'You're a little late lads, the job's done', an A Company tom said as they arrived.

'Yeah it's about time you lot fucking turned up!' the Patrols boys joked. It was always the way when you turned up later than the boys already on the ground. B Company however was still in the UK.

Arriving back in Bastion I was surprised to see how the camp had come on. The cookhouse and living accommodation was up but not so much ready. Most of the toilets were still broke and nearly all of the air-con units weren't working properly too, which was handy as it was 45 degrees plus and moving up fast as the summer approached. But giving them their dues, it was taking shape and most of our stores and equipment had arrived or was on its way. At least we could get our grips out of the ISO containers and set up our bed spaces to make it our home for the next five months.

Patrols were now busy; our WMIKS were in shit state from the move and they needed to be fully operational within days as the CO wanted us on the ground. I too wanted to be back on the ground, that's what we were here for and the more we were sat around shaking our dicks the more bullshit came out from the higher ranks. So if we weren't jacking up our WMIKS we were on the range outside camp test firing the .50 heavy machine guns which seemed to be experiencing problems. They were fine before we left. The .50 were having stoppages all the time and we could not pin-point the fault as we only had a small amount of .50mm ammunition, so obviously a very small amount of it was used for test firing: nowhere near enough to fully test the weapons since they arrived here in Afghan. We passed this up, complaining that we needed more ammunition, especially .50 Cal, more to test fire properly and rectify the issues but also more to take out on the ground. The experience we all had in Patrols told us that if we were ambushed we would need a lot more ammo than this, four or five boxes of 100 rounds per box per gun was a joke. It wouldn't last ten minutes in a fire fight. The 9mm pistols were becoming a problem too; there were only a small amount in country and the high-ranking officers and NCOs in the stores and desk jobs had taken them as they didn't want to carry their longs around all day. For us the drivers were the main priority to have a short as it would be impossible to fire a long whilst driving. If we got caught up in the narrow streets a driver could not operate anything but a short in these close conditions. It seemed that it was just a massive challenge to get anything: spare kit and equipment for the wagons, swing arms for the GPMGs and ammunition of course. One thing that had come in was ballistic matting. As the WMIK had no armour this ballistic matting would give us a small amount of protection. It wasn't much but better than nothing. Still not happy with the ammunition and the working of the .50 Cal we were to be sent on the ground, it would take a few life-threatening encounters to get someone to sort this out.

The WMIKS were adjusted for our personal needs, adding extra pieces of equipment and stripping other bits. We taped up all the lights to stop reflection as we don't use lights even at night, it's all done off NVG. Like I mentioned before, they had kit and equipment everywhere. At this time we had around 800 rounds for the GPMG and 400 or 500 for the .50 –not a great deal. We spent all day in the sun arranging the kit so it was in the best position; all of us liked things in different places like our GPS system, ammo and other personal things and had our own way of doing things. Water was the next thing, the amount of water we would carry depending on the task although we always aimed off and took a little more. For a mission lasting a few days we would carry around six boxes of water plus two jerry cans, for a two week mission around 12–14 boxes of water which takes up a lot of room in the back. Later on in the tour us Patrols found ourselves on the ground between 10 and 21 days at any one time, with or without a re-supply. The .50 Cals and GPMGs always went on last along with our bergens that held all the necessary kit like a sleeping bag, poncho, week's worth of food, spare clothing and OP kit, etc, in case we had to tab in to an OP on foot or bug out from the vehicles. That's if we had time to get them, if not we had grab bags which held important pieces of kit like maps, radios, a small amount of water, night and TI sights and extra ammo which were always with arm's reach. This was enough kit to last 24hrs or more. We also took two jerry cans of fuel just in case, giving the WMIK's an extra 40-50 litres of diesel, providing us with even more patrol range on the ground. The vehicles were very heavy now and we hadn't fully tested the WMIK's abilities in the Afghanistan terrain, and with this load it would put a lot more strain on the vehicles.

Within days we received our first orders. Our mission was to find and prove routes to the north and south of the A1 heading east to Gereshk. Having only conducted foot patrols around the Gereshk area we had no real idea of what the terrain was like to and from Gereshk, but that was one of our jobs. The night before we moved out I sat in the cookhouse, brew in hand and planned a route, looking closely at the maps that weren't very detailed at a scale of 1:100,000. The ground around Bastion looked flat and from what I had seen from the ranges while test firing it was just that. To the north-east it looked higher with a lot of small but steep features, the south east flat but with a lot of small wadi systems and farm areas. We had decided to keep south of the A1 road on the route out, and north on the route back in to Bastion.

The Battle group was still not fully operational. The 7 RHA were getting ready to move to FOB Robinson helping the Yanks when they needed artillery as they patrolled around Sangin, and more importantly to stop the camp being overrun which had looked close to happening a few times. A Company were now training in Bastion and had taken on the role of Ops 1 which meant that any mission would have A Company as the main effort. C Company now had the job of holding Gereshk while B Company was due to deploy very soon. Until that happened the battalion were limited on what it could do.

It was still dark as we woke and loaded our vehicles with the remaining bits of kit. We had requested ISO containers so we could lock the WMIKs up on a night like a mini garage and therefore have the wagons almost ready to drive straight out. Until more came in this could not happen, so till then once the vehicles had anything like ammo on board the 28 of us in Patrols would take turns to stag on our WMIKs until we were ready to go out, something we could have done without before an Op. After the usual final brief by the boss, Swanny, we mounted up and began heading for the front gate.

Moving out into the open we changed the formation of the patrol best suited for the ground, as this was open terrain and our mission to find good routes to Gereshk for ourselves and others we spread out into arrowhead formation, ground dictating. On the big open plains we could afford to push out a little more as long as we kept in range of our weapon systems enabling us to support each other. Any more and the teams could not mutually support one another.

We started moving from the flat open ground to the steep hilly features among the wadis. The WMIKs handled the ground well and our patrol techniques came together in a very short space of time. The ground was hard, covered with fist-sized rocks and as we ventured into higher ground, the slopes were steeper and tight to navigate with more small wadis passing through them —easy for our WMIKs but impossible for larger vehicles and re-supply convoys to cross and pass through. We decided to push further south off the high ground and into the flatter open area but this gave us a few other problems. Really we wanted to keep away from any habitation like the small local farms. The ground around these areas were ploughed fields, a mixture of green and straw coloured plants which they used to grow – I can only presume poppies (opium poppy fields). There were also small buildings that weren't even marked on the maps, these we plotted as it could prove important for patrols moving around the area.

My team pushed slowly over the hard terrain covering the left flank of the patrol. I directed Lee over a piece of ground with Johnny following behind off to my rear left. Breaking the horizon I came face to face with an old man about 20m to our front right, we were both surprised to see each other I think. He definitely wasn't expecting us. Looking behind him I could see two black tents, obviously his home. We slowly pressed on past him giving him a little wave and getting one in return. An old woman and small child were watching from the small opening of the tent. It's amazing how people still live like this although it was probably in better condition than some of the houses we had passed. The women and child were taking a sly look at who these strangers were, the old man saw this and began shouting and waving his arm as if to get them back in the tent and they soon did.

Muslims have laws strange to us. I found from country to country things change in different ways. With the influence of westerners, especially the Americans, countries like Kuwait and Oman and small parts of Jordan and other countries have changed a lot from the traditional Muslim ways and have brought in this new western style. Afghanistan is probably the strongest in its beliefs I would think. Back in England before deploying we were briefed on typical Muslim greetings and ways of acting so not to upset their beliefs and religion. One of these was not to make eye contact, talk with or touch any Muslim women. It was a big no-no. This is why we would see women running away as we approached them or in this case the old man shouting at his wife or daughter to get inside and out of sight. This puts a whole new meaning to the old expression 'lock up your wives and daughters the Paras are on the piss'. On being told this back in the UK I was overcome with rage. From my experiences of Iraq this was the same there, however it wound me up as the people of Iraq would stare, touch and make comments about the young female medics and RMP girls who would accompany us on some of the patrols. 'One rule for one and one rule for another' sprang to mind.

Other big insults would include not talking to the village elder when entering a settlement. Talking to a younger member would upset a lot of people and only our elder could speak to their elder. In Afghan most older men had beards: a sign of wisdom, age and experience. They looked down on us as we were clean-shaven, or at least some of the time, and as we were mostly young lads – even our boss was only in his late twenties. Another reason why I didn't like this shaving on Operations rule especially if we were going back on the ground. There were a lot of other small rules that we had to try and keep to in order to keep these at present friendly locals friendly, like not showing them the soles of our feet which were in contact with the ground, this in their eyes was dirty and furthest away from their god Allah. However I didn't really give a fuck about keeping some of these people onside with their laws, it's not as if they give a flying fuck about our law back in the UK. They can sit in the streets of London and burn our British flag and get away with it.

On the map we had planned to move between two small settlements, but as we patrolled through we soon realised that there was no real gap as far as the farms and fields were concerned, it all joined together. This slowed our movement massively and due to large ditches and ploughed fields we were channelled on their tracks to get through the farmlands, this took our patrol very close to the buildings which I wasn't too happy about and also made the patrol vulnerable as it closed us down into single file at a slow pace.

Breaking back into the open was a relief and we soon found ourselves looking at the watchtower of FOB Price just visible above the horizon. We had one last obstacle to cross before getting into Gereshk: a large wadi which sat between us and the camp about 400m in width. We sat on the edge of this big wadi and scanned the ground ahead; the A1 was visible around 500m to our front left. Large pillar foundations held up the road across the wadi. In the wadi there were three vehicles sitting with people moving around on the wadi floor. It didn't seem that they would cause any threat and looked as if they were clearing and marking something. We began to patrol down and then it became obvious what it was that they were doing, clearing the wadi of mines: it was a mine clearance team. I watched as Ray lead the convoy through, there was a lane set out with coloured poles on a gravel track that ran across towards these men.

'The route looks clear', Ray said over the radio. Well you'll find out soon enough, I thought.

'Yeah, fuck going through that first!' Lee joked. He was right. Just because it was marked didn't really mean this had been properly cleared. They just stood and watched as we drove through the wadi. It would be the last time we plot a route through this, I said to myself. If this group of mine clearance personnel hadn't been there or if this was a night patrol we would have gone straight through the minefield and suffered the same fate as the PF lads. We had requested maps with mined areas as Afghanistan is one of the most mined countries in the world after the invasion of the Russians, yet we were patrolling into these unknown and possibly mined areas. For us the threat of IEDs at this time was quite low because most of our movement was cross country, however the mine threat was now high. A young Pathfinder engineer had lost his leg in a mine blast a few weeks ago and two others also injured while out patrolling on vehicles identical to these. Who would be next? The thought was always in the back of our heads as we moved into virgin territory. It still is to this day as I escort clients from one target to the next. It also meant that we were losing blokes without exchanging rounds in a fire fight, another thing to worry about on top of the Taliban threat.

Moving into Gereshk we parked up the vehicles and cleaned up the guns, got ourselves fully scoffed and brewed; the lads managed to use the internet computers that they had just installed as there were still none in Bastion, before getting their heads down near the wagons for the night. While the blokes rested, me and Ray planned a route back, this time to the north of the A1.

Back at Bastion we had a hot debrief or Chinese parliament and discussed the routes we had used and the drills we had used on the ground. We had a set of patrol skills in place and SOP for our movement; however this was different terrain from the UK and even Oman. For us it was still a learning curve and a chance to adapt and improve our skills to this new terrain. Find out what was best for us and use it to our advantage.

The north was a much better route, maybe not for large convoys but definitely for us, the WMIKs could easily blend in and pass through the small wadis and re-entrants without incident and I explained to the other commanders that if we continued to move to the north when leaving Bastion then once we moved into the bedrocked dunes and out of sight it would be hard to know exactly where we would come out, which direction and which destination we were heading for. It had been good to get out and examine the local area, driving through the Afghanistan wilderness and finding our bearings and finding easier ways to get to and from Gereshk.

Within 24hrs another mission came up, this time the target was Now Zad. We knew some information on this place from what PF had told us, we also knew that the Gurkhas were helping to protect the camp (fort/ANP station). At this time the intelligence picture showed that it was all quiet up there and the Gurkhas hadn't been under any sort of threat so far. I knew this would change the more we interrupted and dominated their area as it was a well known Taliban stronghold.

Again we went through the usual pre-deployment checks and orders as well as map studies and planning. The next day saw the Patrols platoon moving from Bastion and towards the A1 and Now Zad.

It was a typical Afghan day, hot as hell. The convoy of seven WMIKs and one Pinzgauer opened up to and dominated the open ground. The A1 was in sight, a long black line of tarmac running from left to right in front of us breaking the flat desert. We had pushed left of Bastion as we left camp and avoided the ANP outstation that sat off the north side of the A1 only 4ks from camp: a position we were not told about which again could have lead to an incident involving a blue on blue fire fight. There seemed to be movement on the road ahead, large Afghan HGV and jingle trucks were using this to get to Bastion, Gereshk and down towards Lashkar Gah. Both flanking teams, me and Ray, moved up and controlled the road allowing the others to pass, not something that needed doing now but something we practised for when we had a bigger convoy with us and we would have to hold the traffic.

Leaving the A1 behind we made good speed over the open desert floor averaging around 100kph; it was that flat for the best part of 30mins. The mountain ranges were clearly visible now ahead of us, sticking up from the flat terrain like jagged teeth. I was quite taken aback by its amazing view on the horizon with the clear blue sky behind them. As we moved north the ground began to change, small wadis would appear from nowhere slowing us down to try and find a good route through. The desert has this effect. You can look out and think that it's all flat as far as the eye can see, you'll be very surprised that it isn't like that here. Although around here wasn't as bad as what we would come up against near Musa Qaleh in the north where we would come across huge wadis over 200m in depth but whether it was 100m or 5m if it was a sheer a drop then we would end up searching for a possible crossing point as he vehicles couldn't cross. We began moving between two sets of mountain ranges towards our destination. I guaranteed that the Taliban would be watching us. We were briefed that a lot of these groups lived in these mountains to avoid detection from the passing US spy planes and fighter jets.

Again I found that small settlements weren't marked on the map and if they were then it was inaccurate and most villages were a lot bigger and spread further across the land. We boxed round most of these small settlements and pressed on till we hit our FRV 7ks south of the town Now Zad; it had taken around 8 hours from Bastion. We harboured up in a small wadi, making our WMIKs disappear from level ground. For the last few hours we had patrolled up this 25–30k wide lane between the mountains which we still had on our east and west flanks. A small set of hills sat off to our right with a group of buildings gathered a further 1k away behind them. I could see a small hill up ahead; as I looked through my binoculars I could make out a sangar emplacement with a small flag flying from it. Looking at the map it became clear that this was the hill that sat just south of the town on its outskirts with the ANP machine gun post that engaged PF a few weeks previous. The boss got Comms with the Gurkhas in the fort and told them to be ready for us moving in. Moments later we got a reply. They had seen suspicious movement right of the hills in some outbuildings and they asked if we would check this out. What they classed as suspicious was a large gathering of males around one building. The Taliban would gather in one building to discuss tactics and possible missions. They were quite open about it and didn't really sneak around as all they were doing was talking and thought the US with all their laws wouldn't touch them. Once the Americans knew these people were connected to the Taliban and these chats would move into the planning of Taliban missions, and then the deaths of UK and US troops, as well as innocent civilians, the authorisation was given to hit these buildings with air strikes. However this was not in place yet and when it did later in the summer the Taliban began sitting children outside their meeting to stop the air strikes from happening, sneaky bastards.

After some short QBO it was agreed that the boss and Ray's team would move forward while mine and Steve's would dominate the high ground, which was the small group of hills to our east that overlooked the buildings, and use the four .50s and four GPMGs to cover the boss and Ray as they swept through onto the suspected target.

I led the four WMIKs to the north side of the hill that overlooked the group of buildings below it. I made my way through using the features to cover my moment so we wouldn't be seen till the last possible moment keeping the element of surprise. We stopped the vehicles short of the top and a few of us went forward to have a look over the ridge. It was near impossible to identify exactly what was going on down there; there was a group of people gathered but that's all we could make out. The boss and Ray came over the radio; they had broken the cover of the features and were now moving across the flat desert towards the objective. Our WMIKs broke the horizon slightly only showing our weapon systems known as 'turret up' effect, this minimised us as a target, keeping the engine block and tyres out of view, but allowed our weapons to fire. The group of people were around 900m away from us and I set the sights on the gun. All we waited for now was the sound of gunfire below or an order over the radio before we unleashed this firepower we had at our fingertips. The radio crackled into life and I aimed onto the centre of these people who were beginning to move away from the four WMIKs heading towards them.

'Stand down lads, it's just women and children', the boss said.

'Stand down lads just a group of tarts having a mothers meeting', I joked.

'Well is there any chance of getting some scoff?' Tomo said.

'Yeah I'm Hank Marvin', Lee butted in. We hadn't eaten all day which is the normal way of life for us while out on the ground. The sun was getting low in the sky and the heat beginning to cool as the four of us moved off the high ground and tagged on the rear of Ray and the boss's call sign as it drove past. We headed for the town a few ks north of us; I kept an eye on the ANP as we circled the hill and began to get channelled into the built-up area.

Our movement went into hard, fast and aggressive drills as we began pepper-potting forward a team at a time covering each other and our flanks as we sped through the town. This is the time you are most vulnerable. As we hit the main strip I saw the front right sangar position overlooking the street and the big steel gate to its right. Steve pushed through with Dale's wagon close behind; they blocked the road as we began moving into the fort complex.

Pulling in we moved to the rear of the main centre building of two floors. This was more like Afghan, this complex old fort looked full of history. We jumped off the WMIKs and orientated ourselves as we moved through the building and onto the rooftop to get a feel for the surrounding grounds. From the rooftop I got my first proper view of this old town of Now Zad; in the low sunset and with the mountains in the background it looked quite spectacular. We had been on the move well over 12 hours now, it was time to scoff up and rest for the night before making our way back to Bastion.

The next morning, we woke and had a quick brief before moving off; it had been a quiet night. Discussing the previous day's potential strike and the move back now to Bastion, we joked at the thought of brassing up the local women. 'That would have gone down as good as the sinking of the *Belgrano*' someone added. Yet weeks later an incident occurred that made me question that day.

Around midday on 11 June the sound of shouting broke this peaceful day in Bastion. It wasn't long before the Chinook helicopters were turning and burning and A Company plus attachments were kitted up and ready to jump on and support a US call sign that had been ambushed between Sangin and Musa Qaleh. The US convoy had been hit as they made their way through a small settlement. The two helis flew at top speed towards the troubled Yanks. As far as we knew they weren't getting engaged and the situation seemed under control but that could change the more these troops sat helpless on the ground and we needed to get their casualties out of there. The Chinooks put down off to a flank with the US providing as much protection as possible while the helis were vulnerable debussing our troops. In minutes the US injured were CAS-E-VAC out of there. Our troops covered the ground in a 360-degree arc and waited while the Yanks sorted their vehicles ready to pull out but they were having major problems. More bad news came in as after the helis took off The Joke informed the OC that no Chinooks would be coming back in tonight for a pick-up. As the sun began to sink some women walked past some of the outer positions, no more than 50m away, dressed in their female dish-dash clothing with their faces covered. The Yanks moved a Humvee up onto the high ground alongside our blokes. Chris W., a full screw, was the commander up there.

'Hey what you doing?' he said to one of the Yanks now standing sky lining himself with a tab in his mouth. 'You're in plain view, pull your vehicle back.'

'We are fine mate', the Yank replied.

'OK, suit yourself', Chris finished. Minutes later as the US soldier sat at the front wheel of his Humvee a massive explosion erupted. The US Humvee exploded into flames, it took a direct hit with an RPG and then everything went noisy around them. Heavy 7.62mm weapons started firing from the location from where the Afghan women had disappeared. Pete McKinley, a tom in A Company, ran forward under fire and dragged the injured Yank back and started first aid while rounds were smacking into the ground in front of him. Pete had kept the Yank alive with his quick initiative and first aid. The so-called women had really been Taliban dressed to disguise themselves to get as close as possible to some of the lads and the US troops and had set up a firing post right in front of their position. The two US soldiers were badly injured one losing an eye in the RPG strike which later resulted in around 10 Paras with small torches on their hands and knees looking for his eyeball later that night. After this incident, I thought that maybe that day in Now Zad the Taliban could have been using the same technique.

The move back to Bastion saw us making another route south through the mountains and back down the flat desert just north of Bastion and the A1. I had led the Patrols platoon tactically throughout the move, but 2k from the safety of the camp something happened making myself and my team act on a split-second instinct.

There had been a strong threat warning, about possible Taliban covert probing to gain intelligence on the Bastion camp defences, and depending on weakness a VBIED or suicide bomb on the camp itself. The main source of entry in my opinion would be to use one of hundreds of dumper trucks that continued moving in and out of the camp daily, bringing in gravel and getting rid of the loose sand and earth that had been dug up whilst the building of this large camp was still being undertaken. These trucks were everywhere and could get very close without even penetrating the camp wire, that's if they weren't already inside. Another option could be to drive directly into a convoy coming in or out of camp or whilst on or moving to the ranges just outside. This had already happened near the base at Lashkar Gah. A VBIED had tried to blow up the rear vehicle of the convoy while on a routine patrol; the rear gunner reacted by shooting the driver before he got too close.

Just 2k short and with Bastion over the next dune I watched as dumper trucks moved all around us, either heading towards the camp or to join the A1. One of these wagons was off to my forward left around 75m out. I did my usual mini

Hitler impression, standing up on my seat and clenching my fist with my arm extended, this is a technique used in the Middle East to stop traffic so the eight WMIKs could pass through, and it was widely used and 90 per cent the time worked.

It didn't stop. I guessed he just wasn't paying attention and I continued doing it while Lee hit his horn. At this point I thought he might have seen these eight tooled up Land Rovers 70m away from him in the open desert; it looked as if the wagon had stopped and so I jumped back into the commander's seat. The truck hadn't, it must have slowed and now looked to be accelerating, still off to our left. At 25m out it swung round and was heading towards the convoy at a 45 degree angle. I took a quick aim and fired a small burst of 7.62mm in front of his nose. This whole incident had escalated in no more than a few seconds and once the truck had traversed towards us, cutting down the distance between us, and my warning burst had failed, I had ran out of options. My gunner Tommo and I opened up on the truck stopping it dead in its tracks. After surrounding the vehicle, it turned out they were legit with the two workers very shook up as you can imagine. If it hadn't been for the large engine block stopping the rounds they would have both been killed. They were lucky.

This I found out was the easiest part of this accident. I had upset a lot of the Head Shed. As I had to explain, verbally and in writing, I was well within my right, for the protection of myself and the lads. If he didn't see us (8 large fighting Land Rovers) and hear the GPMGs 7.62mm warning shots being fired right in front of him, then they shouldn't allow blind, deaf locals driving heavy goods vehicles. Believe me you know when 7.62mm is whizzing past you and if it had been a suicide bomber and if it had got any closer then some ballistic matting wouldn't have done shit and they would be burying half of the Patrols platoon that day. I wasn't taking that chance and even if the locals had been killed by us then it was tough shit in my opinion, it would have been too late if we were blown to pieces and I expressed my anger to people, who yet again are not in that situation but having a go at us on the ground from behind a desk.

After having it out with the Head Shed and getting a slap on the wrist I wasn't flavour of the month; nothing new there. It was my belief that the RSM (Bish) already had an attitude with me and the feeling was more than mutual.

Late one afternoon we got a warning order for a mission to the Sangin valley. Settling down for orders the next day there was a buzz of excitement in the air. We had heard a lot about the Sangin valley and its town, and apart from 7 RHA being airlifted into the FOB Robinson, nobody had been moving in and around the area. That was till we were sent up there. The job was simple, to support and recce in front of an ANA and US call sign that were due to re-supply and replace the troops that had been in the area for the past few months. I'm not exactly sure where they were coming from but they were heading down the A1 to Gereshk from the west in the early morning hoping to cross before first light, move across country to a major track that ran north, then on this to the FOB south east of Sangin. Tactics vary between units among the British army and more so between nations.

Using main routes just seemed madness. At this time not many units were crossing the Gereshk Bridge as most US convoys were moving to and from Sangin from the south east direction, Lashkar Gah and Kandahar mostly, and therefore did not need to cross the Helmand River. However British troops would have to and that was why Gereshk became a necessary holding area. There still wasn't much traffic moving in these areas but we definitely weren't sticking on the main routes unless we absolutely had to. The convoy had their own protection made up of US armoured vehicles so Patrols would move through the small settlements and the open deserts to the west of their route which was the major threat area along the Helmand River. Once we had provided a screen we would then settle in the FOB before receiving more orders to conduct patrols around the Sangin area.

We woke very early that morning and prepped the wagons and weapons under head torches, it was already sticky hot. After a last minute brew and G2 update (intelligence report in case there was anything to be aware of in the area), we mounted the vehicles and lined up ready to move out. We had moved from Bastion to Gereshk the day before. My WMIK was first, and then Johnny followed by the boss's and a couple of supporting Pinzgauers holding a interpreter, medics, MFCs and engineers, then Ray, Gaz, Steve and then Dale. I fitted my Para lid (airborne helmet) and adjusted the night sight over my left eye. I always used my left as my right eye was my main eye used for looking through the weapon sights, plus I also needed to keep the night vision as it takes anything from 30–45 minutes to gain full night vision once infected by a light source.

We rolled out of camp and headed across the dark open ground. Light discipline was fully enforced; one glimmer of light would give away our position. I had spotted a route through the desert, between the tribal watchtowers to join the A1 as close to the edge of the town as possible. I thought they would be reluctant to place an IED anywhere that could cause injury to the local people so I used that to my advantage, plus limiting our movement on the road itself. I had no idea how long the convoy had been on the road and the distance they had to travel, but it doesn't take much for a Taliban dicker to pick them up and pass this information forward for an IED team to place one somewhere along the A1, the same tactics the insurgents used in Iraq. In the eyes of the Taliban the convoy were heading to one of two places, Gereshk FOB or a few ks further to the bridge crossing point. This is the reason I was keeping well away and joining the A1 as late as possible.

We slowly passed the towers undetected and came to the outskirts of the town, and again more outbuildings. I could see the A1 behind them sitting up on an embankment; the desert floor seemed to be a few metres below the A1 and the town making it darker than dark. I continued to push through and soon realised I had entered a huge open compound. There was no way through.

Bollocks, I thought, it was only when I got really close I could see the walls that had blended in with the embankment; even my driver could not see it, it was that dark. I turned the patrol around and headed back out and boxed around them. It was hard to identify things with the poor light but I still knew there would be a slagging in store for me later.

I jumped on to the A1 with the other WMIKs following behind, looking back into the desert it would have been impossible to have seen us coming with the dark backdrop of the desert. I looked up the A1 to the west to see a large convoy of lights coming down the road some several ks back.

'Well there's the Yanks', I joked. This was followed by someone singing the Christmas Coca-cola advert 'how many days are coming, how many days are coming'. They couldn't advertise themselves any more, to be honest. There were a few people around even in these early hours as we headed down the main road, small lights hanging off stalls and buildings lighting some of the road. We had definitely gained the element of surprise again by sneaking up and now we flew through the town at top speed to keep this. I pulled my torch out as it came clear just how much we were undetected when a few motorbikes and cars nearly ploughed into us. They nearly shit when I switched the torch on and they realised there was a heavily armed Land Rover screaming towards them with three angry paratroopers sitting on it.

Over the main bridge it was an option to debus and walk the vehicles through but due to the momentum and pitch blackness I just pressed on. It was almost as if we had a invisible cloak over us. On the east of the bridge there was two large towers, it was a ANP checkpoint controlling the movement over the bridge and a further two outposts further up the A1 heading north within the next 15ks. Passing the ANP at the bridge they looked at us in complete surprise, a quick wave and we had passed them and disappeared once more. The A1 running north just after the bridge and ANP was the most dangerous area of this VP. With disused outbuildings either side of it, it was a major choke point channelling vehicles into the bridge location from the north, a prime location for an IED and I was proved right as it became the major IED hotspot in the area some time later. An IED is an improvised explosive device, this could be anything from a couple of 105mm shells tied together with some P4 or it could be something much larger like 400lb of HE. We were fully aware of these from our experiences in Iraq; most were strong enough to destroy low level armoured vehicles. We had no armour at all so the risk to us was even greater; even a very quickly placed and poor IED would, in my opinion, have had devastating effects against us.

As it was still dark, our first time and considering the stealth in which we had got into the town I didn't want to fuck about debussing and looking for tracks and so we continued and soon passed without incident. However I brought it up later that we should never do that again. It was the first time we had used it and the first time in many weeks since other units had passed though but I knew that soon this would be the MSR for all convoys running to Sangin and further afield. We had taken our chances but next time we wouldn't be so fortunate. If other units wanted to set patterns and run that route then they could by all means, but I and the other lads were not.

Running north in single file I saw the ANP outstation on the high ground to my 2 o'clock position. It seemed quiet with no movement up there as I watched through my NGV but what I did not notice was the little guardbox at the side of the road until it was too late. The sky was starting to lighten but at ground level it was still really dark. About 50m out Lee saw it.

'What's that, Scotty?' I looked down the road and saw the box shaped guard hut no bigger than 6ft high and 2½ft in width with the shape of a figure next to it, I knew it was an ANP sentry, but our hearts missed a beat when I saw the shape moving into a kneeling position ready to take a shot. I pushed the GPMG round but it was too late for both me and the ANP, we were on top of him. I had obviously took him by surprise and then just as he reacted he must have seen the other vehicles speeding up behind me and shit himself. I know I probably would have. Jesus, I thought.

'That cunt was going to open fire', Lee said.

'Yeah same, fucking dickhead', I replied. 'All call signs watch out for the ANP sentry on our right side' I called over the radio.

'He's probably hiding in that box now', Lee joked. By the time we got to the other ANP station it was almost fully daylight. There was a small stream just in front of the station so we couldn't move off the road until we had passed this as the road was the only crossing over the stream. This was a large outpost and the furthest north position apart from the ANP in various towns that had their own ANP locations and due to this there was a lot of police presence here, four vehicles sat outside and two DShK (Dushka) heavy machine gun posts on top of the roof.

. We moved through the checkpoint and I pushed the convoy over the stream and began moving across country in a north-east direction; the light was coming thick and fast and once we had moved over the desert floor well out of sight of the ANP, and anything else for that matter, we set the WMIKs in all round defence, changed our weapons' sights and kit from night operations to day.

I began to relax a little now; the way I saw it the two biggest threats were the crossing point at Gereshk and moving into the FOB and around the Sangin area. That's not to say we wouldn't get hit anywhere in between but it wasn't as likely, as I could choose my own route. We started pushing out and began our clearance north; the boss had been given an update that the US and ANA were past the bridge and well on their way so we could crack on. Not only were we clearing the route and protecting the convoys' exposed left flank but we were also recceing dangerous and no-go areas, new routes, crossing points and anything else that came up.

The sun was already high and strong and we had learned that with it the extreme heat would kick in very early on. One good thing was the wind which cooled us slightly as we moved but once we went static we soon found it ridiculously hot especially with no overhead cover to shield us. Shemaghs were used a lot between the blokes. Shemaghs were the local Arab headdress and ideal for all seasons in the desert. If not then baseball caps and desert hats were worn to keep the sun off; if you didn't cover up then in a few days you would pay the price with sunburn and sunstroke. During the heat of the day and even more so in the summer our weapons got that hot that if you caught your arm on it then it would leave a burn mark. Sometime we had to wear gloves or at least keep our hands on the weapon to stop it from heating up along with the steering wheel and other pieces of kit that were heated by the sun.

The ground was a mixture of terrains, going from the flat bedrock and good going surface to soft sand, from soft sand to the slow and bumpy fields surrounding the small settlements to dried-up wadi beds and the steep hardened dunes. We kept as far away from the green zones (long grass and trees) as possible as this was ideal for ambushes. We were learning fast, we had no choice. Higher ground was often the better but exposed us for miles around, not exactly what we wanted. Moving between the dunes providing a covered route with harder ground but was hard on the vehicles. The green belt, river edges and around settlements being the worse as they were ideal ambush locations. On this route we had no choice, it had to been cleared and we were to attract the enemy's attention so as not to hit the convoy.

We kept well in front of the convoy; sometimes we could see them through the binoculars but mostly it was just a slight dust trail in the distance as they raced along the main desert track, using radios to keep in touch with one another. The patrol was taking forever, constantly stopping and starting. The US convoy were having technical problems therefore slowing our movement to push on: we couldn't afford to be too far away. We stopped just off a tack and we put the WMIKs in all round defence while we waited for the word of US and ANA to get themselves free after being stuck in soft sand several ks back.

Jay was Ray's gunner, a young small-framed lad with a high-pitched voice. He went behind the WMIK to have what we call a 'tactical shit' (when you have to go you have to go). One thing you have to get used to in the army and that's doing everything in front of each other, including curling one out. At 17 years old I never thought about this till my first exercise when I watched Nick W., a friend of mine, take a dump in the shit trench right by the platoon lines, in front of around 30 blokes scoffing up and he finished off by wiping shit all up his back; nice. Even with all the other vehicles and blokes around Jay tried to get a little privacy by leaning up against the WMIKs back end. Just as he hit the critical point Ray and Dog Head drove off a few metres leaving Jay out in the open still fully kitted up, helmet on finishing his duties with the rest of us chucking rocks at him.

By the time we closed on the FOB around 17 hours after moving from the dark surroundings of Gereshk the light was beginning to fade. Navigating for me was quite easy, I tried my best to box round any VP and use the ground to my advantage. Around 30ks north of Gereshk was a saddle-shaped feature in the middle of the open ground east of a town called Hyderabad, a well known Taliban stronghold. Hyderabad and the other small towns that hugged the Helmand River were in the flat regions with rich vegetation surrounding it. This tit-shaped hill stood out from miles around, good for navigation like I said but also an ideal dicking location for the Taliban to watch this open passageway between the river and the large mountain range on the far east. I used it to navigate but had to keep my distance too. I scanned my frontage as we got channelled into the southern part of Sangin. I lead the Patrols between the sparse farm buildings, the team covering each other as we moved and bounded forward until we reached FOB Robinson.

FOB Robinson was on the high ground overlooking the east of the town. On our approach the main entrance was up a steep hill around 200m high; to the right were a load of disused houses and outbuildings with narrow streets and then further desert, to the left barren open ground before dropping into the valley that we now sat in. Moving into the FOB we positioned the WMIKs up on the ramps along the outer walls: these were ramps to enable vehicles to fire over the walls. For the first time in 18–19 hours we could relax, with a chance to get some scoff and admin ourselves with the last of the remaining light.

Inside the FOB were two separate areas divided by the hesco walls; we stayed in the northern compound. We sat protecting the north and western arcs which was the main area of threat to the camp: they wanted our large .50 Cals over the walls. The 7 RHA lads sat to the rear, their 105mm artillery guns ready to drop shells on any Taliban advances. The centre held a building hosting the US military, officers and stores equipment. FOB Robinson was a basic set out, a camp from which operations could be mounted. As we settled into night routine the boss received further orders for a patrol tomorrow. We gathered round one of the WMIKs in the dark.

'Good effort there lads, it's been a long day. Tomorrow the CO wants us to move into the east of the town to set up a FUP for a US call sign that will patrol some of the town and then find and recce a number of routes into the town the following day', he said. 'However we are not to get that close, he does not want any contact with the enemy, any signs of a "come on" leading us into a possible ambush then we are to withdraw immediately.'

This was for a couple of reasons. One, we (the Battle group) were not fully up to strength and we had little supporting assets to back our platoon, and two, we again had limited air support, Apaches, to support us with their weapons, and definitely the more important reason, in case of CAS-E-VAC. Nobody was keen on doing anything without knowing that the IRT with the medical team was coming in to get us. This wasn't like the movies where helicopters come flying over the horizon to get you out and save the day. It's my belief that the RAF had four Chinooks in theatre for the whole of south Afghanistan. Later I heard it was seven but I think this was bollocks as one always seemed to be grounded for some reason and I never saw more than four at any one time. I believe it was like turning up at RAF Lyneham for a parachute descent, and the RAF turn round and say it was cancelled due to no airframes although we could see about ten parked on the tarmac, and they had brought the old cardboard cut-outs with them. So we believed anyway. If another Chinook was in Kandahar and the other two on a task and we took trauma casualties on a mission then basically we were fucked. We would be on our own, we could kiss goodbye to the golden hour. (It's estimated that if any major casualties were not back in a medical centre or surgery within an hour then your time was up.) Not exactly a warm feeling to think if things went tits up, we would be left to fend for ourselves and get ourselves out of there. I could not believe that in this day and age as part of the proud 16 Air

Assault Brigade and high tech army we only had a few Chinooks and if these couldn't fly or one got knocked out of the sky then the whole of the ground operations would come to a halt. That in my eyes was a fucking joke.

In Patrols we had always planned and trained for the worst case scenario as we mostly operated in front of the Battle group with little or no support but it did make you think, What if…?

We settled into our night in FOB Robinson and took turns to stag on during the night watching the ground between the camp and the Sangin town. Stag is where one team member watches the arcs we had been given while the others slept next to the WMIKs. When sleeping we always remained in our desert kit, weapons within arm's reach and belt kit either next to us or used as a pillar. The blokes were quite ball-bagged and even the few 107mm rockets that the Taliban fired just over our heads had trouble waking us; luckily these missed the walls by a few metres and continued to fly a good couple of hundred metres further south. As for any attack, we guessed that with our presence, the convoy of heavily armed vehicles that had moved into the FOB and the large 105mm artillery guns, they would leave it and have a couple of days off.

That morning, the boss gave us a set of orders for the mission ahead. In the early morning sun it was already close to 40 degrees; most of us kept our tops off to try and get some tan; the sun had one use I suppose before it would start burning you like an army chief with scoff. One thing had changed though, our mission. We were to push a little more into Sangin, hopefully trying to coax the Taliban into an engagement, this was a bit different from the old 'Don't get engaged'. The top brass wanted to know if there were any Taliban present and we were the guinea pigs I thought, laughing at the previous night's brief.

The boss asked Ray to plot a route and lead us around the east edges of town. Me, Steve, Ray and the boss looked more at the map and aerial photos for routes in. We could only see a few routes according to the map. We needed eyes on the ground to locate more and prove these ones we had marked from the maps. We packed our equipment, re-oiled the weapons and made sure our radios and vehicles were good to go before rolling out of the camp and down the steep hill. Apart from the personal weapons, longs and Minimi, seven .50 Cal machine guns and seven GPMGs – which was a hell of a lot of firepower to have on board – we also had the three 105mm artillery guns assigned to us as we were the only patrol on the ground.

A few of us in the platoon, myself included, were trained in calling in artillery, important and essential when forward of all other troops and with limited support; artillery was all we would have. We also had two main FAC and FOO with us, their main jobs were to co-ordinate fast air and artillery if we needed it. However we were also trained just in case a team was cut off, operating ahead or on its own tasking away from the FOO and FAC.

Bomb-bursting out of the camp and into the open terrain our eyes were peeled, watching for any glimmer of light representing a sight of a weapon or binoculars. We kept the spacing and avoided bunching up. Ray led us out to the north-east away from the town, passing through a few small farm buildings before changing direction and heading north-west. Movement was sometimes slow and hard going through the farmland. As Sangin was such a dodgy environment we were operating under war fighting rules of engagement: something that had not been granted since 2003 in Iraq. We moved through open ground to the north-east of the FOB early that morning before punching through a few small re-entrants and small valleys that ran east-north-east towards Sangin town. Again we tried to mask our movement as best we could, dog-legging to and from different valleys. We commanders had carried out a map study the previous night and morning and had pin-pointed a decent position on the map in which to carry out our task, however we all knew from years of experience that in reality things are never quite as easy as that. The ground wasn't as good, and it took several small team recces pushing further in to locate a better FUP and overwatch position.

A few hours later we found a suitable position. The FUP itself was in a small valley between a few high features, the entrance and certain parts of the high ground protected by our different Patrol teams, protecting it from all angles. The overwatch position was on a forward facing spur looking north-west into town with the boss's platoon HQ behind just out of view. I didn't think it was too wise to dominate this ground too early. For us to push up and overwatch the town was a double-edged weapon. The Taliban and everyone else would see us, static and vulnerable on the high ground. I could understand moving into this location once the US convoy/patrol had moved through but we had compromised ourselves and the FUP in the dead ground to our south-east if we sat here for several hours, and as far as overlooking the ground went we couldn't really see that much. The town was almost totally made up of one-storey buildings and sunk into the low lands. Being all one level makes it harder to distinguish and locate anything in the town giving reference points for fire support.

My team pushed up to a valley entrance, leaving the vehicles in dead ground and pushing to the ridge on foot. I knew this position was close to the edge of town but it was a little too close for comfort during daylight hours with outbuildings only 75m away. The only thing keeping us apart was the sand-coloured hills that we now held. We tried to keep as low a profile as possible as it would be several hours before the Yanks came through us and moved into town. The area was now secure but we now had the job of recceing a route in to the FUP. My team was tasked with this as the others held their different areas of responsibility and marked up DF positions in case of attack.

I moved to the platoon HQ for a face-to-face with the boss. He gave me a grid where I would meet our US partners and then I would lead them here to the FUP. Time was ticking to recce the area and due to moving out as a single team our movement had become slow. When moving as a large group we could afford to move at a steady pace, this was known as Green. Moving through a more hostile area like this it moved into Amber and Red. Teams moved forward and secured the ground and allowed another team to push through, bound up to another piece of ground and secure that, a leapfrog method. If any team got hit then hopefully the team static could provide fire to enable the team in front to get out of the shit or vice versa from behind or left and right. Moving as a team was the same only a little more dangerous with only one vehicle supporting the other.

My WMIK and Bradder's bounced from valley to valley and ground to ground. After a few hours of moving around I had a few options in which to bring the US fighting column through. I now had to prove the route and make sure it was good. After patrolling this, boxing round farm areas and avoiding other inhabitants I briefed the boss on my intended route. It was good, completely isolated from any local areas and meant the convoy would be undetected passing into the FUP. With only a little time before the convoy reached the RV I had to push on and secure that area but I would take another route to get there, I didn't want my primary route over-used, all it would take is a vehicle or goat herder to pass through and compromise it.

I moved my team into a small re-entrant overwatching the RV and waited five minutes before the given time to move out. I didn't like sitting out in the open with just my two WMIKs. In minutes Luke saw the dust clouds of the convoy heading towards us. Like most American troops they had come out of FOB Robinson and took the main track all the way to this allotted RV. If it had been up to them they would have just rolled straight through the town on the main road – something they did once they left our FUP. I had a quick face-to-face with their commander, a typical gung ho Yank.

'Hi I'm Scotty', I said introducing myself.

'What in the hell you mean, Scotty? What in the hell does that mean?' the Yank replied.

Here we go again, I thought.

'Just follow us, we haven't got much time', I said as I pushed back up the route towards our platoon HQ and FUP. I moved the convoy of Humvees into the FUP, for now this was their secure location. A chance to carry out some final battle prep, if they did that type of stuff; they were more interested in opening cans of coke, hi-fiveing each other and gobbing off about how 'warry' they all were. I pushed their commander up to our boss before moving back to their convoy.

There were three Brit lads with them; I went over to have a chat to them, even though they were Crap Hats I though I'd try and be nice. I should have known better. Officers, not my favourite set of people.

The US commander came back down.

'Hey, I'm moving in 10 minutes, which way is the best way?' he said.

I pointed out different entry locations and left him to brief his men. On hearing his route I had a bit of a giggle; his route was just as I had thought, taking one of the main routes straight through town. Crack on, I thought.

We moved up on the overwatch position as they were pushing into town and protected them as much as possible. Within 30 minutes we were well out of weapons' range and view, there was nothing else we could do to help them. Just as we began to pull out I heard a lot of small arms firing from the direction of Sangin but no tracer to locate the position or anything over the radio asking for assistance so we continued to pull back to the FOB.

The next day we moved back into the Sangin area, taking a different route closer to town but further north. As we moved there was a large feature on our left between us and the town. Our interpreter had picked up communications between locals in the area within the short distance we had come. We had hand held scanners which we could tune in and listen to conversations via mobiles and insecure hand held radios - our interpreter would then translate it for us. The latter was the main Taliban method of communicating with one another. They had picked up our trail and were watching us as we picked our way through. I and the blokes were chuffed with that; at least they knew that they could pull the trigger if the shit went down knowing fine well there were Taliban targets out there.

We had patrolled down past the feature and had come to a small valley to our left dividing the two high features; the feature on the right of the valley curved round and was directly in front of us. One of the blokes had spotted something up on the high ground to our front.

'What you got?' the boss barked over the radio.

'Not sure, possible dicker in the rocks', the voice said. We pushed the teams out as best we could including teams on the high ground to our left; the possible dicker on the hill was around 1200m away. Just then I saw him among a few rocks, definitely a male, there was no other reason to be up there apart from relaying information on us. Everyone else we had passed just carried on working or walking past; yes they took a bit of interest but they weren't hiding like this bloke, this was definitely a dicker or possible Taliban MFC. We didn't take any chances, within minutes two rounds from the 105mm came screaming over our heads.

'Sort by 100m', I said. The next few were spot on only 50–75m from him, that got him running and the radio traffic stopped. We backed out of this channelled and now compromised area and moved into outskirts of the town further north. The routes were very channelled and narrow, large enough for one vehicle in width. Everywhere I had been in south Afghanistan so far was like this once in an area of habitation: a maze of desert tracks between old sand-coloured walls and buildings, quiet.

After several hours' recceing possible entry locations the only route we could see was a dry wadi bed, it sat almost dead centre to the town running in from the east all the way through the centre and onto the Helmand River on the western edge of town, although we could not see this far with the naked eye. It was around 300m across; the down side obviously was we would be fully exposed. Wadis are dry river beds and so normally have shingle and stony surfaces and deep banks either side. This was no exception. The edges of the town followed the wadi along until it hit a small bridge at the centre of town some 600–700m from our overwatch location. The buildings and high compound wall overlooking the wadi made this route extremely venerable with no escape routes – ideal killing ground for an ambush in my eyes – but again the only main route for convoys of large vehicles to gain access to the town. In my estimation as long as they were plenty of supporting troops, foot and mobile, top cover up it could be used, and it was at a later date.

As we recced entry and exit routes into the wadi, as the banks either side were mostly steep and impossible to negotiate, the support vehicle holding the FAC, medic and engineers etc. got stuck, this resulted in burning out the clutch while trying to free it. This was not a good place to be stuck; we were on the southern edge of the wadi bank at the back of an old single-storey farm building 600m from the main town. All the fields around the farm building to our rear were freshly harvested; several large bundles of poppies were in different areas of the farm complex. I pushed my team out to protect the northern flank; my team had very little cover exposed on the wadi floor just off one of the fields. My team watched the walls some 500m to our front while the other teams moved into position to protect the stranded vehicle. I jumped off the WMIK and moved to the pile of poppies and picked a poppy up. I thought it strange that this simple thing was the main source of producing heroin. These poppy fields were very important for the Taliban. Afghanistan was the biggest suppliers of heroin in the world; over 80% of the world's supply came from Afghan. The Taliban controlled these fields, the movement and change from plant to drug. Without this, their income would be seriously undermined. Before we left England we had been told in simple terms that our job was to rid the country of Taliban and take and control the poppy fields. As we arrived in Afghanistan this had changed, realising that to do that, taking away the farmers' only income, would only turn the locals against us: not exactly what we wanted.

The vehicle was totally U/S. We now had a few options; first we could blow it and leave it here, or two, try and pull it out and tow it back to FOB Robinson. The second choice was a non-starter, it wasn't going anywhere and this was not the place to be towing a vehicle around in anyway. The boss got Comms back to The Joke and advised them of our problem and intentions. The vehicle was being stripped of equipment and set with explosives as he spoke, while the rest of us held our ground and watched our arcs. The way we saw it the wagon was a replaceable item, blowing it seemed the only option. However The Joke told the boss that this would not happen. A helicopter was coming in to pick it up. I was now at the boss's WMIK finding out what was going on.

'Somebody needs to get gripped up there', Chalky replied. Chalky was the boss's driver, a L/Cpl and the main signaller for the Patrols platoon. We often joked that he would sort the boss's outrageous admin for him and was generally Swanny's bat boy, a little joke we had going on the boss.

The heli wasn't due in for a good while, so we took off the P4 explosives and rigged the vehicle with the underslung netting to enable the heli to carry the vehicle under her belly. So for now we were sitting ducks, still on the outskirts of town and now a large static target, not something any of us were pleased about. We now risked the lives of the blokes to protect a downed vehicle for an extraction that could be replaced back at Bastion.

The same mistake happened on 11 June where the British forces lost their first bloke, Captain Jim Philippson of the 7 RHA. When I later heard the facts I was disgusted with what had happened. A UAV had gone down west of Sangin town and over the Helmand River. Command had decided to send a mix-and-matched force out into a Taliban stronghold from FOB Robinson to recover it. It was no job for these people, as most were not proper infantrymen - they were artillery and signallers. And why risk lives for a piece of kit that could have easily been blown up by Apache helicopter and replaced, just like the vehicle we had now surrounded? Listening to more of the story, I was shocked to learn that the troops had used the local river boat to cross the Helmand River and also to return - talk about channelling themselves and setting a pattern! This was why they were ambushed as they returned back to the eastern back on the return boat journey. As I said before, the Taliban were switched-on people, they knew that a QRF rescue team would be sent out to help them and they could only come from FOB Robinson. Captain Jim Philippson was killed as he led the rescue party out of FOB Robinson in a separate ambush they had placed for the QRF. This was the first of many a sad day for the battle group here in south Afghanistan.

Sitting around watching the buildings to our front I was just waiting to see a couple of shooters popping up. I briefed the team to keep alert; the Taliban would definitely be planning something, to think they wouldn't would be foolish. I just hoped the CH47 got here first. This was a major stronghold and we were now pissing around in their back yard. Just as the light started to fade we received information that the Chinook was coming in. The interpreter also picked Comms between Taliban leaders, they were trying to confirm exactly where we were, how many of us there were, and how and where to get in and set up an ambush. Time wasn't on our side and neither was light. With the Chinook inbound this was a delicate moment.

'OK the obvious is figures two, lads', the Boss said over the radio. (Obvious because we all knew what was coming but still did not want to give anything away over the radio in case the Taliban were listening in like we were with them.) It looked like the Chinook had brought in support too; two Apache attack aircraft had escorted it here and were now hovering around 1000ft above us like vultures watching for prey. I felt a little better now. We had practised calling these strike aircraft in onto mock enemy positions back in Oman. The firepower was impressive; however, the accuracy was not. As the build up training went on they began to improve and zero their weapon system much to the slaggings of us lot every time they missed.

'Useless fuckers', one of the lads said as I began re-thinking a story back in Oman earlier that year. Lying down in the rocks in the darkness we couldn't even see the helicopters; it was down to night vision goggles and lighting the target up with an IR laser as we practised calling the Apaches onto their targets.

'What was wrong with that?' one of the RAF safety officers said behind us after the Apache turned off after its attack run.

'Oh fucking mega if I called them in on that target, but they were supposed to be hitting target 3500m north of it', one of our boys said. We all fell apart laughing in the darkness with the RAF safety staff saying nothing.

The Chinook came in over the top of my team, settled down and quickly dropped off the IRT; don't know why when we had seven WMIKs sitting out with heavy weapons but I guessed the RAF thought having another eight soldiers with rifles would be safer. The three helicopters circled until they got the green light to pick them up. Within a few more minutes the Chinook picked up the team and the Pinz and lifted up. The vehicle swung underneath the CH47 then disappeared into the fading light. I believe if it hadn't been for the Apaches above then we would have been hit that day.

Us Patrols began moving off almost immediately after the Chinook took off, using the presence of the Apaches to mask our movement out and back as far as possible till the sky fell completely dark. We had managed to get back to our old overwatch position from the previous day; we had been around this ground a lot in those few hours so even at night we were confident in moving around here and knew some of the routes through the small hills and valleys. The only things we was nervous about were the obvious: Taliban moving in to cut us off and that ANA that had moved into this area earlier on. As we moved in complete darkness we could be mistaken as a Taliban fighting patrol. We switched to night optics and night patrol skills and slowly patrolled with caution through the tight valleys. We had been warned not to go out or patrol at night as it was far too dangerous; we had little choice now and to be honest preferred it. Patrols were used to operating in the dark, for us it was normal and probably a lot safer although very dangerous, and from past experience on exercises could pass our enemy within metres of each other.

It was a tense few hours on the journey back and the strain of the day began to take its toll on us all. Our eyes under the strain of the NVG were beginning to play tricks on us, thinking a rock on a hill top was a Taliban fighter in a fire position or suchlike. We had to be completely certain on what things were; if we fired into the open we were giving away our position, into the town a chance of hitting civilians and back towards the camp a chance of a blue on blue. A few kilometres out from the FOB we hit a built-up area, derelict but highly dangerous and being so close to the FOB an ideal ambush area for late returning patrols or attacks on camp.

We crept down the small streets completely channelled, dark and eerie still. I didn't like this at all and I wasn't the only one. Ray who led our patrol whispered into the radio that he was out of the edge of the built-up area and close to the camp entrance with its eastern wall on his right.

Crack, Crack, Crack!

The night sky lit up with red tracer in front of us. I gripped the pistol grip of my GPMG and pushed my shoulder into the stock expecting the whole world to erupt at any second.

'Boss, the Afghan sangar guards have fired warning shots at us', Ray said.

'OK, push forward', the boss said, 'wait one I'm putting out blue light.' We all did the same; this was to indicate we were friendly troops although we didn't expect the Afghan soldiers to know this.

'Push forward', the boss snapped.

'Boss I've got a bloke pointing an RPG at me so get fucked', Ray snapped back. This had now turned into a Mexican stand-off until they realised who we were. After a few heart-pumping minutes we were allowed through into the safety of the camp. Back in the FOB I and some of the other lads had a bit of a joke about this although one stray round or Ray engaging would have caused a major fire fight. It had been a long couple of days and I think we had been quite lucky not to have been hit whilst out on patrol or coming back into camp, yet we all felt that we could stay here a little longer.

All of the Patrols were keen to stop up here, we had no accommodation and were living by our vehicles but there was definitely more scope for action and decent jobs to be done, and that was proved in the last few days. Back in Bastion was the opposite with more room for bullshit in and around the Head Shed.

The boss was told to bring the Patrols back to Bastion and await further orders, this he tried to argue as it would be easy for us to mount from here for future Sangin tasking, plus I didn't like the thoughts of crossing that bridge at Gereshk too much but this was to no joy. The boss asked me to plan a route south this time keeping clear of the populated areas back to Gereshk then on to Bastion.

The following morning we left just as it came light. It wasn't too hot then and we all wanted to get a lot of the hard graft done before the major heat kicked in. My route took us well to the east, there was no point making ourselves targets and I wanted any dickers watching us to think we were heading north-east or east as if travelling to Musa Qaleh or elsewhere.

After moving through the high features which were bare barren bedrock dunes I began heading the patrol south through the flat open plains coming in on the top of the A1 and Gereshk from the north-east and taking the bridge by surprise. That was my plan anyway. The route east took several hours, navigating and boxing round vulnerable areas and between and over the dunes. Once I thought it was safe I changed direction into the flat open terrain miles from anywhere. I slowed the pace of the patrol before reaching the A1 and scanned the road ahead for possible IED that could be placed on there. We passed the first of the ANP outposts, again they looked surprised to see us and all came out to have a good look. I minimised the movement on the road and jumped off the A1 to the south and used the hilly terrain to make our way to the bridge as soon as we cleared the small stream at the ANP position, limiting the time we would be exposed on the road.

The boss told me to find an area to harbour the platoon up for while. I found an ideal location on the map, 2ks south of the road. We would be covered by sitting in dead ground and it would be impossible to see us from anywhere but the features to the south which looked completely remote. We had instructed C Company to hold and secure the bridge before crossing, a recommendation from ourselves as it was a big IED threat for any military movement, but with ground troops in the area it would make it a lot safer for anyone crossing this.

Unfortunately the message got though too late for C Company to mount an Op to secure it in time for us crossing. We would now have to wait for them to get on the ground which could take several hours. I didn't like this and advised the boss to use the element of surprise, push through and get clear before somebody clicked on to what we were about to do. The decision was already made by the higher command to wait for supporting troops to cover the VP(bridge), a decision made by people in a tent a couple of hundred kilometres away who weren't even on the ground. I thought that was shite, it was our bollocks on the line and our decision to make. The boss pushed us onto high ground to overwatch it, another decision I wasn't happy about; we were now advertising the fact that we were there and at some point would have to cross the bridge. It was obvious to anybody watching us what our intensions would be and gave the Taliban plenty of time to locate an IED. We had spread out across the features sky lining ourselves against the evening light looking back on Gereshk town. I wasn't happy and I had made the other commanders aware of it but there was no point in arguing between ourselves. We just had to get on with it.

I sat on the WMIK with Tommo and Lee watching the light fading over the town and eating some good old biscuit browns and beef paste from my rations. There was something about Afghanistan at this time of day unlike any place I had visited before: strange and mystical with a large amount of history and secrets surrounding it. I watched through the binoculars at the steady stream of HGVs passing through the large towers and over the bridge about 2ks below and to our front. With the traffic flowing it gave me a little more confidence in our ability to cross, blending in with the Afghans without being blown to pieces.

Johnny came over to my WMIK on foot, we stood at the front of the vehicle discussing the situation and talking general bollocks. It was nice for the heat to have died down a few degrees from the constant scorching sun. One thing about the Middle East is, when the sun begins to go down it becomes dark very quickly and being close to the river it also brought out the mozzies. Within a few minutes the four of us at my WMIK were surrounded by darkness. We all went into night routine, again using our night viewing goggles and sights. The boss gave the order to start moving back into the low land and towards the A1.

The Patrols never wore helmets when out on patrol and we were forever getting picked up by the higher ranks although we never paid any attention. It wasn't a case of looking alley (a Para slang for looking good) and not wanting to wear them, it was just the fact that it was unprofessional, for us anyway. If you constantly wore a helmet while moving on the WMIK on patrol and in some cases that was 20 hours plus in 45–50 degree temperatures you would soon find yourself going down with heatstroke with your head cooking like a roasted spud in the oven. However in situations like this, a quick drive over any vulnerable area or forward onto a recce, then yes we would wear them, we knew where and when to place on our lids.

Lee moved our WMIK down the features to the road, because it was dark and we never used lights we had to be very careful on the speed we travelled, one small movement and we could easily be rolling down the feature leaving all of our crew dead or badly injured. This had happened many times before during training and again later in the tour. As I had mentioned the WMIK was a top heavy vehicle especially due to the .50 sitting on the top. The gunner holding it was exposed as too was the commander's head due to raising his seat to operate the GPMG. The head of the commander and the gunner cleared the roll cage and bar to be able to control the guns properly. The driver was the only person protected by the roll cage; if we rolled there was a possibility of serious injury or death but with all that was going on it was the least of our worries.

We turned left on the tarmac and headed down to the bridge. I could see the lights at this side of the bridge at the checkpoint in the distance as we travelled through the derelict buildings either side of us. All of sudden I got this horrible feeling running through me. Something was definitely wrong here. For one as I scanned ahead there was nobody on the road but us: the HGVs were being held at the checkpoint a kilometre or so to our front, their lights static. I didn't like this one bit; there was just a weird eerie feeling to this and like I said before this was a perfect location for an ambush and IED. My six senses were setting off alarm bells in my head.

'Boss this is Scotty, this looks dodgy as fuck.' This he was probably already aware of but he either didn't hear me or chose not to answer. I gripped the butt of the GPMG and sank a little lower into my seat; I had visions of getting blown up at any moment.

'Come on,' I said 'let's get out of here. Tommo, you see anything?'

'Nah it's quiet', he answered.

'Yeah, too quiet', Lee replied. My heart was racing as we neared the bridge.

'Come on,' I growled 'get fucking through.' We passed the ANP checkpoint.

'These look friendly', Gaz said over the radio.

Yeah just a bit, I thought, he was taking the piss. There were no smiles or waves from any of them unlike before. We passed the long line of HGVs and headed over the bridge. As we got over this I saw a young C Company soldier just off the road in a fire position; they had secured the western bank but not the east which we deemed the more dangerous; but I understood that to do that would mean either exposing ground troops to the IED treat or landing troops on the eastern side of the river by heli.

We got through the town and made our way to FOB Price; I was starting to relax again. That last few hours had been a little dodgy but just as we did a burst of RPK machine gun fire shot through our patrol. My heart jumped and I swung the gun round. It was the tribal outpost firing a warning shot.

'It's OK lads, just the tribal guards making sure we are friendlies', the boss said.

'Why can't they just stop us like everybody else?' Dale's voice said over the radio.

'Yeah I nearly shit there', Lee said.

'Me too, they are pissing me off firing off warning shots all the shagging time', I replied. Ten minutes later we were back in the security of the FOB. It was a relief to be off the ground, just because of crossing that VP (Gereshk Bridge). Speaking to the lads later about sitting out in the open waiting for darkness and moving through that choke point to the bridge, I told them of my gut feeling I had while we crossed, I wasn't the only person feeling like that and soon I was to learn just how lucky we had been.

A few weeks later the HCR (Household Cavalry) who had been attached to the Battle group were to escort a convoy of ANA over the bridge. The Household Cavalry moved around in Scimitar and Spartan tanks, small armoured recce tracked tanks with a 30mm cannon on the front. The HCR decided to place the ANA pickup trucks in between and to the rear of their Scimitar tanks giving them as much protection as possible. Unfortunately as they drove over the bridge and through the stretch with the derelicts on the eastern bank an IED had been placed on the side of the road, it detonated and took out one of the ANA pick-up trucks that were carrying several Afghan soldiers on the back, and they all died.

When I heard the news I sat in the cookhouse back at Bastion and thought of that particular time we had moved through and boxed round the threat area, it could have quite easily been us that were hit, and like the ANA pick-up trucks we wouldn't have stood a chance, and if it had been a command wire or timer used to activate the IED then it would have been. I believe we had rolled past this due to the combat indicators we received; one thing was for sure, we had been very lucky.

Experience, combat indicators and a sixth sense often tell you when things aren't right. This had been one of those moments and through my time in Afghan and during my Close Protection work in Iraq I would see this so many times again. One recent time that sticks out in my mind relates to the incident above. While working CP in Iraq I was the lead scout driver for a three-vehicle move from Basra to Talil in southern Iraq. Our job was bringing two US clients back with us on the return leg. As we approached a major junction called (codenamed) A55 I turned to Rocky and informed him that it was a little quiet in the area, which it should not have been. There had been a lot of work by the side of the road these last few weeks; however, today there wasn't a soul about. The machinery was still there but no workers, no passing traffic, it was dead. I didn't like it and Rocky agreed. Rocky was a very experienced guy, 43, a small and bald fella who we nicknamed the mini Buddha. He had spent a lot of time in the Foreign Legion, Royal Irish and then about ten years CP all over the world from Africa to here. A guy I really liked and admired although to see us you would have thought we hated each other as we constantly slagging each other off or stitching each other up. We decided there and then to pull off the road and cross country it around the junction. We didn't think much more about it as we picked up our clients and headed back to Basra on another route. On return we were a little shocked to find that the next call sign through that area (A55) was a Romanian army patrol moving out from Talil with a lot more armour than we had. It passed through A55 and triggered off an EFP which penetrated the lead wagon killing all three on board. We had been very lucky.

Chapter 6

Op MUTAY, 7.62mm Mayhem

Like I said, this Afghanistan tour so far was a quiet one apart from a few small incidents, but we realised that we were now being targeted and there was definitely a large threat out there; something big was just around the corner. Patrols were busy, pushed out onto several recces around the area and we were glad to be away from all the bullshit that was brewing back in Bastion. We had been back and forth to Gereshk, Sangin and Now Zad on different missions, mostly route recces, enemy probing and dominating the ground as we were the only coalition mobile forces operating in these areas at this time, apart from the odd US and Canadian patrol or convoy.

On 2 June we received orders to move to Now Zad for an Op that was planned for 4 June. Again we went through our orders process and pre-deployment checks before loading our WMIK Land Rovers and pushing out into the desert. With more idea of the ground the journey up didn't take as long as on some of the previous missions and we knew exactly where all the VP, small farms, wadis and settlements were as well as desert tracks that we could use. On the flat open plains before we reached the mountains the patrol went firm for one of many tyre changes we had now encountered. Due to the large boulders that litter the bedrock surface and the wadis' floor our tyres were often getting ripped to shreds, another reason why each WMIK carried two spare tyres each. We had done that many tyre changes that I reckon we could have given any F1 racing team a run for their money for speed and they didn't have the worry of being shot at either.

My two WMIKs pushed up to the left flank just in front of a desert track that ran in diagonally in front of us through our patrol. Tommo gave me a heads up that something was approaching in the flat open desert.

'Scotty I've got a dust cloud coming in from our front left but I can't make out what it is', he said, using the .50 Cal SUSA to try and identify it. I looked up from my map and looked through the binos.

'Whatever it is it's travelling at some speed', I said. We could see for miles and there was nothing but this cloud of sand racing towards us. We continued to watch it as it got closer; it was on the track immediately to our front and posed no risk to the other call signs 300–400m to our right doing the tyre change. At around 200m out I managed to focus in on the fast mover.

'What the fuck?' I said out loud.

'What is it?' Lee said.

'Nah, it can't be', I chuckled, again speaking out aloud to myself. With the amount of dust flying up all I could see was a bloke sitting cross-legged on top of the dust cloud as if in a meditation prayer.

'What the fuck is it?' Lee said, missing out. Tommo answered before I could.

'Some twat on a magic carpet!' he laughed out.

'What?' Lee shouted. I also began pissing myself laughing.

'Yeah it's some rag head flying in on his carpet by the looks of it.' Even up until about 40m out the car was almost invisible due to the sand and dust it was kicking up. One of the passengers was sitting on the roof crossed-legged as if meditating. It did for a moment look as if he was just flying away down the desert: a strange but funny start to the patrol.

'Now why couldn't we be issued them?' I shouted back to Tommo. Another thing they do over in Iraq and Afghanistan is strap coffins to the roof of their cars. Funeral directors and hearses are in short supply over there. I have witnessed this a few times and always made the comment of being able to clean up round here, make a bit of dollar by following the Patrols about and cleaning their dead.

We got into Now Zad from the south doing our usual fast and aggressive leap frogging (bounding) drills into the camp. From here it was a chance to clean up our weapons and kit before getting some scoff and head down. We put the vehicles around the main two-storey building in our teams and settled for the remainder of the evening.

In the army on operations or exercise you have two main meals per day: breakfast consisting of a boil-in-the-bag of bacon and beans, corned beef hash or sausages and beans; the latter was always a favourite with me mixed with some curry powder. The water was normally used for a brew. Dinner was just a snack of biscuit browns and paste and tea and was the main meal of the day: something that was going to keep you going till breakfast the next morning and sometimes longer. Us Paras especially took pride in our scoff; no boil-in-the-bags would happen in the evenings, it was our only proper meal so had to be good, and it had to be an all-in-one. An all-in-one would be a concoction of your main meal from the ration pack: chicken and pasta for example mixed with noodles, soup, garlic, pepper and loads of chilli or curry powder, the hotter the better. After a few exercises in the Reg you either become a mini chef or you go hungry. I remember being on junior Brecon in Wales on my full screw (Cpl) course with mixed units (or Hats as we called them), who had never done or heard of this 'all-in-one'. Hats are the term the Paras gave to anybody that wasn't Para Reg with the exception of the Marines, which were Sea Hats. I'm sure Marcus, Shortey and Gav, a few of the lads I have recently worked with on the CP circuit, will love that remark. Some of them were decent lads but there was also a lot of dross mixed in. Not only did they not have a clue about soldiering and tactics but many of them didn't know how to cook an all-in-one either. Ever heard the expression 'an army fights on its stomach'? One lad from some Scottish regiment actually keeled over due to lack of food intake on our final exercise; it turned out that he lived on chocolate and sweets, he never touched the rations because he 'didn't like them'.

Just to put a bit of background on Hats and Paras, I'll elaborate further. Us Paras were normally hated by every other regiment in the British army as well as Navy and RAF, till they worked with us anyway. There was always inter-regimental shit between units like the Signals and Airborne Signals (216) but the Paras are on everybody's shit list. We hated all of them in return and for not being as good as us and part of the airborne brotherhood that we had joined. They believed we had a chip on our shoulders and in a way they were right. As a young tom in 3 Para I, like many others, wouldn't even speak to a Hat, it's the way we had been brought through training. We were the top dogs at everything we did, we always had to be better and to prove a point, and it's what makes us different. I have now met lots of blokes from different units who have later admitted once we had worked with them that, yes, we are better. We were pushed to our limits and trained harder than any other unit. We had operational experience worldwide unlike many other units and so many times I and others would have to help them out or they would ask us to do a particular job because they knew it would get done. Most of the lads I had spoken to would say, 'Well I was going to join the Paras but …'. Some lads got attached to us and stayed, not wanting to return to their own units. In 2001 we got an attachment of Guards that had passed P-COY and joined us on a two-year rotation: around thirty men from all five Guards regiments. I became close with a few of these and a lot transferred not wanting to be RTU back to the Guards, although, saying that, it took a while for them to fit in. At first being Hats they were outcasts and constantly slagged. Blokes even used to get onto their platoon floor and shit all over it and smear it on the walls until after they were tested and trusted. Others just transferred from their original regiment to become part of the Paras. As I got older and attended courses I realised that they are not all bad soldiers and they all had different jobs to do, signallers, mechanics, gunners, chefs, logistics and medics. Medics I began appreciating very quickly because if it all goes wrong they are the lads and lasses patching you up. Medics I had a real respect for and still have, having worked closely to them as a team medic in Iraq on CP work. Paras were the first into any action since the start of the regiment back in WW2 and it was still the same to this day. And because of this approach the other infantry regiments hated us.

Tonight wasn't any different and I cooked up one of my specials, beef in pepperoni noodles with enough curry powder to kill a platoon of Crap Hats and after shooting the shit with the lads over a brew it was time for some good quality head down. With only a bit of roll mat as my bed and poncho liner thrown over me to prevent the mozzies from chewing my face off I settled down for the night wondering what tomorrow would bring …

The rest of the convoy had started pushing through, firing as they went. The two Pinzgauer vehicles moved next, the interpreter, signaller and FOOs keeping as low as possible as there wasn't any heavy weapons on board. I watched them speed through the gap ahead just as I heard the sound of Chinooks coming in.

'Shit the helis are inbound!' I shouted. I got a horrible gut feeling through my body, everything could go wrong at this critical stage without any of us being in a place to protect them coming off the CH47 onto the HLS.

'OK, let's move!' I shouted. Lee put his foot down and we moved from the protection of the wall. Moving into the open I could see the open gateway that led into the orchard field. My GPMG was swung fully round to the left, butt in the shoulder and my index finger taking a slight bit of pressure on the trigger. Movement caught my eye, two figures running through the field from left to right. I let off a quick burst and looked over the top to observe my strike, more movement over to my far left got me back over the gun. I squeezed off a further burst just as the Taliban fired back, 7.62mm flying past us over our heads as we got into the other alley ahead of us. Once the whole of Patrols were in the tight alleyway we had to stop all movement, we couldn't push on any further till we knew exactly what was going on, but then again we didn't want to stick around in the contact area either, the group of Taliban were still round the corner.

I jumped off the WMIK.

'Everyone OK?' I shouted back to Johnny. I got the thumbs up back.

'Tommo, Luke, stay up top', again I got the thumbs up as they struggled to look over the wall. So far we had got through without any casualties; it seemed that we had hit a group of Taliban leaving the area or getting into an ambush position, not somewhere we should stick around in. This tight alleyway had lots of little open doorways either side in the high mud walls that now enclosed us. We needed to get away from this ambush site and quick, we were sitting ducks here, I thought as I clicked my safety off my long and checked and cleared a few of the doorways close to my Patrol. Obviously I wasn't the only one thinking this, the boss had got Ray to patrol forward now. Ray led another three lads down the track on foot scanning the route ahead in case there was another ambush set up waiting before we could push the vehicles on. The commanders did the same, walking in front of their WMIKs we started pushing south out of the contact area. I could hear the sound of gunfire to our east in the direction of the HLS where A Company had put down only a few minutes ago.

I was starting to think that it was all going wrong, we had been hit and we had to look at getting back into the cordon location, and now it sounded like A Company were under attack too. At this point we had no idea what was going on in there. Pushing down the track we came to an open section of ground. The wall on our right continued straight down along the track; there was also a track that ran left as soon as we entered the open ground with another high wall running along it dividing the orchard fields. To our left was a ploughed field with a few sparse trees and then another high wall about 50–75m out which the track to our left ran up to, forming a T junction that ran along the wall to our left. We pushed the vehicles into the open ground in all round defence so we could establish exactly where we were and where we needed to go as this encounter with the Taliban had changed our plans.

I checked my GPS and map; we weren't far from the location that my team was supposed to be holding. I looked round trying to put the tracks and walls to the air photo and map but it didn't exactly measure up. It was just a maze of tracks, walls and fields that looked different on the photos. A large heavy engine broke my concentration. For a second I thought it was an armoured vehicle approaching from the east. I positioned myself behind the gun again along with everyone else. The noise grew louder, just behind the wall 50m to our front. My heart was pumping fast.

They can't have armoured vehicles, I thought, they just can't. Intelligence had never said and we definitely didn't have armour around here. A large vehicle moved into sight from our front left only slightly visible through the sparse trees.

Everyone was twitchy now and we were ready to open up on anything that moved. There was a large pause while we tried to work out what it was. The vehicle was red in colour showing only bits of its bodywork through the sparse trees; it slowly followed the track next to the wall at the opposite side of the open ground we now dominated. 'Dresh!!! Dresh!!!' somebody shouted which meant 'Stop' in Pashtu. The vehicle was a large tractor but due to the trees we couldn't work out who was on board. The tractor came to a stop from another call of 'Dresh' and a warning shot by the Boss or Ray's team further up to my right.

'Boss this is Scotty, I'm going to push forward and clear the vehicle', I said over the PRR.

'OK Scotty, careful and watch though flanks', he replied.

'Johnny can you get up on the far wall and cover my left as I move?'

'Yeah, got that Scotty.' In seconds Johnny and Brett had moved up the track next to the wall to our left. Once they looked in a good position me and Tommo began pepper-potting or fire-and-manoeuver (one man covering or firing while the other ran forward) across the open ground to the tractor. As I got close to the vehicle I realised it was a family: a middle-aged man and woman with one teenage son and a further three smaller children aged around five or six. I guessed they were just trying to escape the fighting that had now erupted around them but I wasn't taking any chances.

'Move!' I shouted as I took a knee next to one of the trees. I caught sight of Tommo out the corner of my right eye coming level with me.

'I got you covered', Johnny said over the PRR. I glanced round to my left; I could see Johnny and Brett at the corner of the wall covering the blind entrance to the field that I would have been exposed to.

'Scotty it's Steve, I got you covered from the rear'. Steve had moved his two WMIKs behind me to cover us.

'Move!' Tommo shouted. I got to my feet and raced forward through the sparse trees only a few metres from me.

'Hands up!' I shouted as I came to slow patrol pace a few metres from the tractor. They were all in a bit of shock and just looked at me.

'Get your fucking hands up!' I screamed; the adrenalin was still pumping through me. They got the hint. 'Off, get off', I gestured. They had a trailer on the back full of bedding and household goods.

'Tommo get that searched, I'll cover these.' I began to calm slightly, they looked very scared and looking at them they posed no threat at all unless they were hiding something or someone. Tommo searched the trailer which was empty of people and weapons and after a quick search of the family we pointed them back to Now Zad and gestured for them to go.

'Yes, yes', the old man said in broken English, 'we go.'

'Just a family trying to get out boss, I'm pushing them through.'

'Roger that Scotty, close in on me once you're back here.' I got back to the WMIK and moved in on the boss who was now at the rear of the column of vehicles in the irrigation ditch with Benney, a tanned-up Kiwi ladies' man who looked a little oriental and was always the butt of many a joke for it, getting the nickname Gurung, a commonly used Gurkha surname. The Arabic version was Muhammad which is widely used, and it seemed that every other Gurkha was called Gurung.

'Boss, Benney Gurung' I nodded as I crawled in on them still a little out of breath from the bit of running about. The boss had his map out.

'That was a bit fruity' pin head Benney joked.

'Just a little', I smiled back. 'Boss I think we need to start moving out of here', I said.

'Yeah', he replied 'just need to work out where the CO wants us.' The CO at this point was circling around us in one of the Chinooks using it as an airborne command station. 'I wanted to push in further where that tractor has come from but the CO wants us to push further south as he thinks the Taliban might try and break out into the open area and wadi to our south' the boss said. I looked at the map the boss had set out in front of him.

'OK then, sorted', I replied, 'we head south.'

'Yeah we will move down this track till we get out in the open then assess the situation from there', he said.

'Any update from A Company?' Benney asked.

'They have been taking some incoming but all seems good at the minute', he answered. I let out a sigh of relief inside, I didn't want them getting brassed up because we couldn't get in to support them. It wasn't our fault we got ambushed and these things happen, but after working with them again I didn't want to let them down.

'The Gurkha patrol that was supposed to be on the east flank has hit trouble too, 1 KIA and a few casualties', he continued.

'Fuck' I mumbled under my breath.

'OK get your guys ready to go', the boss said, folding his map.

'Boss, the CO is on the dog and bone', Chalkie shouted from the WMIK.

'OK, I'm coming over.' I got out of the ditch and ran back to my team. After giving the team a set of QBOs we began moving off again back down the track enclosed by two high walls either side, not ideal for our mobile call sign but we had little choice now. Us commanders were walking in front of the WMIKs again trying to give them a little more protection. Ray's whole team was nearly all dismounted, patrolling in front of the line of vehicles.

'Boss we are coming to the end of the high walls, the track carries on and the ground opens up', Ray announced over the radio.

'Ok, just have a look to see if it's safe to push on, Ray. Steve, Dale, how's our six (rear) looking?' the boss said.

'Yeah, it's Ok at the moment, Boss', Dale replied. After a few minutes Ray got back on the net.

'The 12 [front] looks clear, Boss, we have ditches either side, grass and straw fields after that. A small wall ran parallel to our left with a large orchard field with lots of trees behind it. A small compound with a building behind it 150m to our front on the track', Ray said, trying to give as much information as possible.

'OK, then push on Ray, everybody keep your eyes peeled there is a lot of Taliban heading our way.'

We moved out into the open; this I wasn't too keen about. The vehicles were channelled and exposed with the only escape route being to our front and we were now moving at a slow pace with us walking them down.

Crack, crack, crack!

'Contact left!' someone shouted. I turned and dropped to one knee and fired off two rounds in the direction of the firing point. Steve and Dale behind me were engaging something. I scrambled into the ditch off to the right of my WMIK.

Where the fuck's the target? I thought. Crack, crack, crack, rounds again flying through our position.

'Fuck', I mumbled as I ducked down for a split second. I jumped up exposing only the top part of my body using the ditch as some part of protection and fired off 7–8 rounds into the direction of the firing and the splash marks from Dale and Steve's guns hitting the walls.

'Scotty we are moving', Lee shouted. I looked over to my right to see the other vehicles driving off down the track at full speed. I jumped out of the ditch and ran round and into the WMIK command seat, putting my long on the bonnet and taking hold of the gun. Lee sped off down the track with the sound of gunfire behind us, and I scanned the wall as we moved. There was a U shape in the wall where the mud had broken away; I had seen it before as we patrolled down and moved into the ditch as it stood out from the rest of the wall. We were almost opposite it now. My eyes came across the same patch of ground just as two figures emerged from there.

'Contact left!' I shouted as I took aim and squeezed off two 5-round bursts at the two men; a small cloud of smoke obscured my sight from the heat of the oil and weapon. It cleared but I couldn't see anybody. Lee slowed as I fired another 20 or 30 rounds into the lower wall in case they were taking cover behind it. The 7.62mm GPMG would penetrate the old rotten mud I thought.

'You fucking got them, Scotty!' Lee shouted as we once again raced forward into the area of the ruin ahead. It didn't register in my head, and it would take a lot longer to too. This battle had only just begun.

We had got through the second contact area, again unscathed. We moved the vehicles around the ruin that sat on our left which formed a little protection from view and fire. Ray's two WMIKs pushed past the ruin to a small track that ran through two high walls facing to the left. The boss parked his up behind the ruin with the two Pinzs; my two vehicles were positioned slightly behind the ruined wall with Steve and Dale's behind me covering back towards the contact point. This was supposed to be an area where we could now slow things down, find out exactly what was going on both here and at A Company's location and then establish a plan on what to do next.

I jumped off the WMIK and moved in on the boss who was now to the rear of the ruin.

'What happened there, Scotty?' the boss said.

'Yeah, cheeky twats opened up on us, must've been moving in the same direction trying to get out' I replied. Steve and Ray had now come in too, all of us kneeling around the boss while the remainder watched for any signs of Taliban.

'Right, we need hold this position' the boss started. 'Possible Taliban moving this way to get out of the way of A Company who are now busy searching the area, we could hear firing coming from their direction.'

The ground was split down, Ray and the boss's team taking the front right of the ruin and surrounding areas while mine and Steve's held the left of the ruin and the rear. I moved up to Dale's WMIK using it as a shield as I scanned the wall back down the track from where we were last engaged. Steve, Dale and the hobbit – young Geordie lad called John – were also standing by the vehicles watching the ground ahead. It had suddenly hit me how hot it was now and how dehydrated I was. With all that had gone on I hadn't drunk any fluids in the last few hours. I began patrolling back to my wagon to get some water. Before I reached it all hell broke loose at the forward right position where Ray and the boss's patrols were, causing me to spin round. I raced off at full speed to the forward edge of the ruined building. There were people shouting down the net about Taliban in their position just over the wall. I couldn't make out exactly what was going on.

'Where's the boss?' I shouted to a lad called Thompson, a jock MT driver who was attached to us and driving one of the Pinzs.

'Don't know', he said. Fucking great, I thought.

'Boss!' I shouted round the corner. He was running back with FLt Carter, the RAF FAC.

'Ray's team is taking heavy incoming along with mine, Lee C. has got my team.' Lee was a good friend of mine, a good drinking buddy, a Mank who looked a bit like Darren Osborn from *Hollyoaks*. He had spent most of his time in Patrols whilst in the army and was a good soldier.

'Scotty, keep holding the rear with Steve in case they flank us', he said, struggling for air. That was enough for me; he obviously had his hands full and had come to get Comms with the CO from his WMIK so I moved back to the rear of the ruin and took on some much needed water. There was nothing else we could do apart from keeping our eyes peeled. No matter how much I wanted to get up there with my Patrol, we still had the rear and left to protect.

'What's going on, Scotty?' Tommo and Lee attacked me with as I came back to the WMIK. 'They have Taliban all over the place and that's about as much as I know at the minute, so keep your eyes over that wall'. That they already knew, what with the stray rounds flying over our heads and the constant firing to our right. 'If they struggle we'll move up there and give support', I continued 'but we can't leave this exposed.'

Just as I finished 7.62mm [rounds] cracked over our heads and between us. Being on the receiving end of incoming rounds, especially 7.62mm, was a scary thing no matter who you are. The loud ear-splitting crack as it flies through the air at the speed of sound and the thump as it continues past.

Shit! I turned and sprinted off towards Steve's WMIK instantaneously which was on the forward edge nearest the wall where the firing seemed to be coming from. I think the Taliban had just popped up and fired a few shots at us, however there was only a few of us here now as most of the blokes had moved into the ruin. They realised this as soon as they fired off the first few shots, knowing that most of our blokes were up at the top end or in the ruin. For some reason, and I don't know why I did this, but I stopped in open ground and turned round.

'Lee? Get my camera and get some pics of this!' I shouted. Like I said I don't know exactly why I did this, it certainly wasn't tactical or something I had planned on saying and doing. An RPG went flying past me through Steve's two WMIKs and then through both of mine; the sandy floor kicked up in front of me as 7.62mm hit the floor all round us. I started sprinting forward again into the rain of bullets that were now being fired; Luke was firing from his .50 but only a few rounds then it would stop, the constant stoppage due, in my opinion, to the faulty rounds. Pete, another young lad from Manchester, wasn't even firing, I believe this was due to the same problem.

I slammed into the WMIKs engine block and began firing over the bonnet of the vehicle as another RPG flew past our heads.

'Tommo, get the fuck over here! Pete, why the fuck aren't you firing?' I shouted. It felt like the whole world had erupted around us and at the minute they had the upper hand unless we got the guns firing. RPGs flying only a few metres past you makes a hell of noise, a large whooshing sound but as long as we didn't hear an explosion then it was all good, it had missed. Tommo jumped off our WMIK that was unable to fire due to Steve's WMIK being in the way where I was and sprinted over to me. Lee at this point took a photo with my camera: a brilliant picture that has been shown everywhere and became one of the main pictures of the Afghanistan tour. The WMIKs set out with me firing over the bonnet of one of them and Tommo running for the .50 Cal. Tommo without fear for his own safety jumped up exposing himself and took control of the .50 firing into the wall only 50m from us from where the Taliban were attacking. He too was firing only a few rounds and then stopping.

'Stoppage!' he shouted. Fuck, it dawned on me that all .50 weren't working properly and I reckoned it was due to the poor ammo: something we had told the Head Shed back at camp and now could mean the difference between kicking arse or getting our arse kicked.

I stepped up to rapid fire again with my personal weapon, one round per second while they cleared their stoppages. I could see the Taliban popping up from different positions on the other side of the wall, their dark turbans, white eyes and beards clearly visible, talk about the film *Zulu* I thought later. 'Wait till you see the whites of their eyes boys' – that and Michael Caine was the only thing missing. I tried along with the lads around me to keep the Taliban heads down and stop them getting accurate shots on us. Their rate of fire was really intense and felt even more as they were only 50m away, a wall and a few vehicles dividing us, and that wasn't going to stop 7.62mm slamming into your body and taking us out. Unlike computer games you don't get a second or third life after getting hit. How, at this stage, none of us were shot was beyond me.

I guessed there was between six and eight fighters there; they had done a good job of flanking us and were seriously taking us on. Tracer flew from my muzzle into the Taliban position. Mag change, I thought; with a bit of a warning from the tracer, the magazine changes were so much faster. I slipped the other mag on, releasing the working parts and fired a further few rounds. The straw and grass to our front was alight now due to the rounds from both sides firing through it, and smoke was beginning to fill the air. Another RPG flew past, a metre or so to my right.

'That was close', I shouted, although I don't think anyone was listening and it was probably to myself. Then just as quick as it had started, it stopped. I couldn't see anybody moving. I guessed that we had won the fire fight and had caused them to back off or move to a different location.

'Watch and shoot!' I shouted, 'they'll be back'. I ran forward from the WMIK to the ruin, I was going to inform the lads in there that the Taliban could be closing in on them. I ran into the ruin. Crack, crack, crack! AK47 rounds flew past me crashing into the wall behind me a foot above my head. Again their rate of fire was phenomenal, sending debris onto my helmet and back of my neck as I ducked down. Later I was to learn that Thompson the MT driver took some video footage of this over the wall of the ruin which went on Sky News a day later, some of the first footage of the fighting in south Afghanistan. I already knew not to underestimate them and this was exactly why. It seemed that they were probing our lines trying to find a weakness and exploit it; they weren't put off or scared of our weapons, that was for sure.

I joined the lads at the wall, a mix of Ray and Steve's team and Brett from mine. I didn't need to tell them of the Taliban fighters, they could see them. I looked over to see four or five Taliban running across in front of us amongst the trees.

Bang, bang, bang, I fired at them. I didn't even watch to see if I'd hit any of them, I ducked back down and ran back to the entrance of the ruin which I had run through a minute ago. The lads outside had been firing again, I needed to see if they were OK. It seemed that everyone was in contact now, from all angles and apart from Ray in the right-hand corner of the ruin I hadn't a clue where the boss and Steve were. Steve should have been at the rear, but he wasn't.

As I stepped out of the doorway I bumped into Dale running up using the ruin walls as cover from the passing rounds. Dale was a funny individual, a good mate who received the nickname Hippo Head because that's exactly what he looked like. He had a thing about getting his cock out, no matter where it was – on the piss, on photos, anywhere – it was his party piece. I'm sure at some point during the contact his cock and ball sack was hanging out somewhere.

'Scotty, you're now platoon Sgt' he said, catching me at the entrance.

'What? What's happened to Steve, is he OK like?' He started laughing.

'He just said tell Scotty he is now the platoon Sgt', Dale said in a slight giggle.

'You're fucking joking me?'

'Nah, over to you, Sarge', Dale laughed as he ran off to the north edge of the ruin dodging the 7.62mm that was flying everywhere. Where the hell is he? I thought. Dale like me knew what he was like, always fucking off and leaving things for others. Now I was the platoon Sgt, I had no idea where Steve was but I was guessing up near the boss, his team left behind and I had no real clue what was going on up ahead.

At this point there was a lot of confusion because the platoon was split and there was so much chat over the net that things were getting cut out and messages lost. The intelligence guy, interpreter, medic and Thompson the MT driver were still by the outer wall of the ruin taking cover.

'Where's Johnny?' I shouted to Luke who was operating the .50.

'On the corner, Scotty', he shouted, still struggling to unblock his .50 Cal. I knew the gunners were having major problems with them, that being the reason Pete wasn't firing before because his .50 was completely fucked. The firing had died down once again at the rear left, and I ran round the corner to seek Johnny. As I turned I nearly shat myself. I was looking down the rear end of 84mm anti-tank weapon just in time to see Johnny tap Van, a South African guy who was Steve's driver, on his head

'Fire!' he shouted.

'No, wait, fuck!' I buried myself into the wall expecting flames to fly over me there and then. I didn't fancy a lack of eyebrows and a sun tan just yet. Like a miracle the 84mm anti-tank weapon that would have normally sent a flame of back blast 10–20m behind it failed to fire, it hadn't worked for some weird reason. I had been lucky again, this time nearly getting taken out by my own mates. It wasn't anybody's fault, these things happened. I could see them both trying to sort it while I got myself back up off the floor. Eventually Johnny and Van decided it was proper fucked and lobbed it forward into a ditch to our front. The firing was still intense from our left as me, Johnny and Van moved back into the ruin to take up fire positions. Again the firing from the rear where our vehicles were had died down, probably due to the punishing .50 that had been raining down on them or shall I say in dribs and drabs due to the stoppages. I wouldn't like to be on the receiving end of it, I can tell you. I got back on the wall and stuck a fresh mag on just as my worst fear came true.

With all the confusion I can't remember whether it was from word of mouth or over the radio PRR that I received the news, but I passed it on all the same.

'Man down, man down', I shouted. I tried to raise the boss and anybody else who was forward of wall that I couldn't reach over the PRR. Still I received nothing. Fuck, I was now the platoon Sgt, I had to start thinking of the CAS-E-VAC plan and getting whoever it is out of there.

I took a quick second to calm myself, a Hamlet cigar moment it's called in the Reg, and to think of a few things involving calling in a 9-liner (CAS-E-VAC procedure) before heading back out the doorway and to the forward edge of the ruined wall where the vehicles still were.

'It's Bash', someone shouted at me.

'Bash, fuck', I muttered. It's a gut-turning reality to know one of your mates is either dead or wounded. Bash was a big built lad in his early twenties from London. He hadn't been with the Patrols long and was Lee C.'s driver. He was into all this Mr Muscle or Mr Universe stuff. He had competed in a few shows and won a lot of awards in his age group. In a few seconds word came down that he was OK and up and fighting again. That was enough for me; if he was up and banging rounds down again he must have been OK. I thought of what the hell had just gone on there; I would only find out the real story after this was over.

There seemed to be a big lull in the battle, all firing had stopped and it had seemed that the Taliban had fucked off. Moving back towards the rear of the ruin where the 84mm had failed to fire, me and Johnny took a knee and talked about what had gone on. Mostly we just laughed, laughing about stupid things that had just happened; maybe it was the nervous adrenalin still flowing. It had happened before some time earlier when I moved round to enter the ruin. The Intelligence guy was up against the wall. He was around early thirty and of a small build and frame. He hadn't joined up for this, he was in the Intelligence Corps not the Paras or infantry, and to but it mildly, he was shitting it. I can't remember who I was speaking to before or if something had come into my head but I can remember that I was laughing about something as rounds were striking the wall above and RPGs were flying over and through our position. I caught his eye as he was squatting against the outer wall, a look of horror on his face. He must've thought I had lost the plot, smiling and laughing away at myself.

The boss and Steve came back in; minutes passed as we commanders all knelt down near the wall discussing what to do next. It was mid-afternoon now, we had been on the go around nine hours and the sun and heat was punishing, sweat mixed with dirt dripping from under our Para lids and down our faces.

I, like many others, thought we should go and conduct a clearance patrol over the wall: we didn't know if they were re-grouping for another attack. Sometimes the best form of defence is attack: a method we used a lot downtown on a Saturday night but it never seemed to wash with local police. The boss agreed and let Steve take some boys up to sweep through the left-hand wall.

'Hang on boss, that's not his job, me or Ray should go', I protested.

'No, Steve can do it', he snapped back. Steve was off, already running round taking the Patrol 2i/c from each team and a few gunners. I got up and stormed off to my WMIK. I was well pissed off. Steve's job along with the 2i/c was to sort ammo and admin out after a major contact, not to conduct clearance patrols, that's what a Patrol commander has to do. I suppose I will have to do his admin, I thought, winding myself up about it. I laughed about this later but with all that going on and all the adrenalin it just snapped me like a Kit-Kat, plus I also wanted to see what damage I had done when I had taken them two blokes down at the wall. Sick I know but also fully satisfying.

Crack, crack, crack: more incoming started from the top of the ruin. Steve was just about to leave with his clearance patrol, a few seconds earlier they would have been caught in the open field. Then seconds later all hell broke loose at our end too, they were throwing everything they had at us, a big counter-attack from all angles.

As the initial few rounds went down Lee C., Bennie and Ray had ran back up to the top of the ruin where their blokes were but now the Taliban concentrated their fire back on this area too. I worked out later that in my opinion they had hit the top end realising that our men would move up and engage them, then again splitting our force just like before. They had seen that, apart from the ruin there was only a handful of lads securing the vehicles to the rear. They were now concentrating their firepower on us; I knew exactly what their intentions were. They were looking to take out our vehicles, our means of escape, long range radios and heavy weapons systems: they were not stupid. I knew what we had to do. I moved into the door way of the ruin.

'My team on me now!' I screamed. The message ran round from bloke to bloke and in seconds all of us, bar Luke and Tommo who were still firing the .50s, along with Pete and the Hobbit at the vehicles, were around me.

'We need to get out there push the WMIKs back up the track and hammer that area', I said. Everyone understood and before I finished speaking I was racing out under the Taliban fire to the vehicles with my team running behind. It wasn't a long run across the open ground but felt a little longer when 7.62mm flowed between us only inches away. I jumped on the WMIK and took hold of the GPMG. I felt a lot safer behind it.

Lee began reversing up the track, Brett doing the same behind us. The two WMIK Land Rovers began slowly reversing up the track exposing ourselves to the Taliban on the wall and building; we were sitting with our left side of the vehicles facing the wall with the compound to the front left of the WMIK. The way I saw it was, by pushing out I was increasing our arcs of fire and also the weapon range. Sitting here half behind the ruin wasn't doing shit. The smoke and fire in the grass from our tracer was thick and pouring into the air, it was obscuring both us and them. This all happened in seconds, I couldn't afford to hang around, it was a command decision I had made on the ground and it was made fast before it was too late. The lads in the ruin were pouring fire into the enemy position trying to attract their fire only 10–15m from the Taliban. I was firing at a rapid rate at the wall and now the compound that was behind the ruin.

Within a few seconds we were getting the upper hand, me and Johnny on the GPMG and Luke and Tommo on the .50 Cals firing as much as possible. Our firepower was unbelievable: a burst of 4–5 rounds from the GPMG followed by a few rounds from the .50 Cal; there was no gap in the firing and it soon took its toll on the enemy, forcing them back.

There was a telegraph pole behind the wall of the compound.

'Scotty, blokes in and around the telegraph pole!' Lee shouted pointing over my shoulder to bring me on as the noise from both sides was terrific. I turned my gun and laid myself on.

'Stoppage!' Tommo shouted. I stepped up my firing, short, sharp bursts of fire with only a split second in between while Tommo tried to clear it. A Taliban fighter popped up trying to take aim with an RPG. I began firing, the first few rounds went into the wall just below him, the next few rounds with the recoil and beaten zone with which it's designed moved up hitting his chest. I kept firing, hitting him in the upper chest, neck and head till he fell backwards. I definitely got that fucker, I thought.

We kept on smashing the area with everything we had; Lee prepped another tin of 200 rounds for the gun as I was almost out of ammo just as an enormous spray of rounds hit the compound. Get in, I thought.

The FAC had called in the Apaches, the first time they had fired in anger. I thought our firepower from the WMIKs was strong; the Apaches' 30mm cannons firing anti-personnel rounds were brilliant unless you were on the receiving end. This became the beginning of the end for the Taliban here. Lee C. had the same idea as us and began moving their vehicles back out of danger as we finished off on the left flank. The smell of death, smoke, gunpowder and burning flesh clung in the air as I scanned for any signs of movement. The call came in to withdraw back, getting some distance between us and the Taliban and allowing the Apaches to do the work as we were still in the Apache danger area (being mistaken for Taliban or at risk of ricochet).

There was a high wall 200m to the rear of the ruin (west back to Now Zad); we made this our ERV. The boss and Ray kept some lads near the ruin to sweep through the compound once the Apaches cleared it. The rest of us in the WMIKs began bounding back, covering our route out towards the ERV to our rear.

I stopped on the edge of the wall till all the vehicles came in; the Apaches were still taking out targets that were retreating now some distance away through the orchards. An explosion erupted at the compound as Bash fired an 84mm into it where some of the Taliban fighters had last been seen; Ray moved his men in and swept the area while the Apaches covered them from above. No bodies were found around the compound but a lot of blood trails could be seen; as for the wall and near the ruin it was impossible to get in there and conduct a search, we could not explore any further into orchard field to follow them up or look for the corpses and casualties of Taliban we had hit here. We learned some time after that these Taliban fighters would not only bring their casualties out of a fire fight but also their dead: something that they would pay dearly for when they met the Patrols platoon again.

It was after 17:00hrs by the time the boys moved back into the vehicles; the Apaches had pulled off letting a new friend come in. A US A10 Thunderbolt had been put on task near to the end of the fight and the extraction of A Company pulling off the ground. The A10, known to many as the Tankbuster, was an amazing piece of kit. Fitted with a 30mm canon it was capable of taking out armoured vehicles and main battle tanks. The noise from this aircraft was frightening enough without the rounds hitting the target. It's hard to explain the noise when the A10 fires its weapon, a strange warr-ing sound that makes you cringe, followed a few seconds later by the sound of small explosions as the armour-piercing rounds tear through everything that moves.

I sat on my WMIK scanning the ground with my binoculars and listening into the Comms as the boss and Ray withdrew back. The A10 that was circling came round on an attack run, swooping down into a low level attack position a few hundred metres off the desert floor: it lined itself up with a target out of sight to us. We watched it closely; it was heading straight for us, full speed. I got a weird gut feeling through my body. For a second it looked like we were the targets. Trying to keep my cool I told Tommo to get the marker panel out and place it on the rear of our WMIK: a luminous coloured panel that was supposed to warn friendly aircraft that we were coalition forces.

As the A10 grew closer I began to shrink slightly. I caught myself saying, 'Don't fucking brass us up for fuck's sake, I haven't survived Taliban ambushes just be taken out by a Yank pilot.' From previous experience and friendly fire incidents I knew what the Yanks were like and the damage that they had done in the past. The pilot started firing just over our heads striking a target 200–300m north-east of us hidden in the trees.

'Thank fuck for that', Tommo let out. Least I wasn't the only one feeling like that, I thought.

The US fast air normally asks for the friendly call sign location, then a bearing and distance to the target followed by the target location (10-fig grid) and description. The fast air will always do a 60-seconds talk on: as they approach the target we must describe as much as we can to the pilot on what to expect during his run in and on the target. Unlike the Apaches who can hover and have more time to locate things on the ground, fast air are travelling at a couple of hundred miles an hour. It is hard for both you and the pilot to do this and for him to understand exactly where the enemy is. Where it gets confusing is the difference between RAF and US procedure. Most of it was the same apart from one big piece. The RAF doesn't ask for a friendly forces grid, in this case the Patrols' location, just a bearing to the enemy and distance so they are aware of the danger from the explosions. The US ask for both a grid of the enemy and friendlies; type in the grids the wrong way round and you now become the target, something that has happened on a few occasions, one being here in Northern Afghanistan in 2001. UK forces called in US fast air during a firefight with the Taliban. The co-ordinates were placed in wrong and the JDAM 1000lb bomb was dropped on the friendly call sign and not the enemy, a mistake that had happened before and will no doubt happen again.

The Chinooks came in extracting the A Company call sign off the ground. That was the end of the Op but we still needed to get back to the Now Zad fort and then Bastion. For us it wasn't over yet. We agreed that to go back through the tight maze of compounds was stupid, plus the light was fading and we never used the same route out if we could help it. All on board, we patrolled south hitting the wadi and then pushed west to the rear of ANP hill before making our way into the fort. By this point we were all quite bollocked, a mix of gunpowder residue, dirt and sweat had turned our faces a dirty colour. We had been up and busy for over 16 hours, most of which was on the ground and around 6 hours in contact, fighting.

We tried to settle and have a quick, hot debrief about what had happened. This was a bit of a waste of time to be honest. That much had gone on in those hours that it was impossible to cover exactly what everybody had seen and done. Some of the guys in Ray and the boss's team didn't even know how serious the fighting was at our positions behind them. Blokes were talking of their own private battles. It's what happens in cases like these; you get the old blinkers on and tunnel vision, focused in on what's happening around you and not what's going on left, right and behind you. It happens to us all.

Later we talked about the Taliban and how hard they fought as we sat around the WMIKs as the night faded. We were feeling the effects of the battle now, losing the adrenalin with which we had been pumped. We all mentioned the contacts we had been involved in and the Taliban fighters we had killed. We estimated that Patrols alone had killed anything between 18 and 22 of them not including the A Company boys and the Gurkhas over on the east flank but we had been lucky too, a lot of it down to the skill and professionalism of the blokes with a bit of luck chucked in too. Patrols should have had one T1 casualty at the very least when Bash had been hit; the Gurkhas had received one or two casualties also.

Just before we left Bastion we were issued with the new Osprey body armour, designed more for mobile and vehicle mounted troops. Unlike the old stuff it had two large Kevlar plates front and back rather than the two small square ones that protected the heart on the old one. The down side was it was heavy, restricted your movement and an arse for things like chest rigs and Ops vests to fit over it, especially if you were already a big lad. I like many others decided against it for now, and stuck to the old one. Bash had decided to go for the new Osprey stuff as well as a few others, and this played a big part in saving his life.

Due to Bash being a big bloke he could not get his South African assault vest over his new body armour and used the five issued pouches that came with the vest for his kit and equipment. They fitted to the vest with the magazine pouches sitting on the front plate where his magazine pouches on his South African rig sat on the sides, leaving his chest and abdomen exposed. During the contact Bash had being firing at the Taliban from a corner of a wall. Normally, and especially in Patrols, when we exchange rounds we try and make ourselves as small a target as possible, normally by getting on one knee if not on the belt buckle. Bash hadn't done this and remained on his feet due to the terrain. The Taliban were firing from the wall with the smoke and fire from the grass between them; two 7.62mm rounds hit him bang centre in his abdomen. The two rounds hit his magazines which saved his life; not only that but if he'd adopted the kneeling fire position, like taught, then he would've received two rounds 7.62mm to the head. The impact took him off his feet and onto the floor; it made his tracer rounds explode and begin burning. Lee C. was next to him and ran to his aid, dragging him back into cover while still under fire (Lee never received anything for his brave actions). It was something that happens in the movies or in books not real life but he had the magazines as proof and was still here to tell the tale.

Another close shave that I wasn't aware of was in the initial contact when they ambushed our patrol. Somehow RPGs had missed Ray and Gaz's WMIKs by inches and again at my position and on the start of another contact at the top end of the ruin when a Taliban fighter fired an RPG from the corner of the wall in which Ewan, a thin-shaped Scots lad, was operating the .50. The firer had shot the RPG from around 10–15m away; it missed his head by a foot. Talk about a short back and sides, we joked later.

Drewi had actually seen the Taliban getting into position at the ruin. Looking over the wall he saw six to seven fighters creeping past. He didn't open fire at the time, about which talking to him later I gave him a little slagging. However, he had done a lot better; not being sure on how many were, there he informed the rest of the lads around him. Holding back from firing and informing the lads had definitely saved lives. Without Dewi spotting them moving in to ambush us I think it could have been a very different day.

Many other things happened that day, but we were all still here to tell the story although many of us thought we shouldn't have been. The next day saw me leading the Patrols back to Bastion. When A Company returned they were given a few beers and praised for a job well done which they rightly deserved. By the time we got back nobody seemed to be interested. It didn't bother me but it would have been nice for some of the younger lads to have been given a pat on the back and a cold beer in the hand.

Chapter 7

A Few Hours in Sangin

There seemed to be very little movement on the ground since the trouble at Now Zad and the rest of 3 Para wanted in on the action. PF had been fighting in Musa Qaleh but very little of what was happening to them had come through at this end. After a few admin days back in Bastion, at which point Bernie and Dave, two more Patrol commanders had arrived, we conducted cleaning weapons and equipment and putting the vehicles in for a much needed service and repair. It seemed to me the old bullshit was straight back in. It was my opinion that it was becoming anal for anybody back in camp, and it's my personal belief that a lot of this was coming from the RSM (still Bish at this time) and the provo. In days I wanted to be back on the ground. Give me cold water and decent rat-packs and send me back out on the ground I thought, this is pissing me off. The Battalion Head Shed were on the case of our own Company bosses and commanders. In their eyes you could not be seen to be doing nothing, it was an operational tour and therefore work. The way I see it is, if it's not broken then don't fix it, and after the admin rest and welfare is the next best thing for any soldier. I think some people had forgot this and also forgotten what had just happened a few days ago back in Now Zad where things could have been a lot worse.

Bish wanted to know why we were sitting around doing nothing in these few days to ourselves. It's called rest and relaxing before going back on the ground, I thought, we could be going weeks without a day off and very soon I was proved right. It got to the point where Steve came in our accommodation – a temperamental air-conditioned tent that was to accommodate six to eight lads with full equipment maximum – but we like most of the others had twelve of us squashed in like marines in a gay bar. I was lying on my camp cot that was my bed for the time I spent in Bastion.

'Why aren't your blokes at the vehicles sorting them out?' he said as he stormed in. I could tell by his approach and attitude that he had been rifled by somebody higher and like shit it was now rolling down hill, to us.

'What's to sort? They are done and have been for the last few days', I answered from my half sleep.

'So you're telling me there is nothing to do to them?' he snapped.

'Yeah that's what I'm telling you, Steve?' he pushed on. 'Tommo, are the radios done, batteries and all?'

'Yeah', he replied, sitting up from his camp cot.

'Weapons and WMIKs were done as soon as we got back and personal kit is personal. If they haven't done it by now then they shouldn't be in the army', I said.

120

'Just get your blokes down on the vehicles', he said heading back for the canvas door.

'What the fuck for?' I snapped.

'Just do it!' he snapped in reply, disappearing. I got the blokes and again asked if it was all done. Yes, was the answer. 'Right, well just fuck off for a brew, gym, internet or wank, just keep away from the Head Shed', I snapped. So every day in camp became a mission in itself, dodging the Head Shed and Steve.

In the next few day news began spreading that an Op was going in on the town of Sangin, nobody yet knew exactly when and for what purpose but the lads of Patrols knew one thing, whoever was going in were going to see some action up there, which was for sure. There had also been a small contingent of men sent up to a place called Kajaki Dam at this stage, mostly made up of support companies, guns, anti-tanks and mortars with sniper attachments, signallers, medics, FAC and half of 5 Platoon B Company. Kajaki Dam was an important area, or it seemed to be for the Taliban anyway. The dam was finished in 1975 and had remained fully operational throughout all the troubles of Afghanistan till this very day, surprisingly. An OMLT team had been sent up to support the area. Eight British soldiers and 20 ANA made up the OMLT team who had now joined the local Afghan force commanded by an ex-US special forces' soldier running the private security for the dam. Even with the OMLT support it was close to being overrun on several occasions. The CO was under pressure to do something: 3 Para was being sent up.

Kajaki was miles from anywhere, north-east from Sangin in the remote rocky features. Our lads had flown in and occupied a piece of high ground just off the dam complex, setting up OPs along the ridge along with the guns and Javelin missiles and mortars out of site to the rear as always. Then they waited for the Taliban to strike the dam complex as it was becoming a recurring action. This time the Paras were waiting. As the Taliban began lobbing in their mortars our lads opened up killing all but a couple of the Taliban fighters, about 10–15 men in all. When we heard back at Bastion I was chuffed with the lads, we seemed to be hammering them at every location, showing the Taliban exactly who they were messing with, again. It was an amazing feeling but I also knew that it wouldn't last forever, at some point we would be on the receiving end, it's a fact of life.

We got more information on what was going on in Sangin. The governor of Helmand, Engineer Daoud, had being pushing for the Battle group to do more and more; we had had B Company in Now Zad that handed over to the Gurkhas just before Op Mutay and now had most of 5 Platoon (B Company) in Kajaki, C Company in Gereshk, PF up in Musa Qaleh. A Company were doing all the Op 1 jobs (offensive operations) and IRT and Patrols were being pushed into all locations as the only mobile force operating and we still weren't full operational. Engineer Daoud must've thought we had three or four fighting battalions not just the fighting 3rd with some attachments here.

Engineer Daoud needed our help. One of his former commanders had been attacked and his bodyguards and family members killed. Not only that but one of the local police chiefs was under threat from the local people for raping a young girl.

'Let them have him', we yelled out on hearing the news. I definitely didn't want to be associated with saving or protecting a rapist and paedophile, I thought we were here to protect the people of Afghanistan and rid them from the Taliban and terror. If they thought we were protecting people like this it would turn everyone against us.

Late on the eve of 20 June we got the green light to mount an Op into Sangin. Patrols were included in the ORBAT much to the delight of our lads and A Company, who were the main strength mainly because we had been the only soldiers in that area.

I woke early on the 21st; our kit was sorted and good to go, apart from the small last minute things. I got dressed and placed on my kit and equipment to the sound of *Bad Moon Rising* as always. It was supposed to be a 12–24 hour Op; however, from previous experience I aimed off for a little longer. Our kit was almost as heavy as before: the Patrol commanders were carrying a 351, a larger radio a lot heavier than the rifle company section commanders' 349 radio, just in case we were used to push out and occupy an OP position. More water was included and just as much ammo as before. We were going in by Chinook helicopters and would then be on foot with the A Company boys once we landed.

We formed up in the darkness making sure we all had the correct equipment and that our weapons were oiled and ready to go. There was no in-depth set of orders, there wasn't time, just a quick mission brief and then QBO on the ground. The CH47s were sitting silently to our front awaiting us. After a quick brief we boarded and waited for the pilots to start the engines. On the way passed we picked up a greenie: a green plastic case in the shape of two tubes joined together which held two 81mm rounds for the mortars. It was an SOP within the Reg that every man carried one if needed and on exiting the Chinook we would drop them off in a pile and then carry on with the task. The mortar lads would then set up the mortar line in the relative safety of the HLS or somewhere next to it, collect their greenies and be ready to support us with the 81mm (whether that was HE, smoke or illumination depended on the task) as we advanced onto the target location.

The two large blades of the CH47 began turning, faster and faster and louder and louder. My team had to squat and kneel in the centre of the airframe, not the most comfortable of places, as the seats were already taken with the support elements that were last to be out. We still didn't know if this Op was going in and by the time we got the green light it was getting slightly light. We took off into the twilight sky; I looked at some of my team giving them a nod or wink. That's all that needed to be said now. Then we were lost in our own little worlds and the mission ahead of us. Who knew what lay ahead for us in the town of Sangin?

The primary HLS was in the large dry wadi west of the town and district centre that was the target and where the injured district commander was holding out surrounded by Taliban. If this was hot then the next HLS would be somewhere on the west bank of the river, miles away from the town. The district centre was a single-storey building right on the western edge of town, surrounded by walls and orchards. To its north was a large two-storey skeleton building that wasn't finished with a large wadi running through the town from east to west, where Patrols had operated some weeks before. To the west was the wadi and Helmand River. East, small buildings that connected to the town along with the wadi and south, fields, orchards and farm and rural complexes.

My back was aching already due to the weight on my back that I couldn't remove and I was losing the feeling in my right leg. I wasn't the only one; we were all uncomfortable in some way, shape or form. The flight time was around 40 mins or so; through the porthole windows I could see the morning sun coming up. Well there goes the element of surprise and cover of darkness to cover our approach, I thought. Instead we were now three large targets setting down in total daylight in an area the Yanks had called a Taliban stronghold and major flashpoint. I like many others presumed the worst on arrival. Visions of getting caught up in the HLS by RPG, mortars and machine gun fire entered my head. Well it was too late now, I thought as we swooped in for the final approach.

My heart was racing; we needed to be off quick. My team was to move to the right on exit and then push forward some 20m before finding some cover in the dry wadi bed. We landed with a thud; the tailgate was almost fully down and in a split second the lads at the front were off and running from the aircraft. Just like parachuting from a C-130 everyone began pushing forward, eager to get off. The noise from the rotors on the Chinook was deafening as I ran off the tailgate and onto the stony surface of the wadi floor. I caught sight of my boys taking cover in the small wadi folds to my front. I jumped down next to them and strained my ears to hear over the sounds of the engines of the helis. In seconds the Chinook was empty, and with an increased sound and strain on the engines causing a powerful down draft the large helicopter gained height and headed back to the safety of the open blue skies.

I couldn't hear any sounds of firing from the direction of the town. I was very surprised. I located the district building in a few seconds, just visible from my position but concentrated my team on watching the south-easterly flank along the wadi bank which was of thick vegetation: an ideal ambush area. A Company were already advancing forward as we sat back and waited for any trouble they might expect. We could then push to their flank and take on any enemy while they suppressed them. It never came. A Company moved in and held the district building as we began moving forward towards the south-east of the target. The heat was starting to kick in: early morning and it was over 40 degrees already. We hit a track that ran along the wadi and green belt (vegetation, orchards and fields). The other Patrols were going to stay on the outside of the building complex securing the outer perimeter as my team got tasked to go inside.

There was a little bridge on the track that a fast-flowing river ran through, past the back of the walls of the district building and onto the Helmand River that curved right as we approached the centre edges of town. I pushed my team in through a break in the wall of the compound and took the western wall. I positioned the boys and began to establish communications with the boss outside.

I hadn't really taken anything in as I had entered apart from the young wounded district chief and his bodyguards but now I had a bit of time to take in my surroundings.

The young Afghan had take rounds to his abdomen and looked in a lot of pain. Our medics were already sorting him out. One of his elder bodyguards, around mid-fifties, had also been hit, shot in the arse but was walking round like it was fuck all. I was quite impressed; these were hard people and I wasn't afraid to say it. The alleged rapist was supposed to be in a different area of the Sangin to the north. I never heard what happened to him but I would like to think he got what he deserved when the locals got hold of him.

The main building was a whitewash-coloured structure with an overhanging stone ledge shielding the front from the sun, with a set of stairs making access to the roof to the left. A couple of small portacabin buildings sat to the rear and it was surrounded by high mud walls. The main ground surrounding this was only around 50m by 30m square. From the front of the main building was a track that made its way through the wall to the main entrance that looked onto the wadi that ran into town; the entrance was at a right angle to the complex. Directly behind this entrance was a half completed building, wood supports still holding up parts of the roof and walls.

My CSM Dave T. had come in on the mission and called me over. He wanted me to take the local Afghan guards with their vehicles and collect the heavy kit that was still on the HLS: mostly the mortars, anti-tanks and guns equipment that was really heavy. Me and my team commandeered the pick-up trucks and raced down to the HLS and helped the boys move their kit. Once back inside my Patrol pushed into the orchard fields at the eastern and southern edges of the complex, still within the confines of the walls. It was quite nice in there, the trees keeping the burning sun off our backs but also making it a lot more humid, trapping the heat in.

I pushed out the team covering the area. Me and Johnny paired off in the centre with Prig who had joined us with a little local boy aged around seven, covering a break in the wall that looked down a small abandoned side street. There was a little stream running through the orchard to our front and for a few seconds while Prig and Johnny chatted to the boy I forgot where I was. Time had flown and it was a really hot day, lying here chilling with Prig and Johnny and a friendly local made me feel like we were in the safest place on earth. It was strange. A quick slagging got me back on the level.

'No funny business with that kid, mind you Prig' I said.

'Do you want to try my helmet?' Prig tried to explain to the boy. I looked at Johnny; both of us began pissing ourselves.

'You fucking what, Prig!' we began, 'try your helmet!!' So the boy did (his Para helmet may I add) and I got a quick photo of it.

The first few days in Sangin were quiet, the OC of A Company set up his command post as soon as he got the command that he was to hold this position and stop it falling into the Taliban hands, something that had changed on the ground. Like I said before, a simple 12–24 hour Op now looked like it was going into something much longer, a few days, a few weeks. Who was to know that it would be held till we handed over to the next regiment to relieve us in October?

In days this place became known as a Platoon House, one of many that became established later in the tour. It was a mini-fortress; the boys had made and erected Sangar positions on the rooftops and around the outer walls made from sandbags, wood, bricks, corrugated iron and anything else they could gather. The gun teams, FAC, anti-tanks and snipers held the rooftop of the highest building that sat to the north and was known as FSG House, from this position you could see a hell of a lot: the wadi, river and western bank to the left, the northern greenery and buildings, the shopfronts that sat to the front right leading into town along the east–west wadi that was re-named the pipe range and then the town to the north-east. The rifle sections manned the sangar positions at ground level around the complex, each section holding a key area and keeping guard from the sangar. This became part of life for the boys on the ground. One man would stag on while the rest rested, slept, ate and conducted admin during the day; at night there were always two lads watching due to tiredness, strain and lack of visibility. Each sangar would have around five or six blokes operating from it and their shift would last 24hrs. Some people might think this was an easy task split between the five or six men; however, add the elements of heat, lack of food and water, constant attacks that were soon to come, no electricity, washing facilities and shit houses, limited equipment (what we had brought in on our backs was our lot) and the fact that if they weren't on guard they were patrolling these dangerous streets, put a lot of strain on the blokes. The main building itself became the HQ and RAP with two mortar teams in the grounds around it. After a lot of blood, sweat and tears the Platoon House of Sangin was becoming a lot more secure.

Sangin was still fairly quiet around 27 June, that was till an Op went in south of the town. The Op was a snatch and grab on a key Taliban leader by SF soldiers. It went wrong resulting in one KIA and another missing. B Company was tasked to support and find the MIA and bring him back, alive if possible. B Company reacted from Bastion and with the mass troops invading and securing the town in minutes of arriving on the ground the Taliban and locals were on the back foot, but they soon realised that the surprise, speed and aggression in which they moved in would not last for long. They had to be fast, find them and get out. They found the bodies of two dead British soldiers and evacuated them out with them. It was an instant blow for all that knew them. From that day many people thought the attitude of the local people in Sangin would change, and they were right. A few pot-shots were fired at the platoon house, what we call shoot and scoots. A few rounds fired at a sangar before they disappeared back into the cover of the town or greenery. At this point they were more than likely watching for our reactions and testing our defences but they were also sniping exposed targets.

Everybody was convinced that a Taliban sniper was operating in the area. A mate of mine (Jim) in the machine gun platoon was on stag one day in the FSG building, he bent down to pick something up that caught his eye. As he ducked down a round cracked and struck the wall where his head had just been.

A chunk of stone from the wall cut into his ear; he was lucky, just like Bash with his magazines.

'Scotty that fucking sniper had his sights on me, if I hadn't dropped down I'd be fucking dead', he told me later.

This story came back to me after an incident in Basra in 2007 while I was a CPO. One of our teams was on its way back in from a job further north; the air station at Basra was restricted on routes in and out making every mission a little nerve racking, vulnerable to EFP and IED at the start and finish of the mission. The team, E3, pushed over a flyover called A1A about a kilometre south from the camp entrance. On approach the lead vehicle was hit by an EFP, the copper chunks that form projectiles tore through the B6 armour like it was nothing, most of it directed to the rear of the vehicle. Kiwi Dave was in the back facing rearwards as the gunner. He bent down to his grab his mobile phone that he had dropped while pulling it out of his pocket. A large amount of copper penetrated the armour and hit him in the head, the armour had slowed it down and his Kevlar helmet kept him alive. If he was upright as usual then it would have taken his face off.

These pot-shots had now turned into attacks. A Company were a static target, and with only limited soldiers to conduct patrols, were vulnerable to attacks. The Taliban took advantage, sneaking into different locations around the complex and attacking in co-ordinated ambushes. At first it was mostly at night but soon it was happening in daylight and around three times a day. They were becoming that intense that air power was also being called in. The Taliban were often close to the walls trying to penetrate a weak spot. The blokes were well into routine by now but due to the increase of attacks there wasn't much scope for rest and sleep. That and the fact that the temperature during the night was mid-thirties making any quiet night hard to sleep anyway.

It was back to basics in Sangin, sandbag sangars on windows and walls, shell scraps and mortar pits, the river for washing kit and our own bodies, ration pack scoffs and ridiculously hot drinking water. Next time you're on holiday somewhere hot – most holiday destinations are around 30–35 degrees so add on another 15–20 degrees –leave your water out in the open sun for an hour of so then drink it, it doesn't taste too good and sometimes makes you feel sick. Imagine having to live on it day in day out. Imagine having to wear full kit all the time, not being able to strip down, go into the air-con building or dunk in the pool to cool off. The temperature was so hot that you could make a decent brew with it; I often chucked a bottle onto the bonnet of my WMIK to make a coffee using the heat off the bonnet.

On the night of 1 July the lads went into night routine; movement was kept to a minimum and the blokes who weren't on duty tried to settle down on the floor in hope for some decent sleep. Just after 21:00hrs a massive explosion broke the silent night. This was followed up with small arms fire and RPG whacking into and over the FSG building that overlooked the pipe range. The highest point of the FSG building was hit, flames and smoke flying from it. It was now an aiming post for the Taliban fighters. The square shaped concrete block sat on top, silhouetted on the roof. It was at the top of the concrete stairwell used to gain access to the roof. As well as being the main access route it also hosted the LEWT team. A couple of attached signallers and an interpreter that were listening in on the Taliban were using it as their work and rest area, mainly because it was the highest and best position to gain radio waves and signals. One of my mates in the mortars, 'Hoss' Cartwright, had been in there too and above them two snipers lay on the wooden beams watching for signs of movement, Taff Hatfield being one of them. At the time it was believed that it was a recoilless rifle that had done the damage. Later it was assessed as a 107mm Chinese rocket. There was a lot of confusion going on and the majority of the blokes on the rooftop were still firing away at the muzzle flashes of the Taliban weapons in the distance to the north.

Messages got passed down that there were casualties; the blokes continued engaging the enemy while Zack Leong the CSM took a work party up to the tower to bring the casualties down. 'Hoss' Cartwright had severe shrapnel wounds in his arse, but he was OK. The other lads in there were not so fortunate. L/Cpl Jabron Hashmi and Cpl Peter Thorpe had taken the brunt of the impact along with the local interpreter. Jabron Hashmi was in a lot of pain but still alive as the rescue party brought him down the stairs but died just as he arrived at the RAP that was in the white building at the rear of the FSG building. Peter Thorpe had died there and then in the tower with the interpreter. The snipers just above the tower had been lucky and received small shrapnel wounds and hearing damage due to the explosion along with some of the other lads on the rooftop. The lads on the rooftop around the tower had somehow survived.

As with all casualties a sit rep had been sent through to Bastion requesting a heli for the P1 casualties (needing surgery and/or possible resuscitation). The two P1 casualties were soon P4, or as it is now known T1, no vital signs shown. There was no need for helis tonight.

I had seen Jabron cutting around in Bastion but didn't know him personally; he seemed a young, quiet lad. Pete was the LEWT commander; a few of us knew him since he had been attached to the Battle group, a good down-to-earth bloke. The 107mm Chinese rocket had initiated the contact; it was a direct hit on the FSG tower that tore through the concrete like it was cardboard leaving a big gaping hole. Pete and Jabron, both Royal Signals attached, were both killed; five others were P2 and P3 casualties. These lads weren't Paras but that didn't matter, they were part of this team. Everyone felt saddened by the loss.

The next day the two KIAs, sealed in body bags, were flown out of Sangin along with the P2 and P3 casualties. The Chinook that had come in to pick them up brought in the CO rover group. Lieutenant Colonel Stuart Tootal our CO had come to see how the boys were doing. He stayed the night in Sangin with the OC Will Pike.

As the light faded over Sangin the CO, RSM (Bish) and some others were up on the rooftop of the HQ helping out with the defences. The Taliban attacked the platoon house again, RPG and machine gun fire flying all over the place.

On 3 July the first elements of B Company prepped themselves for the takeover of Sangin platoon house from the A Company boys. It was a large Op involving everyone already in Sangin to secure the area for the two Chinooks coming in. It was also a chance to bring in more water, food, ammo and medical supplies. The two CH47 came in from the south-west and used the HLS in the wadi as before. Half of B Company and attachments picked up their kit and patrolled into the platoon house. Before last light B Company took over the guard of the camp allowing everyone who had been their since 21 June to rest.

At this time I, Dave E. and Bernie M. settled outside of the small box-shaped concrete room close to the gate that looked back onto the HQ building. Trees shaded the sun over the doorway of our little home while we sat and cooked up some spicy scoff. We sat and took the piss out of one another and talked general bollocks, mostly related to drink, sex, scrapping, jumping and making up and spreading shit (only banter) about each other: your typical Para's conversation really. Dave was a 24yrs full screw and a good mate, we had served in A Company together a few moons ago, people said we looked slightly alike but Dave was definitely the chubbier and less attractive one (it's OK, you can thank me later, Dave). Me and Dave spent a lot of time together and were constantly slagging each other or fucking about in some way. One of my old screws from depot, Steve, called us the Chuckle Brothers as we were always pissing about and arguing. Bernie was also a full screw and Patrol commander, I had also first met him while serving in A Company. A bit older with more years experience than me and Dave, he was a good soldier with a lot of knowledge and also one of the best tabbers I had come across. Tabbing (Tactical advance to battle) was an expression used for getting from the DZ or HLS to the FRV or target with kit on your back at speed. Bernie was also known as the mountain goat, even by Paratrooper standards he would out-tab 95 per cent of the battalion.

As the light faded into pure darkness our laughs turned to whispers.

'Come on, shall we go and see Dan, Charlie and Prig?' I said.

'Yeah fuck it, it beats listening to your shite all night', Dave replied. The three of us ran across the small 50m gap to the HQ building taking with us our fighting order. 1 Platoon were under the overhang, around 30 of them lying on the floor. In the left-hand corner was Prig, Charlie and Bryan so we went over and joined them getting ourselves as comfortable as possible on the hard floor under the overhang. During the early days of Afghanistan I had worked alongside Prig and Charlie as the 3 Section commander under big Dan and Hugo Farmer back in Gereshk. When my team went back to Patrols where it belonged Bryan Budd came back to command 3 Section. I had known Bryan a few years and met him when I first turned up at battalion before he moved to PF. He was an extremely well-liked bloke, calm and cool and a very professional soldier. He left 3 Para for PF and had now come back; his combat experience and soldiering skills were welcomed by all especially by 1 Platoon whom he worked under. I lay next to Bryan and Charlie and we sat and talked about old times and the tour here and now. I didn't realise it at the time but it was the last time I would have a chat to Bry and one of the last times I would see him alive.

BOOM! An explosion erupted next to the HQ, my heart missed a beat and the shock wave that passed through my body was immense.

'What the fuck was that?' All hell broke loose on top of the roof and at the north and eastern sangars. The GPMG and .50 were banging away. Everyone scrambled for their body armour, Para lids and weapons which were always within arm's reach. Shall I go up to one of the sangars and lend a hand, I thought? I suppose I just wanted to do something but I quickly realised that I would be in the way and could quite easily be shot by the sangar positions as I moved through the darkness.

After 5–10mins the incoming stopped but our mortars began throwing up illumination and HE. Everybody remained alert expecting more incoming. I still didn't know if it was a mortar or what that had hit the camp, whatever it was it was loud and fucking powerful.

'I think it hit our room' Dave said.

'Fuck me, we would have been in there a half hour ago, mate', I replied.

'Yeah I know, that was lucky', Dave answered laughing. The next morning we discovered that the wall of the room we had been staying in was also part of the outer wall that ran along to the gateway; it had been hit with a 107mm Chinese rocket, the same weaponry that killed Pete Thorpe and Jabron Hashmi. The room was still intact but had been damaged. I reckoned that if we had been in there we would have been injured, probably receiving shrapnel wounds from the concrete and internal bleeding due to the blast, which happens a lot, and also due to the echo from the concrete probably had our earsdrums blown out.

Nearly a year to the day the same thing happened to me again. I had just come over to Baghdad and was leaving the villa that we were staying at. As myself and another operator walked to the door an almighty explosion erupted, smashing the windows and taking us off our feet. A 107 or 122mm rocket had been fired into the IZ from insurgents which had flown directly past the front door and taken down the wall behind it. Three seconds later it would have cut us in half as we left the villa. We had been really lucky. I had to have a quick word with myself thinking that maybe all the shit from Afghan was following me as I had only been in Baghdad around a week, but after half an hour I just laughed it off, and cracked on.

I placed my PRR onto the channel operated by the fellas on the roof hoping to find out more. I could hear a conversation between the OC and one of the anti-tank observers.

'We have a vehicle on the extreme east', a voice said.

'Hit it', the OC replied.

'Roger', came the reply. A few seconds later a loud whooshing sound broke out; this time instead of coming towards us it was heading away. The vehicle had been close to the firing point of the contact; it was almost definitely moving the source of that explosion that had hit us minutes before, whether it was a mortar base plate or recoilless rifle. That and the fact that a warning had gone out after the first few attacks on the platoon house that there was a 'no move at night policy' in Sangin town. Anybody moving at night was seen to be a threat and Taliban and would be taken down. The snipers were having a field day, every few hours you would hear a 338 sniper rifle firing into the darkness. Seconds later a message came from the rooftop, target destroyed. Anti-tanks hit the vehicle with a Javelin missile, one of the first ever to be used in anger by the British army.

We tried to sleep but it just wasn't happening for me, I was wide awake and hotter than a fatty in bin liner.

'Dave, you awake?' I whispered. I got no answer. 'Fuck it, I'm going on the roof.' I still had my body armour on; I put on my chest rig and Para lid and grabbed my weapon and made my way over to the break in the wall that led into the FSG building. I passed a few of the blokes stagging on at the windows of the building and made my way up the concrete stairs. You find that in temperatures like these the heat gets trapped in the buildings and that is why it's sometimes advisable to sleep outside. The boys in the FSG building (mainly the attachments of 3 Para snipers, machine guns, anti-tanks, FAC, MFC and signallers) couldn't. I got on the top which was quite refreshing and moved over to a GPMG sangar. From there I watched out with the boys till first light. The rest of the night had been quiet apart from the odd sniper shot and mortar round being fired and I moved back to my kit still down at the little concrete room.

From then on the attacks on Sangin platoon house became worse, the attacks harder and more often. On several occasions JDAMS had to be dropped on the other side of the wall to stop the Taliban penetrating the compound. It was funny, here was us a small band of men inside a little compound fighting for in some cases our lives thousands of miles away from home in the ridiculous heat and living in bunkers or the floor, and drinking and eating hot, sickly food and water and there are prisoners back in the UK wingeing about not getting treated correctly. They have decent food, accommodation, TV and pool tables, etc. Fuck me they have it easy, we thought, they want to build prisons in Sangin or better still get the fuckers over here for a few days then see what they want to winge about after that. This was the same after 1 Para had moved from their Dover base. They decided to use it for the holding of illegal immigrants. They complained and after an investigation went ahead they decided it wasn't suitable for them. Hang on a minute, it was good enough for a battalion of Her Majesty Paratroopers so why not illegal immigrants, who to be honest should not have any say in the matter. And guess what, we were at war and still paying our taxes so they could be put up in five star hotels. That, just like prisoners wingeing and complaining, really pissed us off. If you didn't fuck up in the first place then you wouldn't be in there, and for the immigrants, then again if you don't like it then fuck off.

That day before A Company were due to move out the OC decided to hold a *shura* (meeting) for the local elders. I stripped down and sat out in the sun and made a bird's eye view (sketch) of the platoon house including all defences, like sangar and claymore positions. The village elders had arrived in the small courtyard of the main HQ building; two of them saw me sketching away and like all Arabs came up to look. Nosy twats, they were all like this. As they began looking in I folded the map over which had the town of Sangin on the other side. They moved away and began talking to one another and I began cracking on with my sketch. Again as soon as my map was out and I put pencil to paper they were back over me.

'Go away', I said, 'GO!' I pointed to the building where the rest of the elders were waiting. They smiled and made some comment in Arabic and the younger of the two leaned in again to my map. 'FUCK OFF!' I shouted as I stood up. They got the message and moved on. I didn't trust any of these people; they could all be Taliban for all we knew and I was marking information on our defences.

The *shura* lasted about an hour; they didn't seem too happy as they began to leave from the main entrance to the north. As they cleared the pipe range and disappeared a massive wave of automatic fire began whacking over our heads from the opposite end of the complex. If that wasn't a set up then I don't know what is, I thought. They were showing who was boss and who had control here. The Taliban had sneaked through the thick vegetation to our rear and began firing once they knew the elders were clear.

The mortars lads began lobbing their 81mm at the firing point. They had put up a good rate of fire on the initial opening, the rounds cracking over our heads as I ran across the courtyard to the wall where Dave and Bernie were seated. I whacked my body armour and chest rig on and listen in to the radio. The GMPG were blazing away from the over the walls. Whoosh! An RPG came right over the compound over our heads missing the wall by inches. The sangar down in the orchard was taking the brunt of it. Around 15mins later it went quiet. Rumours of a casualty came round and it turned out that an ANA had been hit in the arm. The blokes on the sangars and roof went straight into their re-org drills, making sure all ammo was reimbursed and there were no casualties while me, Dave and Bernie got ready to join Dan's platoon who were getting kitted up to sweep the area for Taliban fighters. On one knee I ensured my kit was sorted, mags were good, tourniquet and FFDs were still attached and easily identified and accessible and grenades still where they should be. I turned my GPS on and laid it on the floor in front of me with my small Sangin map. I checked my weapon again, mag securely fitted, round chambered and my sights on 300m. Now we just waited for the off.

I began going through my actions on, what if this happens, what if that happens, what if I get shot, what if my mate gets shot, a million and one things running through my head. When you get ambushed like we had in Now Zad you don't have time to think of all the little things that could go wrong, with the years of training you hope it is enough to get you through and you just go with sheer bollocks and soldiering skills at the time. Everything goes that quick that you don't have time to worry. However when you are about to go into an area that had just been full of Taliban and you're waiting for the first crack of firing your mind often begins to run away with you.

We waited at the wall waiting to go, only be told to stand down. They had pulled back but it looked as though they were still lurking, possibly in a ambush waiting for us to make our clearance patrol. The last thing anyone wanted was more casualties and KIA. The mortars continued dropping 81mm into the area, the MFC Mark Wright and his mates were doing a good job and spotted Taliban not far from the contact point, they closed the mortar rounds around them and on top till all the movement had stopped.

Feeling a little keen a few of us volunteered to help stag on the FSG building; a couple of extra bodies could make a big difference for people having extra down time. The sun and heat was at its maximum, slowly cooking all of us as we moved about, constantly pissing with sweat with nowhere to cool ourselves. It makes you appreciate air-con and cool water and some of the basics we normally have back home.

I moved up into the FSG building relieving Bernie from his stag rotation. It had been the first time I paid any attention to the large concrete stairwell as I moved up them. Bloodstains were clearly visible from the night of 1 July. I got myself on my haunches and settled into my stag; my view was mainly to the north and west of the district centre: the river looked amazing, clear light blue and refreshing. There were people walking and riding over the small crooked wooden bridge. You wouldn't think a few hours ago this place was like a scene from *Zulu*. As time passed I kept scanning the ground in my arcs; time was ticking and I was thinking of getting some scoff on the go after this when I realised that it was very quiet, another combat indicator which we had began switching onto before most attacks. Very different from Iraq where they are quite happy to kill innocent men, women and children around a IED or ambush when a British patrol moves past.

A huge boom erupted overhead, I could only think it was 107mm that had gone high and missed the target: us. From the north and north-east direction 7.62mm came screaming in; our guns reacted, firing on rapid to win the fire fight and keep the enemy's heads down. The noise, like always, is deafening especially from inside the building. There were fire control orders and target indications being shouted from the roof. I turned to see Andy K. from Snipers running up the stairs.

'Here we go again, Scotty', he said.

'Yeah lucky I wasn't scoffing up or I would fucking snap', I shouted up the stairs behind him. Andy had joined 3 Para just after me and again we had served in A Company together. I remember on an airborne exercise jumping into a DZ somewhere in the UK. Andy had been on the other side of the aircraft to me. Unknown to us, we must have been the same number down the line in the jump queue, but with myself on port and Andy on starboard. As I exited the C-130 we came face-to-face with each other, almost getting entangled in each other's parachutes and rigging lines. I managed to resolve this by putting my size 11 boot into his face, although once clear we continued to slag and blame each other for being a sky mong until we hit the ground. I think most of snipers and Patrols had come from A Company. A 24 yrs screw with ginger hair, although that wasn't his fault, we had always been close mates, he was a good sniper. Andy and the other snipers here were doing a mega job of hitting Taliban fighters sneaking forward.

Crack, crack, crack; a few stray rounds hit the side of the building a few metres from me. I pushed myself into the corner and scanned the greenery to my front. Where the fuck did that come from? Crack, crack, crack, crack, crack, crack! More automatic fire hit the wall, this time a little closer. 'Why the fucking twats …' I caught myself saying. I spotted the foliage moving over to my right; I began firing just as Minimi gunner a floor above me opened up. I could see at least three crawling through the tree line and out of sight. I continued pumping rounds into the area for a few seconds in an aim to catch one of them or all three. I stopped firing and looked at possible areas where they would expose again to take further pot shots at us or escape. I waited but they never reappeared.

Aircraft screamed overhead making their presence known to all. A set of A10 had been operating in the area when the main FAC called for air power. The Taliban automatically knew to silence their weapons, make a run for it or hide. They normally hid as movement would be picked up, but unfortunately for them they obviously didn't realise the technology these boys had up there. Moving or not, most of them would be turned to dust in the next minute or so. They came diving in one at a time smashing the wood line to the north-east now known as Wombat Wood, the firepower was amazing yet terrifying at the same time. Fuck being in their shoes, I thought. Blokes now put their weapons to one side and grabbed their cameras while they hammered the area with their 30mm cannon lighting up the area, followed up with a few minutes' pause. The Taliban thought the A10 had possibly returned to base. We knew different, a 30-second count got past, around 10 seconds followed.

'Keep down!' someone shouted from the rooftop. The buildings to the north just erupted into a puff of smoke and rubble with a shock wave and huge booming noise following a split second after. Cheers came from all who was watching.

'That will keep the fuckers quiet for a bit', someone shouted over the cheers.

I came off my busy stag and settled back down beside the shade of the trees. Nobody really talked of the constant attacks that were now happening; it was part of the Sangin routine now. I stripped off my body armour and helmet, the sweat dripping off me and began to set my gas burner running while I prepped my mess tin and rations. A Company were told they were moving back to Bastion within the hour, or at least some of them. Chinooks would be en route soon to pick them up.

A message came back from Bastion that there was a need for me, Dave and Bernie to fly out with A Company also. There were missions happening elsewhere very soon which needed the three of us. 1 Platoon was also told they were staying behind and due to fly out the next day due to lack of air power (Chinooks). I rammed the rest of my scoff down my neck and got my shit together and said my goodbyes to my mates in B Company who would now have a hard few weeks ahead: the last four or five attacks in the 48 hours had already proved the fact. We tagged on the back of 2 Platoon and patrolled out to the south-west; the HLS was south-west of the complex next to another compound. We used the high wall and trees to shield us from the sun and view from any locals and waited for the choppers.

The lads from B Company and 1 Platoon pushed forward securing the HLS and areas south and east of it in the thick dangerous greenery, something that had to happen in order to protect the CH47 during taking off and landing. Some lads from Support Company, guns, tanks and mortars used this opportunity to use the river and get a wash 50m from where we waited. The fast flowing river was used only when protection was out as it was just on the outside of the platoon house; we had put a vehicle towstrap and rope out, attached to the side, so you could hang on or connect yourselves to it while washing without worrying about getting swept away. That would be all you need, swimming past the Taliban flashing your arse off and you wouldn't want them getting the wrong idea.

The sound of blades caught my ear; I looked up and saw two Apaches already hovering above us at a great height, covering the town as the CH47 came low and fast. The sound grew louder and we started venturing out into the open, scanning as we moved as this the most likely time to get hit. The Chinook came in at a pace swinging its huge arse round and settling down. We raced on and I noticed that the loadies were a little panicky; they didn't want to stay on the ground too long. Packed with Paratroopers we took off and headed out of Sangin and the safety of camp Bastion.

Back in our tents we dropped our kit and took a shower and generally de-grunged ourselves. There was little time to chill however; Patrols were getting a warning order to protect a convoy into Musa Qaleh in the next few hours.

Chapter 8

A Fallen Paratrooper

Again we went through the usual process of getting ready for the long move. It would be our longest yet. Musa Qaleh was situated north-east of Bastion, around 65ks in a straight line: however, that never happened. Deception plans, dog-legs, VP and the ground would decide the route. It had become the furthest outpost (platoon house) that the Battle group operated from. More and more trouble was brewing from up there and PF were on their own. They had gone up to support the ANP and ANA. They too had gone from a few days' Op to now a lengthier operation. They couldn't just leave now. After several attempted helicopter re-supplies all of which had to pull off due to intense fire, a cross-country vehicle supply was the only option.

After the big kick-off about the .50 Cal weapons not firing correctly in Now Zad, little had been done. PF were also having dramas up north and at last something was getting sorted. The Canadians and Estonians were selling the British army .50 Cal ammunition. It was ridiculous that this couldn't be solved ourselves and we had to sponge off other countries, as whoever had ordered the ammo had, in my opinion, gone for some cheap shit and the low grade of ammo was causing the problems, but at least we were getting it from elsewhere. Patrols had actually pre-empted this and had begged, borrowed and stolen around 200 to 300 hundred rounds per gun off our foreign counterparts. Not a lot but hopefully enough to get us through an initial contact and out of any killing zone that we may have entered. We knew that if we did not, next time could be a lot worse, we weren't waiting for some pencil pusher up north to get the ball rolling.

What had happened in Now Zad, Sangin, Kajaki and now Musa Qaleh had made the top brass realise this was no ordinary Iraq, Kosovo or Northern Ireland tour. I also began seeing more kit and equipment coming through the stores, TI was the big thing, TI sights for personal weapons and the .50 Cals were like rocking horse shit yet here they were (one TI per .50 Cal and one Viper TI per team). The new body armour and swing arms for the WMIK along with run-flat tyres we also accommodated. Also more ammo was coming in and we could eventually operate with our 'full scales' ammunition: which for us was as much as we could get hold of. About time; but again a little too late in my eyes.

I sat in the cookhouse with a brew and looked over my map; none of us had been any further north than Now Zad. Now Zad and Musa Qaleh were only 25ks away from each other but large wadis and mountain ranges separated them. Musa Qaleh had made up the right tip of the inverted 'triangle of death' as it was now known, a phrase used by the Yanks. Now Zad was at the left and Sangin at the bottom tip of the inverted triangle. Musa Qaleh had a large influx of Taliban coming down from Baghran that sat further north and also Sangin which was almost directly south about 35ks; all three sat along the Helmand River and looked as if they were mutually supporting each other along with Now Zad to their west.

My route would take us over the A1 and through the flat, open plains towards Now Zad; reaching the mountains I would then skirt round to the north-east boxing round the little settlements and farmlands and negotiate the large wadis coming off from the mountains. From map studies I looked for ground that would not be too steep or high, trying to pin-point crossing points using the contour lines from the map as an aid. It wasn't a problem for us, the WMIKs had proved they could handle a lot worse terrain, but a lot more difficult for the large HGVs with metal containers of equipment on the back. We briefed the logistic commanders on our actions – for them it was simple if they came under attack: they were to follow the boss's WMIK to a safe location away from the fire fight. Patrols would navigate recce forward, clear obstacles and protect the convoy if under fire. We also prepared ourselves for a long stay in Musa Qaleh just in case. I had a feeling that Patrols being the same size, strength and job role would take over from PF allowing them to return with the convoy to Bastion for admin and rest.

There was news in that a TIC (team in contact) was happening up in Sangin, not much of a surprise at the time, it was happening three times a day on average but this one was a little different. There was a little more of a flap in the air. The rest of the handover between A and B Company was due today as me, Bernie, Dave and 2 Platoon had pulled out the day before; the CH47 had already left to bring out the rest of A Company home as I had heard the noisy fuckers from my pit (bed space). Until I found out exactly what was going on there was little we could do and we continued our planning for the mission.

A few hours later one of the Patrols lads came in and told me of the news. Damien Jackson or Jacko as he was known had been KIA while on patrol.

'You sure?' I said.

'Definitely, Scotty.' I stopped and let it sink in for a few seconds. Jacko was a member of 1 Platoon A Company, a young blond-haired lad of 19yrs. It was a shock to the system. He was a fellow Mackam and devoted Sunderland supporter; we always talked about how our team was doing and told each other the results when someone would email from back home. I and other members of the Patrols platoon had worked alongside him when attached to 1 Platoon earlier on in the tour. I was gutted not only for Jacko but also his family and his best mates within the Company. A young lad and professional Paratrooper who had paid the ultimate sacrifice for his mates. I wanted to hear the full story of what had happened but that would have to wait, the lads who were there needed time to let it sink in and to sort themselves out.

We all respected the need to keep our gobs shut after a death of a friend. We had all been there and unfortunately have to go through it many times over, whether it was here or in our operations worldwide. In the army and CP world we deal with it day in day out. There is always a mate or bloke you know off doing something somewhere that gets killed. It never gets any easier but we respect each other's silence giving ourselves a chance to deal with it in our own way. It's only when some idiot back home asked if any of your lads were killed, or when they say 'Did you know that a Para guy has died' etc. They don't realise the Paras are a close knit family. They fail to realise that it's a very small world and they are our mates, part of the blood clot.

Again we sat for orders, all of us now on a downer following a loss of a fellow Paratrooper, and explained the mission ahead. Once we were happy the rest of the night was ours.

Early the next morning before the sun came up we scoffed up and loaded our bergens, weapons and other kit onto the WMIKs. We rolled forward onto the main track where the convoy was parked; it was a quite a large convoy made up of HGV, Pinzgauers and Land Rovers. I knew it was going to be a long day and that the large vehicles would struggle moving cross the harsh rocky and uneven ground, but I would rather have that and get everyone up there in on piece than get IED somewhere on a nice long comfortable road.

If it was only Patrols moving then we could hide our movement as we boxed round VP and use the ground to get ourselves to our objective. Now we had a convoy to bring up, we would have protect them and not just hide ourselves, hiding them. This was near impossible too but still better moving cross country giving onlookers no real idea of our route, destination, RV and entry point.

After a few stop starts we began moving out and headed north. Crossing the A1 got us a lot of attention. As per our SOP for normal large patrols we blocked the road allowing the large convoy through. The ANP were also out and watching us disappear from the high ground. I continued pushing directly north looking like we were heading for Now Zad till we reached the mountains.

So far so good, I thought: a wrong thing to say. The ground from here became a lot harder, the Patrol teams worked non-stop pushing in front of the convoy and finding and securing wadis. On a few occasions we would have to stop the whole convoy while the two teams up front (mine and Bernie's) pushed left and right sometimes 4 or 5ks to find ideal crossing locations. As this was our first mission up here we could afford to use ready made crossings (tracks) but I tried to avoid them and we wouldn't be stupid enough to keep using them especially close to settlements and habitats.

The large HGVs began struggling and due to the intense weather a few began to overheat, stopping the convoy with our Patrols pushed to their exposed flanks. These stop starts were starting to wind everyone up but there was nothing we could do. Sitting in the hot sun was beginning to do my head in too, we had already used our cold water that we had managed to get from the chefs and were back onto the hot stuff. Placing a bottle in a wet sock cooled it down quite a bit, only trouble was using extra water to soak the sock, but it worked as long as it remained wet – something we had used in the invasion of Iraq back in 2003.

I wrapped my shemagh around my head in an effort to keep off the burning sun. In conditions like this anything metal was scalding, conducting the heat. Tape was strapped onto the weapons to stop us burning our hands and arms when picking them up and anything else that would be touched after being left in the sun. Another useful idea we had was bringing out foldaway chairs. If out in the open desert we could angle the WMIKs giving a fair amount of shade to one side. As one bloke took stag watching the open desert, the rest could sit in the shade against the WMIK. It was ideal, not exactly tactical but in the open desert we would have a lot of warning of anything approaching. It was another thing to make our lives that little more comfortable.

We pushed on and cleared the mountains and small pockets of farmland. We now had two large wadis to cross to get to our RV that we were to meet the PF at. The wadis were huge and in some cases 100–200m in depth, the biggest we had come across. This caused problems, but again we found some areas to cross. Our front two Patrol teams (my two and Bernie's two) pushed over the wadis first, clearing them and proving the route. Steve, a team from 7 RHA and the boss's team held the high ground overlooking the wadi; if we got in the shit down here they could provide fire support from the banks of the wadi. It was always a vunerable time, they were natural obstacles and choke points for us and if we were hit clearing these in the deep wadi we would be trapped. We always tried to overwatch the area first, looking for any tell-tale signs of a possible ambush. If we did get caught out the Taliban would be firing down from the high ground onto us as we would have to E+E back to the friendly side with Steve, Lee's and Tom's team covering us. The name of the game as always was to keep them guessing, choosing different routes and crossing points and not going for the easy (locals') crossing.

It had been hard work and the sun was dropping in the sky as we sat on the furthest wadi looking back, covering the convoy moving through beneath us. An Arabic voice was blasting down my earpiece.

'Who the fuck's that?' I said.

'Fuck knows but I've got it too', Tommo said. We passed it up through the boss.

'I think there is someone on this net', I said. A lot of other boys had heard it too and it had seemed that the Taliban had compromised our PRR system and were not just listening but also communicating. Not a secure net and available on eBay, it wasn't surprising.

It was a chat net for us but we never let any vital information go over it. We used codewords for different things like wadis. Any vital and important information we would always stop and have a face-to-face. Information passed by The Joke to the boss was by a secure means.

After changing to an internal channel on the PRR we kept pushing on but with a lot more corrosion, we were close to Musa Qaleh and they were obviously watching us or had spotted us during our journey. The sun was rapidly dropping and we were yet to reach the RV with the PF call sign. The convoy positioned itself into a desert box, a square formation that held the HGV and Land Rovers in a three-vehicle column with a HQ element. Our Patrols then moved to each of the four corners some 400m away providing early warning and protection for the convoy. My two WMIKs hosted the left-hand corner.

'Thank fuck that's over', Johnny said, joining me at my WMIK and jumping off.

'Yeah it's been a long day but it ain't finished yet, so get some quick scoff down ya fellas I'm off for a brief with the boss.'

'OK mate I'll sort things here mate', Johnny replied. The rest of the team ran round getting some much need scoff, admin and night patrol kit done before light completely disappeared. I tabbed over to the boss's wagon to meet with him, Bernie, Steve and Dave. Ray had gone on leave the previous week.

'OK lads, well we got here in one piece anyway', the boss said.

'Yeah that was an epic', Steve piped up.

'Surprised we got here to be honest, with all them HGV breaking down', Dave continued.

'I've just managed to get Comms with PF, they have been hit just outside of the Musa Qaleh platoon house', Tom said cutting our little spell of winning. Again my heart skipped a beat. Don't say more KIA, I thought. I was waiting for the old 'get ready to go in and help them out', and fucking right too.

'The fire fight has died down and there are no PF casualties but they can't risk coming out again' the boss, Tom, said.

'Mega, looks like we are going to have a hard battle getting this convoy in then', I said, taking a look over the boss's shoulder at the large desert box now sitting here.

'Well the last update I received is that the Taliban have placed a few IED and ambushes on the main routes into Musa Qaleh, they know we are coming', Tom said, watching our reaction. I looked round at the rest of the boys, none of us said anything but we were all thinking the same thing. I didn't give a fuck about mixing it with the Taliban face to face, weapon to weapon. We had done it on a few occasions now but with a few IEDs we didn't stand a chance. With no armoured protection we would be blown to pieces and like in Iraq they could do it from a great distance away without us even seeing a Taliban fighter. Fucking cowards. If it had been only us Patrols going in then we could make our own route through, doing the usual escorting of the vehicles through the green belt (farms, fields and orchards) but to escort a convoy would mean using main tracks and roads and your's truly clearing the route.

'I'm going to get back in Comms with 0 [The Joke] and find out what's happening' Tom finished. With that we left, going back to our teams. I whispered and briefed the fellas in the darkness, not a sound was made by them when I told them of the plan. It was just one of those things, if it had to go in it had to go in. We were all big boys and knew the risks.

Within a half hour of darkness passing we mounted up again and headed for another harbour location. This was an SOP by the Patrols platoon; once static before last light we would conduct admin, briefs and scoff. Once darkness fell we would creep out in a different direction and move a few ks further out from our target, to a position me and Bernie had located during the move and therefore already recced and cleared. Anyone watching during daylight would have our position and could easily DF us. We were moving under darkness as we believed that very few Taliban soldiers would have night vision and thermal imaging equipment and wouldn't know the exact whereabouts of our harbour.

During the night and as your vision becomes limited your other senses become more alert. Ever wondered why you hear more during the night when lying awake in bed? To reduce sound the drivers would normally creep off slowly in second gear keeping the revs of the diesel engine as low as they could.

Me and Bernie slowly moved off and pushed right using NGV to find our way. The drivers of the HGVs didn't have much tactical experience, revving their wagons and slight flashes of light coming from inside the cabs.

'Boss, tell them to cut the noise down and kill all lights for fuck sake', I snapped.

'What the fuck are they on?' Tommo and Lee jumped in. I knew that operating like this was new to them, most of them were just logistic drivers and the first or second time they had been out of Bastion, but they had to realise this was real. If the Taliban could they would try and hit us even out here in the Cud's.

The boss must've got a grip of them and they didn't do too bad the remainder of the short journey. Again we harboured up and I closed into the boss while Johnny set up the stag position and list of who was on and when on the far left of the desert box. It had been a long old day and being in the sun all day drains you even more. I expected that a few teams would be getting pushed forward to recce possible entry locations but the CO back at Bastion had other ideas. With the information that The Joke had received from PF and some which we had too, it was beginning to look like a suicide mission. PF were around the same fighting strength as us (Patrols): eight to ten WMIKs; after their ambush and then follow up on the platoon house it looked like they would not be venturing out in a while and advised us of the same. They were near enough surrounded and the routes laid with IEDs. Their advice was not to even try.

Orders were to harbour for the night and PF would reassess the situation and inform the CO in the morning. For the remainder of the night we either took our few hours on stag watching out or tried sleeping in the warm sweaty air. My stag gave me the opportunity to rehydrate myself, something I always did. Even sitting in a WMIK with all your kit on you were losing a lot of body fluid with all the body armour and chest rigs hanging off you. PF were sending up flares from their position lighting up the area around their camp. I used the ambient light to look further with my NGV, scanning the ground to our frontage. When on stag we would use the outer WMIKs .50 Cal turret to stag on from; the lads would conduct admin and sleep around the other or in-between.

I kept on thinking of the mission tomorrow; I didn't fancy a daylight move as they would see us coming a mile off. Looking at the blackened shapes of my team sleeping I wondered whether all of us would return from this Op. Not something I wanted to think of but something that was always in the back of my mind. Like I mentioned before sometimes it's harder building ourselves up for an Op with everything bouncing round your head. Any soldier will tell you that his biggest fear is the not knowing how he will react under fire – will I freeze, cower, piss myself? We had all proved that we hadn't and so now the worry was a little different. What will happen, what do I do if this happens? Will we hit an IED, lose a leg, arm, get blown from the vehicle and be caught while the others withdraw? A million things rattle through you, whereas when it happens you react to it and take everything as it comes and that's exactly what does happen, and to be honest a lot easier to handle. I tried to forget all that shit and I thought of what my family and friends were doing back home.

We woke before first light and packed away our gear; by the time the sun rose all we had to do was scoff up and then move. I moved into the boss once again. There had been a lot of chat over the net that night and due to little support we were instructed back to Bastion and for Patrols another Op into Sangin.

Although we didn't show it we were all relieved about the job being sacked. It could have been a disaster and a lot of us would not have been here today, that I was sure about. Bernie's team took the nav position allowing myself to chill a bit and cover my arcs. Again we headed south this time using a different route; everything was going to plan until we hit a large amount of farmland, not marked on the map. It was impossible to box round this, it was huge. The convoy was up our arse, we had no choice but to push through.

I didn't like it too much but felt a bit better once our air cover came overhead. Two Apaches had been put on call for any problems we could encounter during our route back; it was worth getting them overhead watching just in case. It worked; the track brought us round the northern edge of the town, far too close for comfort. I locked off my gun, placed my long on my lap and drew my 9mm short. I was the third WMIK and began thinking back to Now Zad a month earlier. Local Afghans came out of the small, narrow side streets and onto the rooftops, some no more than 15ft away. Everyone was twitchy as we moved through. One shot, harsh movement or aggressive look would trigger it off. I caught sight of the end of the village. Not far, I thought, a few hundred metres. As always each of us would call out possible targets around us, 11 o'clock two pax (persons) in doorway, 9 o'clock four pax in the alleyway, no weapons seen, and so on.

'9 o'clock one pax on rooftop', I called up. He definitely wasn't friendly, dressed in a brown dish-dash and black turban with a large dark beard. He watched us closely with an evil intent in his eyes. I made eye contact and kept the stare, he looked at the sky above and the helicopters that now circled us. I knew what he was thinking, if it hadn't been for the Apaches then it would be a different story. I agreed. They were very hostile here and it showed. This would definitely be placed into the patrol report for future convoys, patrols and missions to avoid.

Our front two teams, four WMIKs broke clean from the town and gained the high ground that overlooked it. I felt a lot safer from here and could now support the convoy if attacked whereas we couldn't before while still in the settlement. After what felt like a week the convoy of large vehicle got clear with Steve and Dale bringing up the rear; it was definitely a tense time.

'OK, push on', the boss said, 'I don't want to hang around here.' The four of us pushed out, spreading out over the frontage. 'Stop, stop, stop!' The boss shouted down the radio. I expected World War Three to kick off over my shoulder.

'What's going on, boss?' Steve shouted.

'We have two suspect Taliban vehicles to your front, pick-up truck with a heavy weapon on board', he said. I pushed a little more forward to gain better vision but still couldn't see anything on the horizon.

'The Apaches want to engage, they are moving into position', Tom called up.

'What's the grid?' Bernie piped up.

'Wait one.' After a pause the boss reeled off some numbers. I checked my GPS; I clocked Johnny at the same time.

'That's fucking us!' he called, shouting over to me.

'Boss that's fucking us, don't fucking engage!' I shouted over the radio.

'OK, roger that', he replied, calm as you like. It was a tense few moments till the Apaches realised their mistakes. After relaxing, thanking our lucky stars and

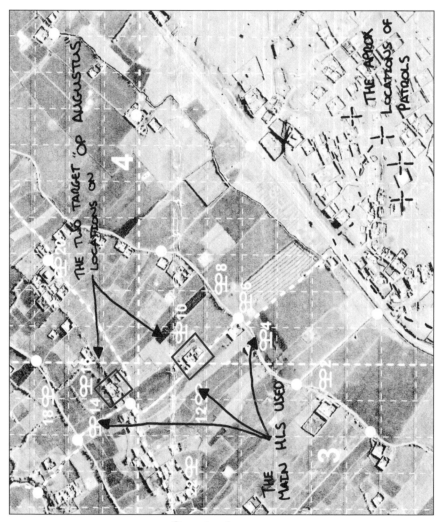

Operation Augustus

slagging off the fly boys above us, we pressed on and back to Bastion. If they had engaged then there wouldn't be much left of us.

It had been a long day, again getting back well after nightfall, making our progress to Bastion over the last few legs even slower but a lot more covert. Just before the A1 crossing we hit an ANP checkpoint that again nearly came to a blue and blue contact. We had clocked them but they seemed well twitchy. One of our lads, Pete, called out 'Britannia, Britannia', something he got slagged for later.

Getting back into camp there was little time for rest, stripping the vehicles of weapons and radios and off to our beds for a few hours. The next day saw Patrols moving straight into post-mission admin and back into pre-mission admin for our next job. As well as all this we commanders were putting together a patrol report as we always did, an in-depth report on the route to and from, ground and terrain, harbour locations, vulnerable areas and choke points and many other details. With the team 2i/c cracking on, me and Bernie were back up The Joke (opium and glue sniffing den) marking and planning a route. On operations you have to let others know of the route you will be taking, this is called a patrol trace. A large operation map of the whole of our AO sits fixed to a table. Before a patrol moves out it must place in a patrol trace indicating where we will be moving. This way we avoid using routes and setting patterns that other call signs like the HCR or PF have used and also shows all Head Shed where we will be on the ground, and in some cases the dangerous areas we will be travelling through. After several hours me and Bernie headed back for some head down before the mission.

Augustus was the operation name for another snatch and grab mission on a top Taliban leader just north of Sangin and I soon found myself sitting in the orders tent sweating my balls off (lack of air-con systems) listening to the CO and A Company OC giving their orders. To be perfectly honest, I remembered the operation names of the early few missions, Mutay, Augustus and the American Mountain thrust (or as the Paras re-named it Op Anal thrust). After that it all just seemed to roll into one.

Patrols became part of almost every operation during our six months and to be truthful I lost track of all the different operations and their operational names. I also lost track on how many times the Patrols found themselves in Now Zad, Sangin, Musa Qaleh and Gereshk, and while on the ground sometimes what day of the week it was. For me as the Battle group got stretched it was just one big Op and we would often be on one mission and then receive orders over the radio to move and conduct another.

A and C Company were being used as heli assault troops landing close by and striking the targets that they had been directed to take. As for Patrols we had a number of jobs. One, we were to push in a few hours before and act as fire support force for the ground troops (A and C Company); two, a last minute reconnaisssance and intelligence picture for the lads coming in on the strike; three, mobile cut-offs and potential opportunity for ambushing escaping Taliban, and last but definitely not least also to aid any CAS-E-VAC that needed to be done. A list full of possible jobs depended on what happens on the ground.

At the end of the orders the rifle companies departed, briefed their blokes and began battle prep for the Op ahead. They had plenty of time before 'wheels up' some 36–48 hours later. However Patrols had to make the long and dangerous journey to the north of Sangin and into position before the mission went in. We were leaving in the next few hours.

Blokes got a quick chance to phone home, clean kit and get to the gym before the whirlwind of admin to follow. This gave me some time to speak to my mates and find out the crack on what had happened up in Sangin on that last day A Company had been on the ground, the day Jacko had died.

It turned out that 1 Platoon had to secure the HLS on that day, the day the rest of A Company was due fly out. Moving into position around the green belt (large grass fields and tree lines) 1 Section caught sight of a few Afghan males around the bridge south of the platoon house. As they approached they were caught in an ambush, a 'come on' by all accounts. Jacko was hit in the abdomen and dragged back into cover by his mates while still under heavy fire. Prig his commander had no choice but to continue winning the fire fight or he could find more of his lads injured. As commanders we all knew this, it's not something we are happy on doing but something that has to be done and it's the job of the reserve section and medics to sort out the casualties. Stuart Giles had been the first medic to treat Jacko before he was CAS-E-VAC back to the platoon house; unfortunately he was unable to do much in those circumstances. Jacko had been fatally wounded and unfortunately died in the fields of Sangin. He would be sorely missed by the rest of the blood clot.

The move was early the next day to Gereshk, minus my driver Lee who had suffered a shoulder injury a few years ago and it still wasn't right. He was trying to build up the muscle and whilst doing some weights damaged his shoulder again resulting in dropping the dumb-bell on his face, not a good thing. That was the end of Lee's tour. Due to a delay we had to spend a night in FOB Price and then, followed by an early start the next morning, up to Sangin. The Patrols platoon pushed north and then east using the folds in the high ground to mask our movement to the FOB. Gereshk hadn't changed much since I had last been there, however the atmosphere on the ground had. Something that I knew would be inevitable.

C Company were feeling somewhat left out, arriving as one of the last rifle companies into Helmand and taking over A Company in Gereshk where they still remained while A, B, Support, PF and Patrols were getting a fair share of the fighting. That was till a few weeks ago when the mood in Gereshk changed. It was on a standard patrol to one of the nearby villages east of Gereshk that changed the view on how things would look around here in the near future.

Elements of C Company met with the elders of the town; accompanying them were two *Sunday Times* news reporters. A few of these had moved up into Sangin platoon house but after the first contact thought it wise to pull out and got on the next available helicopter back to Bastion. The Gereshk area was known as a more peaceful area and so the news crew joined the soldiers on routine patrols

Andy W. and Dave on board a CH-47 flying out of Sangin, June 2006.

Even with faces disguised, the strain is visible as blokes
from A Company and Patrols fly out of Sangin.

Patrols liaise with ANA before a night recce south of Now Zad.

Patrols, on the all-round defence in dead ground somewhere
in Taliban country, during an admin halt.

The author and Patrols use folds in the desert to hide themselves in a FRV, south of Now Zad, June 2006.

Looking through the author's NVG back at his WMIK, Brett and Tommo as he leads them to the north of Sangin through the Taliban's backyard, July 2006.

The author crosses a river in the dangerous backstreets of Sangin town.

Johnny and I rest after house raids in Sangin town, July 2006.

Sangin platoon house with makeshift sangars. Like Now Zad and
Musa Qaleh platoon houses, these were held by approximately 80
men miles from any support and under frequent attack.

A view from the Patrols position protecting the HLS
after a snatch and grab mission in Sangin.

More sick humour but also a very real dilemma that happened
on a daily basis inside the Sangin platoon house.

The view from a WMIK of Sangin's backstreets. Moving through
places like this was always extremely dangerous.

Anyone for a taxi!? Chalkie, Sticks and myself looking very happy.

Bernie leading his WMIK across the Helmand river back to our overwatch position after being in the Garmsir district centre.

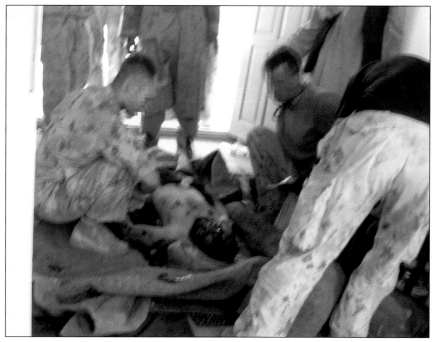

Canadian and Patrols medics help injured ANA soldiers after a contact,
Garmsir, July 2006.

Kiwi and Tom talk to local elders, Garmsir, July 2006.

there. The main group had pushed into the outskirts of town while the vehicles harboured up in the surrounding area and provided an overwatch.

On arrival Major Paul Blair the OC was asked by one of the elders to come back in a few days as all the locals were at prayer. He was also asked to leave at the opposite end of the village by the village elders who were present. In my eyes two major combat indicators had just sprung to mind although the patrol had not picked up on this at the time. Firstly the Afghan prayer day was on a Friday not a Tuesday, and secondly, why ask the patrol to leave through an area that was obviously channelled leaving the patrol vulnerable and exposed? I was amazed that they were going to take the route offered by the elder.

The Taliban ambushed the group in two separate areas: the team in the town and the vehicles in the overwatch, showing the organisation of the Taliban, this time helped by the villagers for one reason or another. The two groups of Paras were cut off from each other but seemed to be more than holding their own in both positions. One of the media was a slim light brown-haired girl called Christina Lamb. During the contact she had jumped in a ditch alongside Kyle D., a young lad from snipers. The Taliban had got a bit close for comfort and Kyle dispatched one of the fighters with his sniper rifle at close range that had sneaked up on him and Christina. After the fighting we all listened even more to find out if he received any special thanks from her for saving her life. I don't think he did.

'A waste of fucking time then', one of lads said, making the rest of us fall around laughing. The Paras began to get the upper hand, killing most of the Taliban in town. The WMIKs that had been part of the convoy in the overwatch moved in and flanked the village, ambushing around ten Taliban in a narrow street preparing to move in on the ground force under Major Blair, killing them all before the soldiers broke contact and made their escape. I had spent a bit of time in C Company and knew a lot of the blokes; it wasn't long before I caught up with H Handlon and Stokesy, two good friends and NCOs in C Company. They asked about the Ops up north in Sangin and Now Zad. They still didn't know if they were going to see any other part of Helmand other than here but had been told they would be part of Op Augustus.

We left Gereshk in the early morning, under darkness: me, Bernie, Ray and Gaz lead followed by Tom all in WMIKs and then the convoy of extra troops and supplies and a few HCR Scimitars, Pinzgauers carried the other troops and stores. Pinzgauers were the same size as Land Rovers and commanded by Captain Mark Eisler. Mark Eisler was a former RSM of 3 Para. He was a tough cookie that had been down south in the Falklands back in 1982. Again we wanted to use the darkness and get over the bridge, driving on NVG. We made our way into town and down towards the ANP checkpoint and bridge.

'Go, firm', Bernie called over the PRR.

'What's going on mate?' I said coming to a stop in the darkness.

'The boss and the convoy isn't behind us Scotty.' I looked back up the street using my NVGs, the town was quiet with only a few small lights on coming from nearby buildings. The four of our WMIKs pulled off the main route; we couldn't get hold of the boss with the PRR.

'What the fuck's going on?' I said to Ray.

'There's a flare just gone up', Ray interrupted. A red mini flare was slowly falling through the sky over the area we had just come from. It was a Patrols SOP that if something had gone wrong and we were out of radio range we send up a mini flare. Something was wrong and I and Bernie headed back off to see what was up while Ray and Gaz stayed put.

As we approached there were vehicles everywhere.

'What's going on?' I said to a silhouetted figure, jumping off my vehicle

'One of the WMIKs has rolled, got a few casualties', he said.

'We need to get the WMIK back upright and the casualties out of there', a voice said over the radio.

'Op-sec, op-sec don't mention anything over this radio it's not secure!' I shouted through my PRR. Again someone called up gobbing off that we had three casualties.

'Fuck sake, op-sec keep the Comms clear', I snapped; someone else also came over the radio saying the same thing. I was almost certain that up in Musa Qaleh the Taliban had infiltrated and listened in on our chat net (PRR), if they did the same here then they would know that we were static and would be for a good while, had a vehicle overturned, men trapped and three casualties. A prime time to co-ordinate an attack on us as we had lost the element of surprise and time was not on our side.

The boys worked hard and finally dragged the boys free as the rest of the vehicles pushed out to protect the rolled WMIK. It turned out that the boss's wagon had overturned while manoeuvring. As I mentioned before, it was hard to get real depth from the NVG and also easy to roll due to the weight of the .50 Cal on the top. When cross country driving we would always try and approach steep obstacles straight on; if you approach from an angle then there is a chance of rolling the vehicle. The driver, Van, suffered back and neck injuries; the boss, Tom, got thrown clear and ended up with his radio antenna through his leg. Geordie A. had been the gunner and when he felt the WMIK beginning to roll dropped further into the gun turret. This and the fact that the .50 Cal took the impact saved Geordie's head from being cracked like a nut; he would certainly have been killed. Due to the injuries we would have to change our ORBAT and we had also lost the surprise element of this mission, so it was cancelled for now and we headed back to Gereshk and for the lads to get looked at. Again it could have been far worse.

In 24 hours we were back on the road, minus Van; he had suspected spinal and nerve injuries. The ORBAT had to change and Johnny stepped up to drive the boss. We moved north of the bridge and RV with a large Canadian call sign in the desert. When these boys went out they went out in force. There must have been about 30 vehicles, mostly the large eight-wheeled armoured LAVs. They were sitting out in the sun drinking coke and playing cards. I didn't know exactly where they were heading but I guessed the same place as us. It wasn't long before we pushed on north again leaving the Canadians to blackjack and more Coca-cola.

Movement was slow, and time was ticking down to get up there and onto target. At this rate we would be patrolling in darkness and that's exactly what happened. As the night fell over the Afghanistan desert our progress slowed. The HCR were also having dramas to our rear, mechanical problems and also making a lot of noise. Tom wanted me, Ray, Bernie and Gaz to push forward, a good tactical bound in front of the convoy and recce a safe route through the Sangin back yard.

The ground was dodgy, lots of ditches, wadis and ploughed fields. It was also potentially dangerous with the amount of Taliban in the area. I got off the WMIK and walked the route ahead of us in the darkness to make sure it was safe for the vehicles to follow. It had been a long day and we all felt quite drained, I was still sweating a lot even though it was now cooling down and my clothes were pissed wet through with the sweat. I felt a little isolated out in front, scanning the route through my NVG and patrolling with caution.

My tired mind was beginning to play tricks on my eyes; I kept thinking something was moving up ahead. Stay focused, I said to myself. It was taking forever and it was also quite tense up front. I crept forward, stopping every 10m to scan ahead and listen in to the surroundings.

'OK, push on', I told Brett who was now my driver. Once I brought him up I would stop, then continue the process again and again. 'Stop there Brett, I've got a small wadi ahead, only 15m wide, just going to clear it mate', I said.

'OK Scotty' I dropped down the uneven slope, almost breaking my ankle in the process. I crossed over and climbed up the other side; I went to press my radio preset switch to tell Brett to cross when something caught my eye. I focused in, another trick maybe. I kept looking in the direction of the movement. Something moved from behind the foliage to my front right. Fuck! I dropped to my knee and brought my weapon up to bear, I was about to squeeze off some rounds when a little desert fox popped up and scuttled off into the wilderness. I let out a deep sigh. I don't think I had taken a breath in those few seconds and it had felt like 10 minutes. I don't think anyone saw me either which was a good thing: this was a big opportunity to slag me. If I had been seen one of the lads could have opened up too, pre-empting my drill. I too could have opened fire causing panic within the convoy and locals or let Taliban know our whereabouts. But the main reason would have been that I would have looked like a tit.

I had done this before while on my final exercise for my L/Cpl course. After five days in the field with only an hour of sleep per night we patrolled to our FRV through the wilderness of the Brecon Beacons for our final attack. We were all ball bagged and I was the lead scout of our eight-man patrol. I noticed another section to my front crossing a fence and then heading down a track that we wanted to take as part of our route, they were making their way to the same RV as us. We carried on patrolling for a few hundred metres then I stopped the patrol. It looked like the other section had stopped up ahead. I pushed up to one of their lads next to a tree. I could see him from the light off the moon.

'Hey up mate, it's Scotty.' I didn't get an answer.

'Mate, you OK?' Still nothing. Arrogant twat, I mumbled. I reached out to touch him and felt the wet bark of the tree. My lazy eyes strained. There was nobody there, just a tree but I could have sworn someone was there.

'Scotty you OK?' I heard behind me in a slight whisper.

'Yeah just scanning ahead', I said. I let out a little giggle. Fuck me, I need some serious head down, I thought.

We pressed on and could see the outer buildings of Sangin town through our night and thermal optics. We were close to the Canadian RV now, their vehicles glowing white on the TI display. We pulled into the RV which was a small patch of dead ground around a couple of hundred metres square. The three Canadian LAVs were going to lead the way into the suburb, as they were a high level of armour. Patrols would follow, then peel off taking a piece of high ground east of the target while the LAVs pushed on towards the north. I felt a little safer with the LAV leading although we all knew the difference if they hit an IED and if we did. They would get a small scratch to the side or maybe a few casualties depending on the amount of explosives, but in our case, well they would still be searching for our arms, legs and parts of our stubbly beards even now. Two ks later with the Canadians clearing the route we pulled off and headed up the steep, narrow back streets to an area of overwatch.

I was pleased to get everyone here in on piece without any contact with the Taliban. That was the name of the game. If my Patrol or the convoy we were leading got constantly ambushed then something was going wrong on my behalf. I would leave the Yanks, Canadians, main convoys and other units to set patterns and take the easy routes mostly resulting in them being blown to pieces or shot at. My aim was to keep them guessing, using different routes and the terrain of the ground in hiding the patrol, box round areas and dog-legging. Dog-legs were a tactic I used a lot: heading off in one direction and then breaking track and begin moving in a totally opposite direction. It had become a bit of a joke in the Patrols.

'Oh here we go again, one of Scotty's special 200-mile dog-legs', the blokes would say. It added a lot onto the journey but paid off in the long run. If you could use the ground it was amazing how much you confuse and deceive the enemy and I believe it saved us on a few occasions.

We had got in around 30mins before the assault team and helicopters. From what we could see there didn't seem much movement in the target area. There wasn't much movement anywhere which was expected as it was still around 3–4am. We had been up and on the move over 24hrs now and it would be a further 20hrs before this Op would be completed and we could find an area to rest. At this moment we didn't actually know where that would be, we only had the Op with its unknown events and the extreme heat that would soon be on us to look forward to.

The boss gave us a heads up that the five CH47s were en route. I heard the distinctive wocka, wocka of the Chinook blades as they came in low to land. This was the most vulnerable time and I now concentrated on the surrounding areas and possible fire positions. The first heli touched down with the others following, the airframe was hard to make out through the night vision. Before the words 'wheels down' went over the net, enemy tracer started flying everywhere lighting the area. Mostly it was in the direction of the Chinooks and LZ, the red and green flashes of light from the tracer rounds flew in all directions from Taliban positions followed quickly by our own guns engaging them in return which was all red.

The sound of machine gun fire deafened the helicopters' noisy engines all round. They were obviously sitting waiting in some sort of defensive role but it was too late, the mission was already green and three of the CH47s were already on the LZ and unloading Paratroopers. It was the first time I had seen the RAF with some balls; they sat and let the troops out under fire instead of fucking off like normal. I could now see tracer firing from the A and C Company soldiers as they began pushing forward to the objective as the large Chinooks pulled out and the Apaches also beginning to rain down their heavy firepower onto the objective. The Taliban didn't know what had hit them, in minutes A and C were sweeping through the target, the sound of rapid fire and grenades could be heard as they pushed and cleared the buildings.

A Chinook had been hit on the LZ but I couldn't see wreckage or hear the crash and assumed it had limped back to Bastion. Later I heard of Taliban fire cutting through the Chinook's fuselage missing the troops by inches. This was unbelievable considering it was packed with around 40 Paras. How nobody had been killed was amazing.

The Apaches sent in hell fires, anti-tank rockets exploding on impact with the target buildings and lighting the dull sky.

It wasn't long before things began to settle, the odd shot or bang but nothing more, as they cordoned the area and located the Taliban leader. The lads on the LZ had been pinned down on landing and took effective fire on their position. Once we began returning fire along with air support the troopers gathered their momentum and pushed the Taliban back. The Taliban leader had guards around his position, not something anyone had identified till it was too late. I believed that we should have been sent in earlier to gain more intelligence and identify enemy positions. Luckily we hadn't lost any men or Chinooks but that might not have been the case. With Patrols conducting a good recce this could have been avoided and the suppressing of targets by either us or air power could have happened before the Chinooks came in, stopping them from being a target.

Rumours of more casualties began circulating: injuries on the LZ. I didn't expect anything else from what I had seen. Two blokes had been shot and two with broken bones, non-life threatening, thank fuck. Good work, lads, I heard myself muttering.

The sun was up as we waited to be re-tasked. But further orders were to hold this ground and support the withdrawal of the ground troops through our position. At this point, the boss Tom Fehley, came out with a typical officer quote in the most camp voice I have ever heard:

'He who holds the high ground holds the key.' You had to be there but the lads never let him forget this and definitely made me piss myself. The rifle companies were due to tab through our location and out to the rear, heading east into the relative safety of the desert and to await a pick-up.

The situation around our teams was getting a little uncomfortable; there was something about it now. A strange feeling and the odd head popping over different walls taking a sly peak at us which always made you feel that something wasn't right. The locals were obviously getting a little neckey and a few warning shots had to be fired to tell them not to even bother trying out and that we still ran this patch of ground for now.

Our four Patrols had pushed out now covering different areas; the centre was a large rocky knoll big enough to hold a few large vehicles that looked down onto the route we had moved up with the Canadians a few hours before and the buildings and compounds that overlooked the target. Left and right had buildings, narrow streets and walls within 50m of us in which some Patrols had now dominated. To our rear were a few compounds and the open rocky desert that pushed up on to a ridge line that travelled north–south which Captain Eisler and his men were occupying. After a few hours the Companies began pulling back, patrolling through our position as we watched ready to engage any follow up.

The blokes were quite fucked after the Op, drained by adrenalin and the heat and sun. After most of the lads had pulled out I pushed up between the buildings and the high ground and started doing a few shuttle runs taking some of the lads closer to the hill on the other side of which was the RV. The HCR in their larger tanks did the same getting more people on board and helping them out while we protected them. It looked like a scene out of *Kelly's Heroes*. The Companies pushed down into the rear slope and headed off towards a HLS between two high features. Once they had almost completely moved into the HLS, Patrols pulled back. Some of the HLS could be seen by the buildings on the outer verges of the town around 400–500m away. This was beginning to get a lot of attention as they knew something was going on as the lads waited for the pick-up. Well, if getting woken at early doors by helicopters and a major fire fight hadn't got enough attention.

Patrols dominated the high ground and protected the lads waiting on the LZ from the surrounding hills. The Chinooks were taking their time; the weather was hot as normal and sitting around was only raising the temperature. We scanned the outer settlements, compounds and surrounding areas for any suspicious activity. My team of two WMIKs held the forward left looking back into the east of Sangin. The sound of rotors came into earshot, growing louder approaching from the relative safety of the east. I watched for any signs of reflection from a weapon sight or optic from the town. There were a few males on top of their flat rooftop watching; each of us pointed their locations to one another so we all knew where they were. The Chinooks touched the valley floor and sat ticking over as the troops ran on board.

Pop, came the distinctive sound of a mortar firing off, most of us heard it.

'Incoming', we all called out. The thing about mortars is once you hear the pop you have only a few seconds depending on range to take cover and even then you have no idea what the targets are. I later gained a lot of experience on being on the receiving end of mortar and rocket attacks while based in Basra as we would get incoming on average around three times a day. A mortar round exploded between two Chinooks, the soft sand luckily absorbing most of the impact. A direct hit would have resulted in catastrophic injuries. Looking round I could see the smoke and sand that had been kicked up still hanging in the air. There were three males off to my front around 700m away, a few buildings into the town, who had climbed onto their rooftop just before the pop of the mortar. One of them had his hands above his brow shielding the sun or holding a set of binoculars, I couldn't make it out for sure. Was he spotting the mortar?

Brett and Tommo immediately shouted, thinking the same as me, believing he could be the spotter for the mortar firer. I could see the wall in which they stood and part of their ground that lay in front. I took aim. I let off two, three to five round bursts in quick succession at the wall beneath them. I watched the strike marks hit the wall, a few missing, two of them by less then half a metre. They jumped and dived off the rooftop like something out of a movie.

'Fuck me, Scotty, that was close', the blokes laughed out. They will never be that lucky again. If I had wanted to I could have cut them down there and then, only problem was I wasn't 100 per cent sure that they were spotting the mortar ready to correct and bring on the next few rounds. However no more mortars fired suggesting to me that they probably had been. If I had been 100 per cent certain then they would not be alive, it was simple.

For A and C Companies the job was done, time to take off their helmets and relax, get back for a hot debrief and a slap on the back for a job well done which was rightly deserved, followed by scoff and rest. For Patrols it was back to the grind and it would be a little later before we could do the same.

It wasn't long before we received further instruction from The Joke. We would be moving back into Sangin platoon house in the next 24hrs for a further operation.

The next few days were spent trying to get into the Sangin platoon house; from our intelligence most of the routes were laid with Taliban ambushes and it wasn't just a case of heading straight in on the main road. Our Patrols kept probing forward but it just wasn't happening. That was till extra troops from B Company pushed out escorted with Apaches on top cover. Once that was in place we managed to get in and re-supply the B Company lads from Captain Eisler's group of vehicles. As always it was a tense and nervous time as we were channelled into the back streets of Sangin. Unable to effectively use our guns we were back to pistols and Minimis. The locals, mainly male in black turbans and dark dish-dash clothing, stood and stared from the streets and shops, hatred and evil in their eyes. The atmosphere was that thick that you could cut it with a knife and they were waiting to take us on, it was like riding into a Wild West high street.

Tommo constantly advised us who was where.

'Two male pax on your three o'clock side street, five pax right-hand side in the shop way.' I knew what they would do if they had got hold of one of us, it wasn't worth thinking about. Do-gooders back in the UK go on about the military mistreating POWs, yet these people here would cut your balls off and stuff them in your mouth before dragging you through the streets for all the locals to finish you off. This was what happened in the past for anyone crossing the Muhammadi and Taliban. For me and the others that wasn't going to happen, we were more than happy to take down any who took us on, it was our job. If we couldn't then we would die trying. This may sound a bit 'Rambo' or 'hard man' talk, but that isn't the case. We were human and when put in that situation we were prepared to do anything to stay alive. It's life or death and at the end of the day it would be, and was us or them.

The vehicles pushed in to the grounds beside the main entrance and the orchards, the only place we could hold up. Once we were sorted I did my usual tour of the platoon house and caught up with my mates in B Company who had now arrived. I met up with Dave S. or Sha-mon (Bo Selecta) as he was called at the front sangar. Dave had previously left and then rejoined the Paras: a funny and likeable bloke.

'Hey up Scotty, how's it going?' he said.

'Better than you lot by the looks of it.'

'Ha-ha yeah! Been living on two rat-packs per day per section mate. Water's nearly out too!' he laughed.

'Fucking hell I knew things were tight but that's a bit shit like', I replied. A rat-pack was a 24hr individual food ration. Here they were living on one rat-pack per three to four blokes. Fucking mad, I thought. Water was also well rationed and they had been using river water and purification tablets to keep some of the bottled water as there just wasn't enough. Not just that, but with constant attacks by the Taliban the ammo was also running low. This was even worse in early September in the Musa Qaleh platoon house: the blokes reckoned they had enough ammo to withstand another 40min contact, that was it. No re-supplies were getting in and visions of Rorke's Drift was entering the heads of the lads trapped inside. Imagine the blokes being overran as they ran out of rounds, they would have been slaughtered. It seemed that we had got here just in time.

It happened again later in the tour and the RAF refused to go in because of the increased threat. Us patrols set up a DZ for a parachute re-supply that we could mark then pick up the supplies (one of Patrols' many roles) and take them into the platoon house. That was after patrolling out under darkness and setting up the DZ with IR lighting that could be seen by the air and giving The Joke a dropping grid and a run in direction after estimating the wind. As always the RAF being 800ft in the air thought they knew better, and dropped it around 4ks out on a totally different run in direction.

'Well fucking done', we snapped.

'What's the fucking point? Dale said. 'I mean why did we even bother risking our necks out here?' Patrols came back empty handed and had to explain to the boys they would have to wait a little longer for their scoff and water as now the

Taliban and locals were enjoying your rat-packs. Eventually US Apaches came in hovering just outside the platoon house as US Chinooks came in and dropped off their underbelly loads.

The RAF was starting to get a bad reputation from the blokes. I remember on one occasion when dropping into Sangin the RAF loadmaster at the tailgate of a CH47 was pushing the lads off to speed them up and minimise the length of time they spent on the ground. We were carrying around 120lbs of kit minimum; it's easy to become off balanced with that weight over you and the unsteady aircraft and sometimes your knees can buckle with just a small trip making it almost impossible to get yourself up off the floor. The loadie standing in just his flight suit and body armour began pulling and pushing on the blokes. I watched as I pulled myself from my seat, a strain in itself, using the side of the heli to hold myself up. Two blokes fell and rolled off the tailgate due to the loadie. It was hot, packed and uncomfortable under this weight; I saw this and was snapping at what he was doing, he wasn't helping at all. I knew they didn't want to be on the ground any longer than they had to, neither did we. But guess what, we would be there a lot longer than them. I wasn't the only one who picked up on this as we waited for the ramp to clear and the visions of dropping my Para lid into his face ran through my head as I pushed on. I didn't have to, someone further up from me gripped the loadie round the neck. After that the struggling blokes were helped rather than pushed around and off the tailgate. He had probably been flapping with being on the ground and had no idea of the weight we were carrying.

I gave Dave a few spare rats that I had in the back of my WMIK and headed on to catch up with Joe D., the Buffalo Bill impersonator. It was never a dull moment with Joe; he always had some tale to tell. Most of it was pure bullshit or what we called 'Joe Gen', in hope to spread rumours about somebody else, or so I would go running off to slag the lad in question but whichever it was always a morale boost. I had known Joe from A Company as young toms, then as L/Cpl together in C Company during the Iraq invasion. His ginger skinhead got him the nickname Zippy Monster and he would often do one of his Zippy impersonations and have me in stitches.

I was still waiting to receive orders on what was happening with the Patrols platoon. Rumours were beginning to circulate about a major Op taking place from here. I guessed just as much as we had seen an increase of Canadians up at FOB Robinson. Later that day we heard of the CO intentions. We were to clear the buildings around the platoon house; clearing the ground of Taliban in an effort to stop the attacks on the platoon house and enable more patrolling to take place.

The next day kicked off early after spending the night by the vehicles. Patrols were back on foot to help the Canadians and A Company who again had come back in by CH47 to take over B Company on holding the Sangin base. It had turned into a Battle group operation. We stripped our kit, water, bombs and bullets; that was all we were taking on the ground, everything else was binned. I looked at my watch, 08:15hrs. I had been awake most of the night due to the heat and a few shoot and scoots on our position, these were nowhere near as intense as the last time I had been in Sangin although Joe and Dave told me that it had been extremely hot (and he wasn't talking about my usual rectum burning scoff either), before our arrival and couldn't believe we made it here in one piece.

My team was up against the wall on their arse and knees and had been for over 15 minutes as the sun beat down. I stood opposite under the sparse trees with Bernie talking through our movement through the streets. I listened in to the radio through the head set on my ear. Once the other Patrols teams got clear of the pharmacy then we were good to go. The pharmacy was around 300–400m across the pipe range. It had become a major contact point where the Taliban would hit the platoon house from. I took my last gulp of water and rotated my finger in a circular motion (we often use hand signals to indicate certain things that was going on especially close to enemy areas) informing the lads to prepare to move.

'OK, let's move', I said to Brett. We sprinted from the safety of the compound and into the open, 10m between each man. We ran till clear of the gateway and then settled into a steady patrol pace. Even from the little sprint I was breathing a little heavy, some due to the weight but most from the nervous adrenalin running through my blood. I looked round over my right shoulder to see the remainder of the patrol exiting the platoon house. We were now half way over the pipe range, a vulnerable and open area. I didn't want to hang around here too long. We reached the other side and patrolled up against the shop fronts, the town was eerily silent. We bounced forward taking fire positions and covering each other as we pushed through the shop fronts and then moved left up a side street and into the town centre.

Already the plan had changed.

'Scotty swing round and head west and for the building close to the foot bridge', Tom came over the net. I knew where he meant, we had covered it in the orders previous but I guessed we needed to clear these first. After a 2min face-to-face in a back street we pushed back out; our target was a set of buildings north of the platoon house, half hidden in the orchard fields just south of Wombat Wood. The tight maze of tracks and streams leading from one compound to another was a dodgy area to patrol, but it had to be done.

'OK boss my team's in position', I whispered over the radio.

'Roger that, how are you Ray?'

'Yeah I'm ready', he called over.

'Stand by, stand by', the boss said. It was all quiet as we waited to react.

'GO!' Ray's team ran in sweeping the small courtyard of the compound; there was no firing.

'OK, Scotty' Ray called.

'Go lads!' Bash and Tommo ran in with me close behind, Ray's team were covering the buildings and some of the outhouses. We swept through the buildings; it was clear. The rooms had been stripped of a lot of their things but some larger items were left. From one of the outbuilding's rooftop we found empty 7.62mm cases, the roof itself looked onto the FSG tower of the platoon house. It had been obviously used as a firing point in the last few days. There was lots of half eaten

US rations, old and ripped clothing, used bloodstained dressings and fresh shit, indicating their presence was recent, maybe only hours.

We moved on, jumping walls and kicking in doors, we had no idea if the Taliban were over one of these walls. As time ticked on we began to get a little lazy in our drills realising all was quiet in and around this close set of buildings. It was only as we patrolled further that I believed we could have had difficulties. A signal came back to halt, the sun couldn't get through the trees that littered the small tracks keeping the heat locked in. We were pissing sweat like a turkey at Christmas time.

'Enemy', Bash whispered. I took a gasp and crept up behind him. Bash went to aim by putting his weapon in the aim from the crack in the wall ahead; I thought it was going to kick off. He dropped his weapon slightly.

'You fucking idiots!' Bash called out. It was the boss's team on the other side of the wall and we had been close to a blue on blue situation. The Canadians had pushed further north and had set up a perimeter around some large three-storey houses that had been used as firing points in previous attacks on the platoon house. We took a few seconds to get some water down our necks and photos of the abandoned buildings. Most of the grounds in and around these hosted hash plants in a massive form. The blokes quickly took pictures of themselves amongst the huge hash plants.

'If only I brought some skins out', the lads joked.

'Yeah I can see the lot of us finishing this tour with around 70kg of hash in our bergens', Dave joined in. I imagined the lot of us patrolling along with huge spliffs in our mouths; after all, the Taliban did.

Jokes aside, we moved on through the town, again operating in our six-man teams a few streets apart. You can often feel a little isolated and lonely out there, you sometimes believe you're on your own without being in sight of the other teams. We all traversed onto the main building that the Canadians had now surrounded in what we called a ring of steel.

There were a lot more troops in this area and you could sense the feeling of being safer especially with our Canadian friends on their armoured LAVs. A quick set of QBO were issued by Tom then we were ready to go in. The LAV was going to smash down the gate and open the way for us as well as a mouse hole charge on the wall for another entry location. The countdown began and again my adrenalin began flowing.

'You know the score lads, fast and aggressive, get in there, clear and inform me what's going on', I said to my team.

'Ten seconds', the call came over the net. We waited patiently thinking only of the job in hand. The LAVs large engine revved up just as the large explosion from the mouse hole charge broke through the wall. The sound of steel against steel screeched as the gates were torn down. We were in.

It was a large building of three levels with grounds all round between it and the large protective wall that separated it from the surrounding streets. It was probably previously owned by some governor or official and one of the best houses in Sangin although that wasn't saying much.

The dust hadn't cleared as we ran in supported by the Canadians; we hit the front door like a herd of bulls, you couldn't clear this in the normal manner it was far too big and open. We could only use mass numbers in order to clear it as fast as we could and hope there wasn't too much resistance. The blokes smashed in through the doors firing a few bursts as they went.

'Room clear', Bash and John shouted.

'OK next team', I would scream, Brett and Tommo already right behind me pushing through Bash and John and onto the next room. It was near the full platoon in there sweeping from the downstairs, up the staircase middle and top floor. The Canadians followed our route entering the house. I stayed on the stairwell between the middle and top floors as Ray and his team finished off the clearance. Sweat was dripping off us all more than ever, the heat seemed trapped in this place. The word got shouted round, floor clear, floor clear, house clear. I took off my Para helmet and relaxed, again there was no sign of life and only a few rounds had been fired but the stressful tension of not knowing what was on the other side of the door was always in your head.

Most of the lads were looking exhausted; it had been a long day even though little action had taken place. Like I said it was the waiting and the constant thinking of what could happen that can take it out of you. I believed it had been the larger presence here, Canadians with their armoured vehicles and fast air in the form of A10s and Apaches that had kept the Taliban at bay. I took a look round checking the rooms; again most of the things were gone. Nearly the entire top floor windows had been shot out with bullet and shrapnel marks covering the walls from what looked like the direction of the FSG tower of the Sangin platoon house. Bloodstains were in most of the top floor rooms and stairwell.

'Looks like we got some of the fuckers a few hours before', I said to Johnny.

'Yeah fucking right', he replied. There were old medical dressings and clothes stained with blood in a few of the rooms. They had obviously taken a hammering when they engaged the FSG and took some .50 and GPMG (airborne) punishment in return.

With the Canadians still dominating the area we could afford to chill slightly; me and Johnny sat on a small garden wall chewing the fat as we waited to patrol back to camp or another tasking. The boss Tom sat on the other side against the house. In seconds he fell asleep, showing the strain of today's activities and giving the boys some ammunition for future slaggings on the boss with photo evidence to go with it.

The sun had dropped but the heat remained as it always did in the Middle East at this time of year. We began our movement back through the streets, our job not over till we were in the platoon house and even then not exactly home sweet home. That night brought a few small skirmishes but nothing major. I found myself up near Dave's front sangar unable to sleep and firing a few shots off on the few occasions the Taliban turned up to play.

Intelligence reported that Sangin, with the presence of this large force, had emptied of the usual amount of Taliban fighters. It also stated that Now Zad and Musa Qaleh were being constantly attacked more than ever and indicated that the Sangin fighters had probably moved to these locations till the heat was off in Sangin. I had seen this before and a tactic in all fields of warfare. They would move to other areas and join in the fight till a major operation switched to there, and then they would return and start again. A game of cat and mouse sprang to mind.

I along with the rest of Patrols was hoping to stay a little longer and support B Company and then A Company as they prepared to take over the platoon house yet again. It wasn't going to happen, and I knew why. We were the only real mobile force still on the ground as far as the Brits were concerned. PF were still trapped in Musa Qaleh and HCR struggling to move as freely as us due to constant breakdowns and their slow movement. Without the Patrols platoon vehicle re-supplies could not take place; operations like Augustus and Mutay and future RIPs (relief in place) for Now Zad, Musa Qaleh and Sangin would be a lot more dangerous for the Chinooks and ground troops and Battle group recces could not happen without us being there.

On arrival to Bastion much had changed, not just to the Bastion base but also the Battle group and the 3rd Battalion. The camp wasn't the dust cloud it once was, it had certainly taken shape. More accommodation, telephone and internet facilities and even a Naafi and bar (no alcohol was sold unfortunately) had opened up. The HLS was now hard surface with shelters for the Apaches and the airstrip for the C-130 was set up, raised and awaiting the tarmac. In fact it had come on that much that by the time I led Patrols back to Bastion I had to box round this large embankment that had risen out of nothing and become the airstrip. Not only that, but someone at the top had now realised how much strain 3 Para was under, they didn't realise how things were going to turn out. One fighting battalion now occupied Gereshk, Sangin, Kajaki Dam and Musa Qaleh as well as mounting recces and operations. I'm not just saying this but I think it was only the Paras who could manage this, once more against the odds just like the old days. One year later three fighting battalions plus attachments were needed to do what we had done in the summer months of 2006. We had asked for 2 Para who were waiting back in Colchester, they were itching to come and join their fellow blood clot members already here.

The blood clot was an expression used by us Paratroopers, something frowned upon by other units outside of this one. It was mainly a jealousy thing, admitted by several blokes I got to know during courses throughout my service.

'You boys stick together constantly,' they would say, 'you can't go for a shit without another Para being there.' If you were a member of 3 Para, 2 or 1 detached on various courses away from the Parachute Regiment it was always good to find fellow members of the airborne brotherhood. Without even knowing the other person, if you catch sight of another maroon beret, you close in on each other and shoot the shit becoming friends in a matter of minutes. The trust in each other's abilities is there automatically, as well as the mutual respect: piss taking and black humour we all have. We are also all put through the same rigorous selection tests and have the same pride and passion in our regiment. As more home in and join the maroon berets our group becomes larger in our own little corner away from the rest of the course or unit. From then on we socialise, train, scoff and generally hang around with each other. The maroon berets close ranks and stick together unlike any other unit I know of, just like a blood clot. This is the reason for its name, that and the colour of our berets. Other airborne units sometime misunderstand this: 7 RHA, 216 Signals, 9 Sqdn engineers and the rest of 16 Air Assault Brigade. These aren't part of the blood clot and definitely not Paratroopers. I need to make this clear as it has become a sore spot for the members of the 1st, 2nd and 3rd battalions. The units above are exactly what they are called, Signals, Royal Horse Artillery and engineers who have passed P-Company and the static line parachute course to enable them to support the fighting men of the 1st, 2nd and 3rd battalions the Parachute Regiment by means of a parachute descent. This we have no problems with and they are good at what they do. Paratroopers or Paras are these fighting soldiers of the 1st, 2nd and 3rd battalions and a parachute course does not change men from the signals, artillery or engineers into Paratroopers. Some of these units call themselves this under false pretences and this would be like us calling ourselves Guards or Green Jackets when we are not. The Marines have the same problem; attachments of signals and engineers passing the Commando course calling themselves Marine, and like us Paras they hate it.

Much to the disappointment of themselves and us, 2 Para were not sent to Afghanistan. I knew of a lot of good soldiers from there. We were to be given a company plus of Fusiliers from Cyprus. As well as these we already had the HCR who had come out a few months previously. Not bad lads at all, and definitely well appreciated later in Sangin protecting the ground troops. Before deploying a platoon of Royal Irish was attached to 3 Para. At the time our boys weren't too impressed about it. If it had to be anyone then it should be a fellow Para platoon from 2 Para. As it turned out it the Royal Irish did a good job and I can easily say were some of the best soldiers I had worked with outside of the Reg. During my time in Afghanistan I didn't work with Royal Irish or 9 Platoon C Company as it was called. But from the courses I had been on and later in the CP world I worked closely with serving and ex-serving Royal Irish lads. They were a good bunch of boys and I think the feeling was mutual to us, especially since the Paras and SF had got some of the Royal Irish boys out when they were kidnapped by the Westside Boys in Sierra Leone in 2000.

Not only had small amounts of support arrived which changed the shape of the Battle group but our RSM had too, having received a promotion: a change for the better in my opinion, I might add. Unseen in the papers and news coverage 3 Para's morale and the Battle group was at rock bottom. Many people were unhappy and like me preferred to be away and on the ground. On the ground the boys grafted, against the odds and in very difficult circumstances fighting often for their lives and their mates. The last thing we needed was bullshit like this. I personally had a clash with him on a few occasions, something that I will not elaborate on too much. I can say it was something over shaving in Bastion after being out on recce patrol for over a week. It was my personal opinion that he needed to go. The man up for the job was RSM Hardy, or Uncle John as he was known to the blokes, a man who had been with the battalion many years in a number of different positions and had the full trust of his men and likewise the respect of his Paratroopers. In days the morale was back up there: amazing how much one turnover can do. With a 'big boy's rules' and 'kick the arse of the Taliban' attitude the lads were back on top form. I think it definitely had an impact on the operations side and the chilled atmosphere in camp.

Chapter 9

A Lucky Escape

It was coming into the middle of summer: temperatures scorching, well over 50 degrees and still over 30 at night. I was intrigued to get a warning order to find that Patrols were being sent on another recce into virgin country. Something that was our bread and butter and would mean operating on our own again and without babysitting others; we could definitely get amongst our job and hopefully some Taliban. Orders came and went as we discussed the ground and area in detail. The mission was to recce routes to the south and the area of Garmsir and liaise with the Canadian forces down there and dominate the ground.

Garmsir was south of Bastion and the major town north of the Pakistan border sitting like most towns along the Helmand River. It was rife with Taliban, all pushing over from Pakistan and then forming up in the town of Garmsir before heading north to other areas like Sangin, Baghran and Now Zad. It was also a main location for the poppies to come through, then being turned in opium and then pushed over the boarder and out of the country.

I, Tom, Ray and Bernie had looked more closely into the mapping that we had on this area. We would be the first British troops in this area. There were no real patrol reports and information to go on, and very little coming from the Canadians. The only thing that was clear was the amount of action in the area. The Canadians wanted us to RV with an armoured convoy in the town of Lash (Lashkar Gah) as it was known to us; this was a non-starter straight away for us, it wasn't too bad an area at the time, however the IED threat on main routes was forever present. The Canadians agreed to meet us near Garmsir itself: less work for themselves and a chance for us to recce routes down to the south of Bastion.

We soon saw ourselves heading south through the open desert and leaving Bastion behind. This time we were loaded with up to two-and-a-half week's worth of equipment. We also took a lot more ammunition, each vehicle holding around 2,000 .50 Cal and over 2,500 7.62mm. With eight WMIKs and one supporting Pinz we were averaging an ammunition state of approx 12,000 .50 Cal rounds, 20,000 7.62mm rounds split down for eight .50 Cal Brownings and eight GPMGs, eight 84mm anti-tank weapons, 200 magazines worth of 5.56mm, 8,000 5.56mm link for the Minimi and around 30 HE and RP grenades. We had more ammunition than most small armies. It was about time and worth carrying as we would be on our own working down around Garmsir. Like our first trip into Sangin MED-E-VAC was also a problem. Only in a worse case scenario would helicopters be sent down here. It felt reassuring, not.

The trip, as always while recceing, was a mixture of fast and slow with a lot of stops and starts, giving the teams a chance to push out individually to recce and secure VP areas. Garmsir was around 40 miles (66ks) south of Bastion on a straight bearing; however, we never used the straight and easy route and it

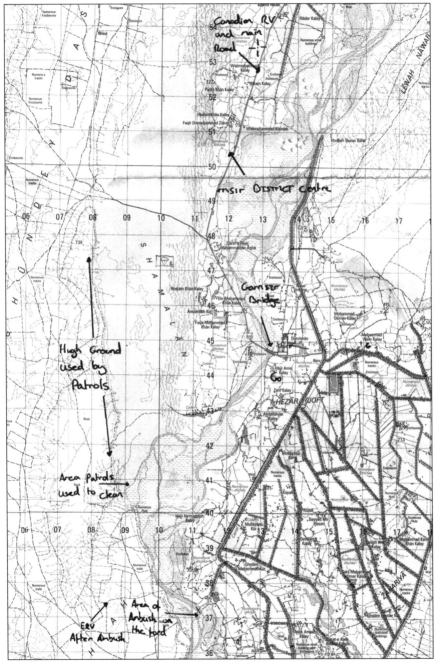

Garmsir

took many hours to get close to the outer settlements and farms to the north-west. We reached the Canadian RV, eight or nine LAVs just off a main track in all round defence. We pushed in and had a face-to-face with their commander. This bloke was straight out of a Hollywood Vietnam film. Our intentions were to push directly into the district centre. The Canadians were happy to lead us in and escort us. This we all agreed on but it wasn't till I sat down ready to go that I thought this could be a bad idea. I hadn't been briefed on the route. We moved onto the main track.

'You reckon we are going to take this all the way in?' I said, looking at the map.

'Looks like it, mate', Brett replied. One LAV was to the front, another between our WMIKs and the last holding the rear. One of the Canadian troops was hanging out of his turret.

'Oh mucker!' I shouted.

'Yeah what's up?' he replied.

'We are not taking this all the way down are we?' I questioned.

'Yeah we cleared it a few hours ago', he said.

'A few hours?' I confirmed.

'Yeah it's fine man', he assured me as he disappeared back into the nice large armoured vehicle. I could hear him battening down the hatches. Fucking easy for you to say, I cursed. I know Brett and Tommo agreed.

'A few hours ago!' Johnny shouted behind me overhearing the conversation.

'I know, mate, what the fuck?' I said. It was too late, we began moving.

'Fingers in ears again then fellas', I joked. To be honest it wasn't a joking matter but hey, what the fuck else could I do? There might be a device out on the road, bearing in mind the Iraqis could place out an IED within minutes once they realised the route we were using. Let's hope the Taliban weren't as experienced in this line of work. No wonder the Yanks and Canadians take so many casualties. It was the same from my experiences of Iraq on the CP front. We could spend hours boxing round VPs and avoiding hot areas. The US just ran straight through. A Yank once told us, 'Speed is camouflage'. We all just burst into laughter. Not even the Yanks and Canadians can out run an IED travelling at around 300–400mph.

A nerve-racking fifteen minutes later we arrived at the bridge. Fuck doing that again, I thought. The bridge was the only crossing point in the area, and held by the ANA and ANP. You can imagine how important this was. Commanders again jumped off and walked the vehicles over and down the main street. This place was a shit hole, worse than any other place I had ever come across. The streets were minging and every building had bomb and bullet damage. This place had taken some severe pounding.

The district centre was up on the left-hand side, behind the main street. Again it was a whitewashed single-storey building with a high wall around it. Unlike Sangin which had a bit more ground in which to defend and manoeuvre, this had none. The walls pushed right up against the building.

'Canny tight in here fellas', I said once we arrived.

'Yeah could be cheeky in here', Lee C. replied. The Canadians didn't think so; they sat in the compound with a large bonfire and had a few other armoured vehicles sitting just outside as the protection. The Canadians told us what was going on in the area. This was a holding position where they could come back to rest and regroup as it sat near the bridge and northern part of town, although a few nights ago they were fighting from this location and were nearly overrun. The strike marks on their LAVs suggested that they were not lying either.

Further in to the south a few Canadian teams in the large armoured LAVs worked alongside the ANA holding back the Taliban. The boss worked on The Joke, asking if we were to push in but orders from the CO indicated that he didn't want any British fighting down here. I felt a little useless: so far we had moved into the district centre when we could be moving to join up with the teams defending the streets a few hundred metres south of us. That evening saw us sitting around with the Yank brothers shooting the shit and scoffing up. They have had a hard time down here and they had been told that we were here to take over. I think there had been a cross in communication somewhere down the line. The Canadians were under the impression that we were here to take over them in the district compound and town, allowing them to pull back to Lash. Not what we have been told, we explained around the fire.

'We are to get a foot on the ground, recce, gain some intelligence and report back.' We also learned that they were pulling back tomorrow and they were glad of it.

Although our tactics were better by far than those of our coalition friends, the loss of vehicles, manning and firepower was going to make a large difference. Plus most of the LAVs had taken a direct hit, either by 7.62mm or RPG; one of them looked like it had taken a little more. One direct hit to the WMIK and it was good night Vienna. Like I explained before, for recce tasks the WMIK was a good bit of kit; however, stick it in a street as a static bunker and you were asking for it. They wouldn't stop shit.

That night we slept next to the vehicles as always and surprisingly had a decent night's sleep from the long and tiring journey down, even with the sound of explosions and firing that rang out at irregular intervals. As I settled into my hammock I thought about the next few days ahead. This could be the last decent night sleep in a while, I thought, better make the most of it.

The smell of burning woke me early. I packed away my hammock and checked over my weapon as the sun rose. All seemed quiet outside the walled compound as the rest of the blokes sorted their shit out. The boss Tom was already on the net talking to the CO and I made my way up onto the roof of the main building with Bennie to take a butchers. Keeping low we monkeys crawled over the rooftop. Smoke was billowing from different locations south of here. The Canadians were sealed in their armour on the streets in their relevant positions that had been held for some time with the ANA moving to and from the bombed-out buildings alongside and behind the LAVs. Using our binos and Bennie's L98 sight we could see the town in depth now spreading itself down out of sight.

'Proper Taliban country in there mate', Bennie said.

'Yeah I fucking bet', I replied. Most of the morning we sat and watched over the town and Tom briefed us on what the CO had said. Lieutenant Colonel Tootal didn't like the idea of holding Patrols in the town. For one it meant defending this position like the Canadians. Two, we would be stuck in here like PF if we came under attack which was 100 per cent certain at some stage and therefore he would lose his eyes and ears on the ground and his nearly only mobile force; and three, we would not have the freedom of movement to conduct our recces around this area: the sole point of Patrols being here.

The boss spoke to us commanders; we agreed that an overwatch position was necessary outside the town. The only place was the ridge line on the west flank out in the open, over the river and around 2ks from the district centre. Not ideal, especially as we discovered that a small US training team would be staying behind with the ANA here in the district centre. There was no way we could overwatch and provide fire support for them but we had few options.

We sat on the WMIKs and did the usual slagging off of each other; there wasn't much else to do, but gunfire broke our banter.

'That was fucking close', someone said. More landing just over the other side of the wall got us moving. We rigged up; an RPG crunched into the wall and elsewhere along with mortars and small arms fire. I could hear screaming from outside and the shout for medics. Come on, get us out there, I thought.

'Come on boss, let's fucking do something!' some of the boys shouted. We were all frustrated and eager to get out there and help out. Tom was on the net, waiting for confirmation.

'Stand down lads', he shouted, 'the CO doesn't want us engaged.'

'Fuck him', we shouted 'blokes are fighting out there.'

'I know lads but unless we are engaged we are not to fire or get involved.' I could tell Tom was snapping too, but he had orders.

'Fucking dicks', Tommo cursed, 'let's get out there, I mean what the fuck are we here for?'

'I know but for now we have to wait lads', I voiced up. The firing was still cracking over our heads, often close with the sound of the Canadians' 30mm cannons firing back; I decided to move back up onto the rooftop.

Don't engage unless you get engaged, I recalled. Suits me, I thought. I crawled onto the roof to the forward edge; Bennie was already there with his L98 A1 sniper rifle along with Kiwi, the odd few rounds and bursts zipping over our heads. It took a while to ID the Taliban fighters but once we located them we began putting some suppressive fire down. Not much though, we didn't want to begin attracting more fire than that was already coming in, but enough to stop the Taliban flanking the ANA and Canadians that they couldn't see or pin down. We were well in our right to open up; they were closing in on the lads on the ground trying to take them on.

The fighting seemed to die down once more, the Taliban retreating back into the comfort of their town to fight another day. The ANA casualties had also pulled back to the district centre. One of the Afghans was asking us to come out and help them, he obviously didn't realise why we weren't helping. I felt completely useless. Ronnie S. was our medic attached to us for the mission. He got in there with the few Canadian medics to lend a hand. They were in a bad way; we asked to help out but there was little we could do. Two of them had deep facial trauma from an RPG blast, another had a tension pneumothorax and he would need a chest drain to get rid of the air that was now collapsing his lung. With limited kit the medics tried their hardest to sort him out, however, making a whole in his chest and lung cavity and applying the chest drain. It did sort his breathing and the discomfort but unfortunately it wasn't enough. He was going to die; I stood and watched him slip away. I didn't know him but in that environment it could easily have been any of us which always made you think. It wasn't the first person I had seen die in front of me and it wouldn't be the last. Unfortunately in this business it was a reality that we were involved in. We just hoped it would never be a fellow soldier, one of our muckers.

The Canadians got ready to pull back and we did the same. I felt like I was letting them down leaving them in here; I knew what was going through their heads. They risked the chance of being overrun now with us leaving and we all knew it. We pulled out and headed over the bridge, the Canadians cracked on up the main road to the north as we pulled west and headed cross-country towards the ridge. I looked back at the LAVs speeding up the road toward Lash, and I cringed. They will never learn, I said at nobody in particular. 'Well, speed is camouflage' Brett said, remembering what the Yanks had once said to us. We all laughed and were glad we weren't part of the circus convoy that they were on.

We settled on the ridge; we were in view of the town but that was the whole point. We were in an overt position which we hoped would stop the constant attacks on the district centre with our presence of being here and our ability to call in air assets, plus they wouldn't know our intentions: but this would only last so long. Although slightly exposed with only a few WMIKs on the ridge keeping eyes on and the remainder out of sight on the reverse slope behind, we settled into routine. From here we had a good view of the bridge and some of the district centre, the Helmand River and the western edge of the town. For us it was a case of settling into routine and awaiting further instructions from The Joke. As darkness fell over the town I wondered what could happen down there. Would the Taliban, now knowing that we had pulled back, and with the Canadians heading north, try and overrun this small group of ANA, ANP and Americans? Time would tell, I suppose.

It didn't take long before a call came in; the American in charge of the training team with the ANA believed the Taliban were going to take the bridge cutting off all re-supplies, support groups and the only escape route for the men inside the district centre. It was around 22:00hrs, a quick set of QBOs issued by Tom to the commanders then passed up to lads were pasted. We needed to get down and provide security for the bridge: we all knew the cost of letting the bridge fall into the hands of the Taliban.

Before leaving Bastion this time we had been given a set of headlight covers for each team. It was just a black plastic headlight cover that fixed over the headlight of the WMIK; we placed one on each WMIK over the right-hand headlight, so providing more light for the driver. It was a good aid to us; however, if the Taliban had night viewing capability then it could be a double-edged weapon as we would give away our position. I only liked to use these in the open and crossing certain obstacles, then they would be turned off to maintain our covertness while sneaking forward.

We slowly drove off the ridge and towards the road just north of the bridge. We had to be extremely careful; there could easily be an ambush in place ready for anybody about to cross this VP at the bridge. There was also a small settlement on our side of the river that looked very still. We patrolled at a snail pace watching for any sign of enemy and keeping our diesel engines at low revs to reduce noise, covering each other as we whispered into the PRR informing the other teams to move once we had got into position of cover. It's a slow but life-saving drill and this was definitely a tense moment for all of us.

Once a few hundred metres from the bridge and settlement, we killed the engines and waited. We were basically a mobile ambush or as it's now known, a fighting patrol. We sat in silence, scanning for any suspicious activity with our fingers on the triggers and waited, but nothing seemed to be going on down there. I guessed that the Yanks in there had been spooked and I didn't blame them. I would be just the same in their shoes. After a while we got the whispered order to withdrawal back to the harbour location on the ridge.

We expected to be involved in a full-scale fire fight that night and again we were all pumped with adrenalin ready for the action to start, only to be disappointed with the absence of our friends 'Terry Taliban' as they were now known. But we were soon to find out they were definitely wanting to play.

The boss Tom wanted to head down towards the district centre during daylight hours, show our presence and hopefully give faith to the ANA and fellow Yanks in the town. We packed up our gear and moved out, again bounding forward and covering each other, towards the bridge. We positioned ourselves on the west side of the bridge close to the settlement. This got a lot of attention from the villagers. Tom decided to take a few lads to one of the houses on the edge of town. Two WMIKs sat in close support behind in case things went wrong. I, Bernie, Kiwi, Tom and Dave patrolled forward and met with a few of the elders of the town who had now come out to see us. The thing with Afghanistan was that we had no idea who was friend or foe, they all dressed the same and it wasn't till they were firing at you that we knew they were our enemy. The elder seemed happy to talk even though he informed us that the Taliban would probably pay him a visit later on once we had left. This I took with a pinch of salt. Either he was not worried about the consequences of talking with the coalition forces or he was Taliban himself and with the percentage of Taliban and the supporters here I thought the latter.

As the boss and the interpreter continued to talk I pushed on with Bernie to give him some protection from the village. There seemed to be a very chilled atmosphere here, it was very strange for an area like this. Some of the ANA with their US commander had come out to see us also: they too seemed in high sprits. The bridge was still under the control of the ANA and ANP; however, the reputation of the ANP was becoming worse and worse in all areas. Intelligence and comments from the locals had definitely made me look on the ANP in a different light. In all areas in the Helmand Province the ANP had ruled under their own iron fist and set of rules: often doing their own thing, causing a lot of upset in the towns. It was my personal belief that this also included taking people away for various reasons who would never be seen again. We were suspicious that some of them were in contact with the Taliban and were passing on information about our movements and what we were up to. Some of these ANP were actually Taliban themselves. This did not surprise me at all. It was the same in Iraq and still is.

The IA (Iraqi Army) along with the ANA are normally of a good quality who have joined to do their job and rid the country of the Taliban and insurgents and been brought in and trained by US and UK forces to operate in another province. The IP (Iraqi Police) and ANP were near the opposite. They look like they are conducting law and order and helping the coalition but due to the high level of Taliban and insurgents (Iraq) influence this wasn't the case. In Iraq nearly every IED and EFP involving PSC patrols were only a few hundred metres from an IP checkpoint: they have either allowed the insurgents to place the device or they had done it themselves and even detonated it. They are so corrupt and were never trusted either back in Afghanistan with the military or in Iraq on CP work.

We talked to the US officer who alongside another few US soldiers were training and commanding the local ANA here in Garmsir.

'I had ten Afghans leave during the night thinking we would be slaughtered', the US officer said. In a way I didn't blame them. We and the Canadians didn't exactly boost them with confidence by fucking off, did we. We got a quick picture of the US officer and some of his Afghan team before escorting them back into their base. Passing the bridge I did the same with the ANP that manned it. I tried to explain that we were always in the local area; hopefully they would think we would be alongside them if they were under attack as I had doubts that any of these men would still be hanging around if the Taliban came.

The signs of previous skirmishes were ever present as we made our tactical move into the district centre. In the mid-afternoon we received further orders, to patrol the area south of the bridge to another small settlement just over the river from Garmsir, interact with the locals and find out their views on the Taliban and obviously make them aware of our presence. We said good luck rather than goodbye to the US officer and his team and patrolled back out over the bridge and on with our task.

Instead of going along the usual main track we pushed cross-country trying to find new routes into the small village which involved a few WMIKs getting stuck in the soft sand. After a few slaggings to and from we managed to gain entry. The village itself was only 500m in length and consisted of only two main roads. It was very quiet which got me thinking straight away, the absence of the normal and presence of the abnormal was beginning to raise its head. I dismounted and asked the boss Tom if this was a good idea due to the quietness of the settlement. After a very quick conflab we pressed on. Mike and I took point. Mike was a young fella of around 19 or 20 years who had not been with Patrols that long. He was from Scotland and a very good gunner for Bernie's WMIK; I would refer to him as the Spice Boy which he would constantly question but if you had seen him down town then you would understand why. The street was too quiet to say the least, but fuck it we were already in here now so we just had to crack on. The street was tight and I and Mike would check ahead, side streets and doorways before Brett and the other WMIKs would slowly follow us up.

As we hit the middle of the town the main track forked into two with a small square that probably marked the centre of the village. It was here when I saw my first local popping his head out of his house on the right-hand fork. I pushed left by direction of Tom and continued the patrol. A few others came out of the right-hand street which we all covered. Nobody waved from either side; I kept both hands on my weapon and slipped the safety off. They looked a little shocked and slightly afraid which I didn't know how to take. Was this good or bad, I thought. Had we took them by surprise and by that given them no chance to set an ambush or place IED if that's their intention or were they trying to bring us into the right-hand track and looking afraid as they knew what to expect once the Taliban had opened up? I could have been completely wrong and the presence of us British was worrying them due to the repercussions from the Taliban. Again I tried to focus and put my head into the usual 'if it happens, it happens and just react to whatever comes our way' attitude. Hard to do, especially as the point vehicle but there was no point in worrying we just had to push on.

Seeing the end of the village was a great relief. With the vehicles clear we pushed into all round defence; it seemed that now clear of the settlement the locals had begun to come out and watch the patrol from the safety of the buildings. After a while a few brave locals ventured out to meet us. The boss also did the same to meet them half way. With the Afghan confidence growing more locals came out to watch. Tom continued to speak to these middle-aged men but I thought this was odd. An old man came walking through the street with the help of some of the others. He did not look best pleased. We had well and truly pissed him off by breaking a major rule with them: tot talking to the elder (male that is). Women do not have any sort of rights in the Middle East, they are very much second class citizens. Western women think they have it hard: they need to take a visit to the Middle East where women involved in or even accused of adultery are stoned to death in the street. This still happens today by the way! Talking to some of the middle-aged men instead was a massive insult. It is a little like meeting your girlfriend's family for the first time. The first person you must speak to is the elder male of the family, either father, grandfather or great-grandfather, depending on who is still alive. If this is not done then you might as well leave, as the insult will probably result in them refusing to speak to you or acknowledge you, and they will banish you from their home. Basics, I said to myself, although none of us had picked up on it till it was too late.

The elder made this clear to the interpreter and had well and truly thrown his teddy in the corner. The two middle-aged men hurried back into the village which raised a few eyebrows on our side. I knew it was probably because of the tongue lashing from the elder but I and the lads still didn't like them running off like that. This could be part of a 'come on' deliberately making a scene and holding us at the outskirts of the village. Either way we all knew it was best to up sticks and fuck off. Tom made the excuses and we continued our patrol to the south-west, back onto the ridge and dropping down into the low lands behind it out of sight of the town and back to an overwatch position about 1k from our harbour of last night.

The CO told us over the radio to stay put for the time being and again wait out for future tasking. For us it meant apart from taking our turn on watching the town and our local area, sitting around in the shade of the WMIK talking shit and looking forward to our main event of the day which for me was scoffing up. The weather was ridiculous now. We were more south, and now at the height of summer it was clocking high 50s to early 60s degrees: it felt a lot hotter than Bastion. Sitting round I thought made it even worse, you find that you sweat even more when sitting still than when moving about unless you were fully kitted up and on foot. Everything was scorching –water, food and anything metal. There was definitely no chance of sleep; it was bad enough during the night when it was still mid-30s, waking to find yourself covered in sweat and more dehydrated.

We weren't getting much feedback for other areas, just the usual 'there's been several TIC' in Sangin or Now Zad but nothing much else. I was wondering if there would maybe be a major operation going to happen down here and that being another purpose for sitting here holding this ground. It made sense and after a few days hanging around all of us wanted to push in to the town and mix it up. Blokes were bored and it was showing, every so often a slagging would start between the teams; we could afford to have two lads from each team away from the vehicles at any one time leaving the two WMIKs with four men, enabling them to move and fire if needed. This meant that we could at least see our mates from our other teams at the opposite side of the harbour, (bearing in mind there was usually a gap between teams) and talk about other things and catching up on stuff. When moving around we had to take our belt kit/chest rig and weapons with us just in case, personal weapons were always within arm's reach anyway. It did mean in relative safety of the desert we could top up our tans and air our feet too. If not on stag we removed our T-shirts and replaced our boots with flip-flops. If they were good enough for the Taliban they were good enough for us.

With the heat it was easy to fall foul to a mild degree of trench foot out here, not as extreme as in wet conditions back in the UK or elsewhere, but with the constant sweating and keeping boots on 24 hours a day 7 days a week, it was causing problems. On major Ops then we had no choice but in mobile harbour locations like this and in the platoon houses of Sangin, Now Zad, Kajaki and Musa Qaleh then we could, and in some cases had to. Injuries due to not powdering feet, changing socks and airing your feet out could bring sections or patrols, platoons and even Companies to a halt rendering them non-mission capable. It was easily neglected.

As mentioned before, scoff was the highlight of the day for all of us. There were no fresh rations and only our imagination to make noodles, powders and menus

A,B,C and D into things worthy of eating. After this it was the commander's brief before we move into night routine. Tom brought us in around his wagon like always.

'OK lads we need to mark a DZ for a re-supply Op for the US team in the town', he started. 'A US C-130 is coming in at 01:30hrs so we need to have it in place; information passed up and secured by then', he continued. 'Any thoughts from the floor?' Ray mentioned an area of open ground, 6–7ks north-east of here before the river. We all agreed it would be an ideal area and also of a size that we could protect. Getting round the map we pin-pointed the middle of the DZ, and then stretched it out into a direction corridor of approx 5 by 2ks. Due to the lack of wind it would be pretty simple and worked to our advantage for the ground we had chosen. The aircraft would run in from the south using the Helmand River as a navigation aid. From there the aircraft would drop their goods at a given grid on the south of the DZ this would ensure that packages would all land in the DZ corridor as the aircraft kept on flying.

Our teams moved out once darkness fell in the usual tactical manner towards the pre-arranged DZ. It was a good choice and we quickly patrolled the outer boundaries to ensure it was clear. There was a small settlement off to our right on the east up against the river that was only a few ks from the DZ; it wouldn't be a problem unless the goods dropped in there. To make life easy for the pilot of the US C-130 we marked the DZ. Everything went smoothly and then my team positioned ourselves on the eastern flank. We watched our arcs and whispered jokes and old stories to ourselves to keep awake and alert.

One good thing about these boring times was hearing about other blokes' backgrounds. Some people's lives and upbringing were strange, I can tell you. It was good to hear stories about the lifestyles that had now brought us all to this point. We were all from different walks of life and different areas of the world that joined up for various reasons. Dropouts from college and school, builders, postmen, window fitters, door-to-door salesmen, one lad had previously been a tramp. Lads from broken and abusive families, orphanages and even jails were amongst our members. Blokes have always got stories to tell, keeping up our morale, whether from Civvy Street or their time in the Reg. It didn't matter what lads were before they joined, but one thing was for certain, the Reg changed you in some way, shape or form. We talked about leave that for some of us was coming up soon and what our plans were on reaching the UK. For me I just wanted to get on the lash, I had personal problems hanging over my head during and before deploying but the more time I spent over here the more I lost interest in them. Getting the blokes back safely and getting down town on the lash was my main concern now especially after what we had been involved in.

Our reminiscing was broken with Tom informing us of the approaching aircraft. Our DZ details and previous recce had been passed up a long time ago and we received an acknowledgment that they understood and it was a green light to go ahead. We scanned the night sky and saw the blackened shape of the large airframe.

'Is it doing a quick recce?' I said out loud.

'Yeah looks like it', Brett said. He was approaching from the west over the desert passing over the DZ on what looked like a quick recce for him. The C-130 passed over the 2k width of DZ passing over our heads and on towards Garmsir.

'Yeah looks like he's having a little look at the DZ', I said. The words hadn't even left my mouth when I saw the black shape of parachutes falling from the night sky.

'They are dropping', Brett said, 'the knobs.'

'You have to be fucking joking', I replied, watching the aircraft disappearing out of view and most of the parachutes drifting into the town. The only words that sprung to mind was 'Muppets'. I couldn't believe it; obviously we had been wasting our time and apart from the main DZ grid they hadn't listened to any of our considerations or the layout of the DZ along with its IR markings. We RVd with the other call signs.

'What the fuck happened there boss?' blokes began.

'Yeah they have dropped it in the wrong place.'

'That's a bit of an understatement', Johnny said.

'Yeah can't wait to tell the Yanks that they have no scoff coming in', Dave laughed.

'What worries me is that there was also some ammo and a TI sight system in with the scoff', Tom said.

'Oh mega, so now they have a TI capability', I snapped. I was pissed; it wouldn't be the last time this would happen to us but I did feel that nobody had bothered to listen to any of us. Why make us mark a DZ just to fuck us off and do their own thing anyway? Imagine if it had been a company of Paras; most of them would be either in the river or battling it out in Garmsir town if they survived the landing amongst the buildings. The remainder of the night we slowly pushed forward on foot collecting some of the US MRE rations that had come loose. I looked back into the town.

'Sorry lads,' I mumbled, 'you will have go hungry till we sort something else out; you can thank your mates for that.'

After heading back up onto the ridge we informed The Joke about the fuck up. A heli was put on to bring in more supplies the next day. This made more sense as they had casualties to be evacuated from the district centre too.

'Why didn't they just do that anyway?' Dale questioned. That morning we pushed back into the district centre and escorted the casualties and ANA out to the HLS for the exchange. After that it was back on our perch (ridge line). Tom thought we could push south and have a little look at the southern part of the town plus he wanted to keep the boys motivated; we all agreed. We had been down here around two weeks and fatigue was setting in. We bounced round to the southern edges of the ridge some 5–6ks from our original position. It was a hot day as always and the blokes seemed a little low; we needed a jolly, a pick-me-up. The Helmand River looked so appetising down there off the ridge, we all wanted to be down there as if we were on some Club 18–30 holiday.

A face-to-face with Tom sorted the problem. We were in a good overwatch position over 2ks from town. Below us a small stream led off from the main river.

The water was only slowly moving and it seemed concealed from the other side so nobody would see us in there. With two teams providing protection from above, the rest of us moved down on foot to the riverbank. Before long after a quick watch over the area we were in the Helmand River.

'Fuck me this is good!' the boys joked. It was and all, so refreshing, and after we had finished pissing around dunking each other or pissing on the back of our fellow mate who was beginning to strip down – which was always a standard thing every time we had to take mixed showers – we washed our kit. I remember back in Bastion after almost every mission, we would all jump in the shower together. In places like these you can't be shy, water and shower facilities were limited. As we all had to, we would wash side by side and it was a standard joke to try and piss on the guy next to you without him knowing. This was even better when down town on the drink, pissing on your mate's or a girl's leg next to you at the bar although most of the time it went down like a salad with a fat chick. When together we got up to some pretty outrageous stuff, always willing to go that step further. No wonder we gained a reputation.

After a while we thought it best to put our wet kit back on and head back and occupy a harbour for the night. Putting back on wet clothes is sometimes a bad move; in environments like this it was fine, they would dry in a half-hour. In the jungle we operated in wet kit because of humidity and constant downpours and only moved into dry kit once inside our bashas; in Europe we had to try and stay dry for fear of going down with exposure.

The sun began to rise as we sorted breakfast; I closed in on Tom to find out what our job was today, or if The Joke had finished off the midnight 'crack' session and asked us to conduct any recces or if we were needed in town. The word on the street was that Garmsir was quiet; I had guessed that as there had been no sound of firing or anything. Two things had disturbed me though: one, a lot of the US team's ANA force had bugged out during the night leaving a very vulnerable and scaled down US/ANA party in there. Why was this? Did they know something we or the US team didn't? It was definitely a combat indicator in my eyes, that something was going to kick off. Two, there was a phantom shitter on the loose. During the night someone had shit right next to our WMIK; the boys were convinced it was me. In Patrols we often had to shit into plastic bags if in a covert operation; however in this environment we could dig small shit pits for the team in a central area. I knew that it wasn't me but the blokes weren't having it. If it were me then I wouldn't be shitting right next to my vehicle on my side would I? I now had to find out who this was; the quest for the phantom shitter was on.

'Reconnaissance aircraft have spotted a possible crossing point over the river down at the southern part of the town', Tom started. He pointed to the map, about 7–8ks from here.

'What, a small bridge?' Steve asked.

'No, from what they said it's a shallow patch of river a bit like a ford, if we find it suitable for a vehicle crossing then it will give the Battle group a second option to get into town of Garmsir', Tom said. It definitely made sense. At some stage there would be some sort of Op down here; from our recces so far there was only the main bridge near the district centre to cross the river and access the town. Talk about a choke point. Unless they brought the engineers to build bridges, which would take time, they were limited. As the heat picked up and the sun began burning down onto our backs we focused in on the map as much as we could. Pin-pointing the rough area where the aircraft believed to have seen this natural ford we began planning a route in.

The ridge dropped off about 1–2ks before the crossing; the map had markings for soft sand but that was mainly it. Looking over to the other side of the river the map showed a few sets of buildings making up the edge of the town. From what we all could see it was well away from the main town centre and looked quite open around the river banks, providing a good access point, and then FUP and start line for us to host for a company assault later in the future.

However, like I mentioned before, it was all well and good on the map but it could be a lot different once we got 'eyes on'.

I briefed my team and likewise the other commanders did the same.

'I did have some good news, though', I said to the boys. 'The CO wanted us back up Bastion for a quick turnaround before been sent up north again.'

'God this place is fucking wank', the boys fired back.

'Yeah get us back up Sangin or Musa Qaleh we are missing out down here. A few admin days back at Bastion wouldn't go amiss either', I said, 'I'm fucking hanging for a good scoff.'

'Yeah and a wank', Brett butted in.

'Nah had one the other day', I said with an evil grin.

'Did you!'

'Yeah did you not wonder why your fringe was sticking up like TinTin?' I said.

'You better had be joking, Scotty, you sick twat', Brett snapped.

Within 10 minutes we were patrolling back on the west side of the ridge out of sight of the town, then swung to the south and began moving in on the target. We sat just off the high ground and scanned the area. It looked deserted, there was definitely not anything on our side of the bank and only a few large compounds on the other. Pushing into the low lands we had to keep to some of the tracks, cannabis plants were all over, it seemed to be everywhere around here and also soft sand. We didn't want to risk getting bogged in.

We slowly patrolled towards the crossing. Ray was leading with Gaz's vehicle behind. They pushed forward and took a butchers.

'I think this is the spot, boss', Ray called. 'Other side looks clear, I will push across.' Tom wanted Ray, Gaz, me and Bernie to go across; once our four WMIKs were holding the ground then he would come over too. The others were under Steve and they would provide protection and fire support from their side of the river. If something went wrong then we could cross as they fired, providing us protection. I reached the river bank just as Gaz was driving through. Bernie was over to my right waiting his turn to cross. We always moved over obstacles like this; nobody moved until the vehicle was clear and in position. It was a Patrols SOP.

Ray and Gaz were over and left and right of the crossing looking into the compounds, buildings and small hash-coloured banks to our front. The river was around 150m across, a gentle steady flow of rapids travelling from left to right. The ford didn't seem that wide, maybe a car and a half's width and around 2–3 feet deep. Bernie told us he was moving over. I got my camera and took a quick picture of his wagon crossing; it looked peaceful, the sun shining and the crystal clear water flowing at our feet.

'OK Scotty, you're good to go', Bernie called over the PRR.

'Brett let's go', I said as I took hold of my GPMG. Brett took his time as the WMIK slid around due to the wet rocks beneath us. Just before we got half way over there was an almighty explosion behind us.

'Fucking hell!' I shouted. I looked over my left shoulder to see the boss's vehicle in a cloud of smoke and shit. I could only see a little bit of their WMIK and my first thoughts were that they were all dead.

'Shit the boss has been hit by an IED', I said. I let out a large sigh, ready to expect the worst when I returned. Brett stopped the WMIK dead on hearing the explosion. I pressed my PRR pre-set radio switch to inform the boys up front when my whole world erupted around me and my WMIK. Machine gun fire ripped into the water to our front, and left. It felt like a scene out of the movie *Saving Private Ryan*.

'Fuck we are in an ambush!' I shouted. Around our heads 7.62mm cracked as I began to engage and return fire. I fired at the compound but I couldn't see anyone: I was just firing in the general direction.

'What do you want me to do Scotty?', Brett shouted as I continued firing. I gave him a quick look.

'What do I want you to do, get the fuck out of here!' I shouted. Brett whacked our vehicle into reverse and accelerated hard. I had spent enough time in the Paras and Patrols to understand that if you were in somebody else's killing zone then you don't hang around in it. Brett got us back onto the river bank and I told him to position us to the right flank while the incoming zipped and cracked round our heads. I couldn't go anywhere else, my mates were still on the other side and we weren't just going to fuck off. Steve, Dale, Dave and Tom began bounding back out of the killing zone, just enough to stop them being zeroed in on but still close enough to provide fire support for the lads on the other side. I caught sight of the smoke signatures from the Taliban's weapons and me and Tommo fired with everything we had. It's the only way to survive an ambush; you have to be more aggressive than them.

I could see the Taliban now, firing from the compounds and the green vegetation over on the left. I aimed on and gave them hell, we all were. The volume of fire from both sides was outrageous. I could see Bernie moving over the ford with Gaz close behind.

'Brett I need another box of link', I shouted. He already had it ready, another box of 200 rounds on and I was firing again. Ray was still engaging from the far side. All of a sudden I heard shots from our right; I looked over to see Brett off the vehicle about 10m away and firing his long.

'What are you doing?', I screamed.

'Getting some rounds down', he replied. Looking back it was funny but at the time fucking mad and stupid with us stuck in the middle of an ambush.

'Get back on this fucking WMIK!' I shouted. As he jumped on more 7.62mm landed around us kicking up dirt zipping past our bodies. They were fucking close.

'They are firing from that building on our right!' they both shouted. A small house was just visible due to hash plants over on the right about 200m away, I could see people running from and around it, and they were definitely engaging us, puff of smoke generated from their AKs and the crack over my head was giving it away. I turned my gun and gave them some 7.62mm belt-fed on rapid. I can see how people can get scared in situations like this however I wasn't, I was more pissed off than anything. Like I mentioned before, I would have been more scared had I known it was going to happen, but here it was too late to worry. Everything happened so fast, I was full of rage and anger which I have never had during a fire fight before. I even remember myself muttering: Why you fucking twats, trying to outflank us are you Terry Taliban? Just as I took a quick look over my GPMG to see where the Taliban fighters had gone to ground, a heat wave flashed past me and Brett and then we were covered in a smoke cloud and dirt. For a second I was stunned, my head in a total daze. We stopped firing and just looked at each other then we looked over to our right just off the WMIK as the smoke cleared. A RPG tailfin was sticking up from the ground no more than 2–3 metres away.

'Fucking hell', Brett shouted. I began firing again; Bernie had now passed us and Gaz too. Bash, Bernie's driver thought me, Brett and Tommo were dead and we nearly were. Our time to move, I thought, as before we were now definitely the target being static for too long as I covered the others over the ford.

'Brett let's go!' I shouted over the sound of Tommo on the .50 Cal. Just as we drove off another mortar landed close by chucking dirt all over us.

'Fucking hell that was close!' Tommo was shouting above us, another RPG and more 7.62mm PKM came streaming in right on top of us grouped together on the bank. Brett began driving out across the bumpy soft sand, each vehicle had no choice but to fnd their own way out as the track was a single lane. The only way I could fire at this stage due to sitting on the left was by tilting the GPMG over to the right, firing right in front of Brett's face; being so bumpy I'm sure I nearly took his face off once or twice. Not something we did in training but this was for real and I had no choice but to keep engaging inches in front of his face to keep our enemies' heads down. We later joked that I could have done him a favour by hitting him.

Brett pushed the WMIK to its limits driving out of the contact area. We reached the hard desert surface that came off from the ridge and spun round. We were still only 100m, if that, from the ford crossing/ambush point. I watched the vehicles extracting each team working together to get out of there. Just then I saw someone fall from the WMIK, he started running behind. I later found out it was Ronnie S. our medic, he was trying to use the vehicle as cover running flat out alongside it while under fire, the Goblin (John R.) was the gunner. I caught sight of him conducting a box change on the move for his .50 Cal, he threw the empty box over his shoulder hitting Ronnie S. in the head. A strange thing to see during an ambush but I still laugh about that to this day. Killed by an ammo tin. Imagine that.

Luckily Ronnie jumped on the next vehicle giving fire support and who had seen Ronnie fall. Again Brett had a box of ammo ready for me, we were still giving the Taliban everything we had, and most of the vehicles had reached the hard surface. We knew once this happened our spacing could increase and we could bound back faster and further.

'Come on!' I shouted impatiently; the Taliban firepower wasn't as strong now as we had more guns firing. Me, Bernie, Steve and Dale were giving it max. Just then I saw four Taliban running across the hilltop left of the furthest left compound. I laid on and began firing; I didn't stop and held it as they continued to run. Three of them dropped down before they reached the compound and I was quite confident that I had taken them down. A few more mortars came thumping in as we started bounding back towards the hills to our rear. Even as we moved back they still lobbed in mortars trying to make a lucky hit.

The boss sighted an ERV just over the rise; we pushed in and went in all round defence. Straight away we were all calm and collected, something we were like anyway but also from our Afghanistan experience. Ammo and our weapons were our first concern, making sure they were ready to go again after we all realised we were still in one piece. Second was the vehicles: and at least five of the WMIKs had taken hits, including mine. Tom's WMIK, the one I thought had took a direct strike and had the initial feeling that they were all dead onboard had been lucky, the mortar had landed right on the rear left, the WMIK tyre and soft sand took the impact, the tyre itself was shredded: how they all walked away was beyond any of us. I noticed that most of our tyres were flat too, we had lost two and some of the other WMIKs one or two also, either by the flying shrapnel or from 7.62. It was lucky we had two spare per vehicle. Something else caught my eye when we changed over the tyres. The spare wheel on my side sat just behind me, there was a chunk of tread missing from it and two small holes, two 7.62mm rounds had passed through the tyre, another foot left and it would have sliced my head in two. I didn't even bother saying anything there and then as in my eyes everyone had been close.

The boss was sending a full contact report back to The Joke telling them exactly what was going on and calling up fast air, as the lads finished off the weapons and vehicles. Still buzzing by our Hollywood contact (any contact that didn't involve any of us being slotted but was close enough to give you a hair cut or change your desert bottoms was a Hollywood contact) we took photo evidence of the ambush and also a few of ourselves with the old classic 'victory' cigar. I checked and sorted my ammo, I had used just under 800 rounds of 7.62mm from my GPMG in the ambush killing zone. Tommo had used around 200–300 rounds before the .50 Cal jammed making him move to his personal weapon, that being the Minimi. Most of the other WMIKs had used up nearly the same: a lot of firepower to be raining down and the only reason we were still alive but we had used nearly half our ammo. Another reason we had asked for so much. It wasn't to wrap round our bodies to take photos of and place them on some gay dating site, we need it; ammo saved our lives, we would have used a lot more if we had been trapped on the other side.

Later that night trying to sleep I thought about the ambush, we were extremely lucky that was for sure, but also it was down to our training. Our contact drills were so slick that our reaction in firepower and movement must have also taken the Taliban by surprise. End of the day they had caught us out, big time. This happens especially in Patrols or any recce force moving into unknown territory. We had been hit in their killing zone, their ground of choice.

I questioned myself on how me, Brett and Tommo had survived as well as some of the others that day. The RPG had been so close to us that I could feel the heat from it passing. Me and Brett could have reached out and touched it, it was so close; and for it to explode only a few feet away, yet we were without a scratch. When you set up an ambush you have a killing zone, you also have the middle axis of a killing zone which you direct most of your firepower onto and also align your mortars onto. When the middle of the patrol hits the middle of the killing zone you trigger the ambush. My WMIK was crossing the ford, the middle of their killing zone, and we were also the fourth WMIK to cross which was the middle of the patrol. The boss's WMIK was also on the edge of the river bank and too in the middle of the killing zone; the first mortar round had landed between us both, starting the ambush. I think they hoped to cut the patrol in two. With vehicles stuck on the far side it could have been an all out bloodbath. Our hard trained contact drills had saved our lives; in an ambush you have to throw everything you have at them. We had done just that by covering each other's movements out of the killing zone.

After reporting back and watching fast air sweep the area we headed for the high ground. Back on the ridge we overwatched the area for a few hours and sorted our shit but all seemed quiet again. There wasn't much chance of them coming out to have a pop but you can never say never. I suggested that once darkness fell we were to push back out of sight, box round and find another harbour some 5ks up the ridge line. Everyone was in agreement and we pushed into position and tried to get some head down.

The next day we left Garmsir behind and headed back to Bastion. It felt good to get back for once and have a few days off. De-gunging (cleaning) yourself is always a plus, and then it was straight down to the cookhouse to eat mass amounts of scoff. It was here we found out from a good source that one of the chefs in the scoff house was taking photos of himself all kitted and tooled up next to armoured and fighting vehicles and in different fire positions pretending he was on the ground, but really he was just behind the cookhouse. The lads found his camera and were about to do the old classic of an old rusty sheriff's badge or cat's arse (arse hole) when we spotted the pictures. He got some much earned abuse from the lads and also earned the nickname Killer to go with it. Something like this has come to my attention again; there is a picture of Dale during the contact in Now Zad that appears in another book misidentifying Dale as another soldier belonging to another unit on a different mission. Sorry to disappoint people but this is in fact Dale W., a member of Patrols platoon, during Op Mutay in June 2006.

Before our move down to Garmsir, PF had moved out of Musa Qaleh; the Danish recce force had decided after several months in Bastion to actually get out and do something. Saying that it was more than what some other countries were doing. Since the Danish recce had been in they realised it wasn't all plain sailing, they were being attacked constantly and the Danish commanders and government were wingeing already. What the fuck did they think our troops were doing down here, having a picnic? An Operation was being put together to reinforce the Danish with support company troops consisting of mortars and guns and also the Royal Irish platoon attached to C Company. Like I said before, the Danish were pushing to get out of there but at the moment they would have to stay put and grit their teeth with the reinforcements.

It was nice to chill in Bastion, after all that went on down in Garmsir. It was a standard thing that once all the admin was sorted, we would stuff our faces then hit the gym (a tent with CV machines and weights) then stuff our faces again. On our lines they had done a good job of our gym, they had bought loads of equipment in for the blokes to train with; it had took a while but it was here now. One thing had pissed me off. There were lots of Hats getting in there, with all the boys on the ground on various missions they had started getting in more and more. Normally I wouldn't have a problem, Hat or not it never bothered me; however, when we first arrived other units like the engineers, logistics and other non-airborne units banned the lads from using their gym. No reason was given and it nearly came close to blows on a few occasions. They just didn't want us in their gym, fucking sad I know but like I said before it was another thing to get over on us. Now our gym was up and by far the best equipped everyone was using our gym, this after what happened to us previously pissed the lads off.

Within a few days we were loaded and re-supplied ready to go once more. Once in position we would wait for the CH47s to come in carrying the ground troops of B and C Company. This was getting bigger than *Ben Hur*. HCR were also on task as well as the Estonians, ourselves and a large logistic convoy. The plan was for the Patrols to locate and protect a HLS close to the western edge of town. The HCR would move in from the south with the logistic convoy of large ISO containers. On wheels down, the rifle companies would advance and clear the buildings on the western edge of the river, through the green belt over the river and again through more of the green belt towards the platoon house. Sounds easy when someone tells you, but we didn't think it would be.

Again it was a long drive up north in the extreme heat; we pushed north then pivoted in right to the south-west of the town. Musa Qaleh sat on the right of the Helmand River; west of the river was a large ridge line like an inverted finger. As it got thinner at the most southern tip it joined up with two large wadi systems that made a Y shape. These wadis were deep; at points a few hundred metres high making movement difficult and very little option for a HLS. HCR were also making their way towards the position. There were already problems happening, just getting in position around Musa Qaleh. One of their vehicles, a Scimitar, hit an anti-tank mine while escorting 7 RHA (gun line) into a suitable firing position. Luckily there were no casualties, just a few very shaken blokes.

We sighted the HLS in the low lands to the south-west of the town and river. It was almost in a horseshoe with large features around to the rear and sides which the Patrols dominated. Several hours later the sound of the Chinooks came in to earshot. It was on. The wave of CH47s touched down unloading B and C Company; we watched from the high ground as they debussed and advanced on the compounds close by. The HCR moved into the south of Musa Qaleh to one of the little settlements on the outskirts.

The Taliban were waiting: as the convoy of HCR pushed down the street they were ambushed. An IED initiated the contact, killing three members simultaneously with only one survivor. The Spartan tank was completely destroyed and just as with us a few days before, it was part of a more complex ambush. The HCR were caught in the middle of RPG and machine gun fire. As they tried to withdraw one of the Scimitars tried to reach the downed Spartan but after intense fire ended up driving into a ditch: they too were now immobilised. They withdrew on foot taking with them the driver of the Spartan who had somehow escaped. Later Patrols and B Company went in to retrieve the dead and destroy the kit on board. The devastation left behind from one IED is unbelievable, something I would have to get used to in the CP world as it became a weekly occurrence. On this occasion Captain Alex Eida, 2nd Lieutenant Ralph Johnson and L/Cpl Ross Nicholls tragically lost their lives.

B and C Company began pushing into the green belt after the order to 'fix bayonets'. This got everyone hyped up, our pulses racing and the tingle of adrenalin flowing through our veins. The sound of metal on metal could be heard as we connected and pushed home the bayonets. Every fighting man is known as a bayonet. Again this doesn't mean Corps or trade soldiers like REME, artillerymen, logistics and chefs. These are fighting troops, the men whose sole purpose is to advance and kill the enemy. That is it.

We all carry bayonets, an 8-inch blade that fits to the end of your personal weapon. Its purpose is to drive into an enemy's gut, chest, throat or face. As we all carry them we are often referred to as bayonets. The order to 'fix bayonets' had not been given on this scale since 1982, for the bloody battles of the Falklands 8000 miles away. The Falklands were a part of the Parachute Regiment's history. Now in Afghanistan we were hearing the same order, ready to advance on the Taliban and even drive a blade into some Afghan fighter.

The Taliban were using the grass and trees to hide them; it was a very dangerous area to advance through. A call came through the radio: Patrols were also needed to push into the green belt. As we found out from Now Zad this was a recipe for disaster. The two rifle companies had spread themselves out along the vast vegetation and moved in, the river was only a few hundred metres forward. On the other side the Danish recce were moving from their platoon house to secure the 300m of road that would join up with the approaching B and C Company lads. It seemed to be going a little too smoothly for us; HCR had been smashed and this seemed far too easy.

It didn't take long before some firing started. Once one call sign got engaged then everyone began getting a slice. Lee C. was one of the first lads from Patrols to receive incoming – 7.62mm thundered over his head mixed in with two RPG, and then we all got some. The worrying thing was that we might hit the advancing Danish or PF lads that were moving towards us. I put it to the Taliban fighters, they had balls: two fighting Para companies plus all the attachments, and heavy weapons supported by mortars with the Danish and PF troops on the other side advancing towards them. It didn't take long before we started locating targets and we began throwing down enormous rates of fire onto their position. Again it was intense and one of the only times we would all rather have been on foot than stuck on our WMIKs: it was far too enclosed for our vehicles.

At one point the Taliban fire was that accurate that we pulled the WMIKs back, to let the lads of B and C Company push on again before we could yet again bound in. The Taliban were yet again focused on the vehicles; without these the relief could not happen, or it would take a hell of a lot longer. Ammo and heavy weapons could not be brought up and CAS-E-VAC would be more difficult on foot.

We all began making progress but it had taken many hours; whoosh – an RPG would fly in front of one of our WMIKs.

'Fuck me that was close', the blokes sighed. The odd automatic burst of gunfire erupted from the deep greenery but we kept pushing in. Eventually we made it to the RV: at last the RIP could take place. The Royal Irish made their way through the Danish protection and likewise PF withdrew through the area we had cleared. All the while sparse firing continued on the flanks amongst the rifle companies and air strikes near the platoon house. The logistics were some of the last to get in and drop their supplies. On return they had to cross the open wadi; one of the WMIKs was escorting them out. Private Andrew Barrie Cutts was on the rear gun and was hit by a single gunshot to the back. Unfortunately for the 19-year-old soldier they was little anyone could do and he died while being CAS-E-VAC out of the area.

After the RIP had been done, Patrols again secured the HLS allowing B and C Company to get off the ground and back to Bastion.

'Lucky fuckers', one of the lads said as they lifted off and disappeared into the blue sky.

Patrolling back wasn't without incident either. Because the area south-west of Musa Qaleh was so channelled it was hard to get through without detection. A small stretch of ground peppered with sparse farm buildings dominated the area. To the west were the mountains and larger settlements and again east more settlements and large wadis to avoid. The sparse waste and farmland became known as the Gauntlet: every time we passed through they would try something, mostly small, but nevertheless they would have a go. Our survey indicated that we had a choice on where to move through. Even in the same area we wouldn't be on the same patch of ground, it was mostly flat and therefore we could use different routes. As we pushed south a few bikers to our rear and flanks caught the attention of the gunners: most definitely dickers. Our WMIKs were well spaced both front and back and left–right. Tommo and Cookie saw the threat at nealy the same time. Two of the bikers stopped and pulled out what they described as long-barrelled weapons, one of which was a possible RPG. Two or three of the gunners opened up while we continued to move, eliminating the threat there and then. Now through the Gauntlet we could push on south and to Bastion.

Chapter 10

VC, Heroes and Funerals

The Battle group had taken a few shakes to say the least; the loss of the three HCR lads and then Andrew Barrie Cutts was a shock. For the lads involved it could have been a lot worse. From my own experiences and also the stories of others our death toll should have been a lot higher and not just in that operation either.

The Battle group was unbelievably stretched. A Company were still in Sangin, as too were some of the Sniper, Signal and Support Company attachments; C Company was in Gereshk but also used for bigger operations and strike Ops. The Royal Irish attachments were mainly in Musa Qaleh now; elements of B Company along with Support Company were in Kajaki Dam and Patrols and PF usually out doing the old Lawrence of Arabia stuff, patrolling the deserts from one platoon house to the next and supporting any mission before and during.

Apart from the lads on the ground in the platoon houses, the rest of us managed to get a small amount of down time. Although this was good, in a few days we were bored. Apart from smashing the gym and scoffing, what else could we do? Sitting round all day in our tents with the air con constantly packing up was breaking our balls.

The blokes kept up our morale with our own fun and games, normally stitching each other up for one reason or another, planned or unplanned. Here were a few examples. To give ourselves more privacy which was obviously hard in a room with around 10–12 lads, some of the lads set up the large mosquito nets, this covered your camp bed and also gave you a little work/admin area. It was like a little wanking den. Snake Eyes had been in his most of the day, minding his own business with his earphones on but when blokes are bored we need entertainment. Snake Eyes was going to keep us amused. One of the lads placed a padlock on his zip making any escape impossible for him. We then collapsed his mosquito net by pulling out his poles, resulting in the netting falling all over him. Once this happened we prodded him with sticks and flipped him from his cam cot which was attached to the mosquito net; he was trapped in a mess of netting much to our amusement. This along with other childish events like awaking the lads from deep sleeps by screaming at them scaring the shit out of them while also videoing: it kept us going for a few hours.

We did at this stage manage to get hold of some vodka and whisky from a lad that should be unnamed. Apart from early on after Op Mutay, where we got around two beers a man, none of us had been on the lash here. For one, we were too busy and two, it wasn't exactly Shagaluf. With the help of our friend we got hold of a few bottles of the devil's juice. After so long off the drink and with the constant workload and heat we were well smashed after a few cupfuls. As I predicted a few dramas were already in the pipeline. It's what happens, and to be

190

GONG FOR A HERO

Honour... Cpl Wright (far right) is to be recommended for the George Cross

Corporal died trying to save injured comrades

EXCLUSIVE
By RUPERT HAMER
in Afghanistan

A PARATROOPER who died trying to save comrades in Afghanistan is to be recommended posthumously for one of Britain's highest bravery medals.

Corporal Mark Wright is expected to receive the George Cross after he

was killed running through a minefield to call for air support when members of a patrol were blown up in Helmand Province.

Cpl Wright, 27, made his fatal run this week when five soldiers from the elite 3rd Battalion, The Parachute Regiment were seriously injured after straying into the unmarked minefield.

Britain's military commander in

Afghanistan, Brigadier Ed Butler, has already praised Cpl Wright's "act of exceptional bravery".

Last night a para source said: "Cpl Wright's actions were an example of the highest standards expected from this regiment. He is an example of the extraordinary courage demonstrated by the troops from 16 Air Assault Brigade throughout this tour." Cpl Wright's family, from

Edinburgh, paid tribute to him yesterday – and revealed how he was due to wed his fiancée Gillian later this year.

They said in a statement: This selfless act is typical of him – he always put others before himself. We are extremely proud of Mark and the profession he chose. He leaves a large empty space in our lives."

If the George Cross is awarded to

him, it will be the first posthumous gallantry award since Col H Jones's Victoria Cross in the 1982 Falklands War. Jones, of 2 Para, was gunned down trying to protect his men from enemy fire near Goose Green.

The George Cross ranks with the Victoria Cross as the nation's highest award for gallantry.

The VC is awarded for acts carried out in combat – whereas Cpl Wright is eligible for the GC because he was not actually in combat at the time.

news@sundaymirror.co.uk

Afghan soldier heroes in line for VC

Corporal Mark Wright: Died

A PARATROOPER killed while trying to rescue wounded comrades from a minefield in Afghanistan could be in line for a posthumous award for gallantry, Army sources have revealed.

Corporal Mark Wright is among 200 British soldiers likely to be recommended for bravery medals, including 'several' who could receive the ultimate recognition of the Victoria Cross.

Corporal Wright, 27, ran into the unmarked minefield to try to assist badly wounded fellow soldiers after two of them triggered explosions, but after helping to

'A very, very brave man'

treat their wounds and calling for help, he stood on a mine and was fatally wounded.

The 200 likely commendations reflect the vicious intensity of fighting against the Taliban over the summer in Helmand Province, where some 4,500 British troops are struggling to oust the enemy from their traditional stronghold.

Commanders have admitted they face the toughest sustained fighting by the British Army in half a century, and the extent of medal commendations makes a nonsense of earlier claims by ministers that the mission was mainly one of reconstruction and aid.

Almost 100 of the award rec-

By **Matthew Hickley**
Defence Correspondent

ommendations involve members of the 3rd Battalion The Parachute Regiment, which forms the core of the infantry battlegroup taking on the Taliban.

Other units in line for medals include RAF Chinook helicopter pilots who have had to land to rescue soldiers under heavy fire.

Soldiers manning remote outposts have found themselves facing several Taliban attacks a day for weeks on end, often with intermittent supplies because of the dangers of travelling by road and the shortage of helicopters.

Army sources spoke of heroics by many soldiers in close-quarter fighting, including bayonet charges. One source said: "We're talking Waterloo stuff here.

Victoria Crosses – the highest award for gallantry in the face of the enemy – are awarded only very rarely. Two were awarded in the 1982 Falklands conflict – both posthumously and both to Para.

None arose from the first Gulf War and only one has been earned in Iraq, by Lance Corporal Johnson Beharry, 27, an armoured vehicle driver who twice saved his comrades from ambushes in 2004.

Now it is understood up to six men are being considered for the ultimate recognition in combat.

Corporal Wright, who was from Edinburgh and was engaged to be married, died on September 6 in northern Helmand. A foot patrol of around half-a-dozen soldiers was climbing a hill to search for a suspected Talibar position and walked into the minefield, probably left over from the Soviet occupation. A

mines w suffered were left Despit mines, a nea charge and c port b
An l lande could fitter he t cue, A ther mer fou an die

VC FOR PARA WHO DIED SAVING PALS

Cpl Bryan's widow to collect Afghan medal

Sacrifice . . . Cpl Budd was killed in a desperate enemy charge

EXCLUSIVE by TOM NEWTON DUNN, Defence Editor

A HERO Para who died in a hail of bullets while saving seven comrades in Afghanistan will today be awarded a posthumous Victoria Cross, The Sun can reveal.

Dad-of-two Corporal Bryan Budd, 29, won the posthumous award of Britain's highest gallantry medal since the Falklands War nearly 25 years ago.

Rifle

There on August 20, Cpl Budd was ...

For Valour . . . Victoria Cross

For bravest of the brave

The Victoria Cross was instituted in 1856 as Britain's supreme gallantry award.

Since then only 1,351 have been awarded, 294 of them to men who died in action.

Most are made of bronze from Russian cannon captured in the Crimean War. They are literally worth their weight ...

Grief . . . his widow Lorena

The Sun Sept — Page Xx

honest just accepted. Obviously we weren't allowed to drink around live weapons, ammunition and grenades which could be a bad move.

As the night went on a few augments kicked off resulting in one lad being dropped. Once while on a tour of the Falkland Islands we had caused that much shit that we were kept away from all the other units. Every drunken night ended in a fight, not always started by us, may I add. So banished from society we drank alone; boredom and the lack of fun resulted in us 'milling' each other. Milling was a test in the P-Company selection for the Paras: two men stand toe to toe and fight for one minute: they don't box, dodge and block, but all-out fight. One minute can last a long time when you have to stand toe to toe with another person and maybe your mate. On P-Company it was a test of aggression, balls and reacting to an order like 'fight', for us that night it was a case of boredom, fun and drunkenness.

A Patrol commander who shall also be anonymous threw a smoke grenade into the air-con unit but luckily it never went off. A few lads ended up being red-eyed which is where lads are pinned down and the arse of a fellow mate would be rubbed onto their face as a punishment; this was normally controlled by Gaz. He had the words 'black' and 'pool' tattooed on his arse cheeks. If one of the younger blokes fucked up then a chant of 'Black-pool' would get shouted around. It was best either to get out of there and not bother going back that night, or to just accept it, as at some stage it was going to happen.

We finished off with pissing through the barrels of the .50 Cals onto unconscious blokes or anyone not paying attention while in a drunken daze, and then letting the Phantom shave a few eyebrows off lads who had creamed in too early. The Phantom has been with our unit years and years, and the Battalion even longer, and seems to be at every piss-up in the Battalion and even at more than one piss-up at a time. The Phantom's identity will always remain top secret. A few years ago he even broke into the old CO office and shit in one of his drawers. My first OC in 3 Para had this happen to him after a massive Company piss-up, but after he sobered up he realised that it was him who put it there in the first place. There weren't many OCs who got up to stuff like that.

Eventually we all fell unconscious in some location, whether floor, bed or toilet, a few lads swamping down but that was nothing special. I never seemed to have much problem but some lads would splash after a couple of tins; it got that bad at one stage that all of Patrols and sniper floors would have at least four or five mattresses outside the rooms all with maps of Africa (piss stains) freshly marked on them. This I could understand, as it's happened to me on a rare occasion; but I recently watched a mate of mine sit and accidentally piss himself (very drunk as he is only 34) while he drunkenly sang a song: the excitement must have taken him over the edge.

It didn't take long for Patrols to be pushed out again, this time into Sangin and Musa Qaleh for more Ops which included escorting supplies and defences for the platoon house of Sangin. The plan was to build a large hesco wall around the front and rear to make a more secure area in which to land the Chinooks. It was always good to chill but at this moment we just wanted to be out on the ground.

The next few weeks were mainly bouncing into Sangin and elsewhere as the platoon houses were being constantly attacked. Before departing Bastion we heard the news from Sangin. As Patrols had been in Garmsir and Musa Qaleh in our own scraps we hadn't really heard much of what was happing elsewhere. Heavy contact between A Company and the Taliban had been getting worse. A Company had lost a few lads through injuries during these confrontations. On one of these patrols Private Eddie E. was hit, taking two rounds to his thigh which nearly cost him his leg. The boys from his section pushed on, keeping the Taliban's heads down as much as possible so they could get Eddie out of there. Stu Giles was the medic for A Company. Stu had originally been an A Company tom before becoming a battalion medic. Without caring for his own safety Stu ran to the aid of Eddie, applying a tourniquet which saved his leg while still in the open and under heavy fire. This action was typical of the Paras, typical of the blood clot, and resulted in Stu Giles receiving the MC. It wasn't just Stu running to the aid of Eddie that was highlighted that day. All the others had played their part too, including Bry Budd and Pete McKinley who had raced forward into the fire fight to suppress the enemy. Normally the instinct is to run away from danger and flying bullets but again it showed the type of breed we were. They knew there was a mate in trouble and blokes will fight to the end for each other. Again this action resulted in Pete McKinley being hit with shrapnel and also having to be CAS-E-VAC but not until he returned to the platoon house on his own two legs.

The HCR had also moved up into Sangin, using their armour and heavy weapons to support all ground Ops in the area. Unfortunately there had been another fatality a week earlier again from the HCR. Sean Tansey was working underneath his armoured vehicle when somehow it rocked off the jack killing him instantly while he conducted maintenance in the Sangin platoon house.

During August the Taliban had upped their game especially around the Sangin area. Patrols were sent out almost every day into the area around the platoon house; on a few occasions they were ambushed and had to call in fast air, mortars and the HCR 30mm cannons for support as they withdrew. One patrol commanded by Hugo Farmer had apprehended two Taliban fighters during a patrol. After the usual bag and tag (tying of hands and covering of their eyes which were standard procedures for POW) they spotted more Taliban closing in which hadn't seen the patrol. Hugo Farmer's men opened fire and after conducting a follow-up the Taliban had slipped away. The two Taliban POWs had been killed in the crossfire.

On 20 August the day started like any other in Sangin. 1 Platoon were sent out plus attachments and a few of our WMIKs to support 9 Squadron engineers to blow holes in compounds in order to make more routes out from the platoon house. Charlie C. commanded 2 Section in support of the 9 Sqn lads. Andy W. pushed out with 3 Section and Bryan Budd 1 Section. As they started their task Bry led his team through a large maize field at which point he caught sight of Taliban fighters. After spotting this he quickly made his estimate: he couldn't afford to let the Taliban slip through. His plan was to sneak through the field and ambush them. As it turned out there were a lot more Taliban than he thought.

On approach Andy W. got engaged patrolling into his position, pinning him down, which also resulted in Bry losing the element of surprise on setting his ambush. Andy reacted keeping the Taliban at bay but as the rounds began to fly the Taliban caught sight of Bry Budd's team. Bry was caught in the open field and came under enormous enemy fire resulting in three of his own lads being dropped. Guy Roberts had been attached from Support Company; he was the main MFC for the platoon and the main bloke responsible for bringing mortars for support. He was now lying on his back having taken a round in his shoulder. Andy L. (or Langers as he was called) was close behind and tried to drag Guy out of the killing area but he too was hit, and so was Craig S. A 7.62mm round hit Langers in the shoulder taking a chunk of flesh off and then, due to Langers being hunched over trying to drag Guy, passed through and skimmed his top lip and nose. Private Halton continued to drag his friends out of the now very much nightmare of a situation.

Bry had three of his own men down around him, as any commander knows this is not good and staying stuck in the middle of the killing zone would only result in more deaths and injuries to his fellow mates. There was only one thing he could do to stop the barrage of enemy fire. Bry charged forward into the unknown, firing as he went, in a last bid to cut down his enemy and to stop his men being slaughtered. Bry knew the risks but still pushed on alone into a hail of 7.62mm bullets. It was the last anyone saw him alive. As he disappeared rounds from both sides began to slow allowing his team to withdraw.

By the time Charlie C. and his team got there the firing had started again. Andy was also still in contact. Briggs, Hugo Farmer's signaller, was hit square in his chest plate knocking him off his feet but that small square Kevlar plate had saved his life, the AK47 round was travelling directly for his heart. Charlie tried to get his men towards Bry but they were under too much fire; as they tried again Charlie was hit in the legs with shrapnel and so to was Hugo Farmer. Those sickening words 'man down, man down' and 'casualty' were the main words going over the net that day.

After a few hours some of the lads got to Bry Budd. He lay out at the side of the maize field surrounded by dead Taliban. Bry had given up his life for his mates; he had led from the front and charged a Taliban ambush in order for his section and his mates to escape: an unbelievable act of courage that earned him the highest bravery award possible, the Victoria Cross (VC).

The loss of yet another guy was a blow, but Bry was a good friend and this hit even more. The loss was unreal.

Within days myself and a few others were sitting on an RAF Tristar bound for home. Not only for Bry's funeral but some of the lads were due their well-earned leave. Two weeks off at home during a six-month tour. For me my tour was over for a small spell, or so everyone thought, including myself. I had terminated my army career before deploying to Afghanistan for a number of reasons. The Head Shed had allowed me to leave theatre a few months earlier to sort out resettlement courses to enable me to find work outside in Civvy Street. After two weeks off and then a few weeks sorting my courses and end of service paperwork I would return to the lines to become a member of the guard service while the lads remained in the desert fighting it out.

The first 72 hours back in the UK were a blur. Andy W. and I were constantly in the boozer drinking cheeky vintos like they were going out of fashion. I didn't even phone family and friends. I just wasn't interested, we were more than happy to get to the bottom of the barrel and being able to talk about things. Unless you had been there we didn't have any interest in talking about what had gone on. One middle-aged guy was in our local, he knew who me and Andy were.

'Well done fellas, we are proud of you lads', he said. It was strange, we didn't want the thanks although he was probably the only ever bloke to say that to me. We just lifted our drinks slightly and got back to business at the bar which instead of the usual Taliban was in the form of a cheeky vinto.

Later back in Afghan we got some news that boiled our piss that much and made us want to tear the town apart, and just proved that the middle-aged bloke we had met was a one off, everyone still hated us. Some of the lads had been sent back home early, one a PF lad. With nothing much to do they stayed around the camp and Colchester, 'block rats' we call it. After hitting a club called the Hippodrome (although it was more like the Gipperdrome after you see some of the states thay get in there) the DJ announced his next song – *A bullet in your gun* – an insult to the men over there dying for this country once more. One of the lads questioned this and got told to fuck off as he (the DJ) didn't give a fuck. Surprisingly he was dropped on the spot. This didn't end here. A few nights later a few more of our lads tried to gain entry, a bit of a slagging match kicked off about why the lads couldn't get in.

'Listen, fuck off back to Afghan', a bouncer said, 'I heard about your lads getting killed and to be honest I hope more of you get it or the lot of you.' This reached us by the jungle drums and caused an uprising. But for now we had to deal with the Taliban, the gobby bouncers would just after wait for us.

Andy picked me up from *The Bull* which had been my home for the last few days and with Charlie C. too Andy drove us up to Scunthorpe where the funeral of Bry Budd was to take place. For the 3–4 hours of driving Andy continued to play *Chasing Cars* by Snow Patrol, a song that reminds me of the sad times of Afghan and more so Bry Budd to this day.

I'm not going to go into much detail about the funeral. I think it's best to be left, although the turnout was unbelievable, proving how much he was thought of and admired. We had more than a good drink for him that day starting off after the service at around 10:30 then drinking till we dropped which in my case was into a middle of a roundabout and many others in cars and other random areas.

With Bry laid to rest I had to think of getting back up north. Within hours of being there I wished I hadn't bothered. Nothing against my family, but I just couldn't talk to anyone. Unless they have been there they will never understand. Down in the local pubs and clubs of Sunderland with my Civvy mates it was as if nothing had happened over in Afghanistan, and in reality in their world nothing had, all was normal. Coming from a war zone where we had been in close quarter fighting to being on the piss on a Friday night was just weird, even a drunk bumping into me was bringing down the red mist, I'm not sure how any of us coped and some didn't. It was alien and I felt totally lost without my blood clot around me. I had nothing to talk about and kept my stories of Afghan to myself as they talked and joked about what the last weekend's antic was.

I decided there and then that I was going back to Afghan. Fuck, why was I staying here laughing and joking while my mates were out there grafting and dying? I wanted to be alongside them; it sounds stupid to put yourself back into that situation but nothing else mattered to me at that time. In less than two weeks of touching down in the UK I was back at RAF Brize Norton and getting ready to go again.

The aircraft was full of Marines; they were beginning to bring in their advance elements to take over from the 3 Para Battle group in a few months. Landing in Kabul the Marines went off for the usual 'in theatre' briefs from the same jobsworth as we had, while I hunted down Michelle Marsh and Lucy Pinder. They had been on my flight and I thought I'd get a picture of them two and be the envy of the blokes back in Bastion. This backfired when I gave my camera to a typical Hat who pressed the power button instead of the one that takes the photos. By the time I realised they were gone, bound for Bastion. If I ever see that Hat again, and you know who you are, then all I'll say is, Stand by, you stitched me right up! A good story did come out of the girls' visit. During a quick meet and greet with the lads in Bastion, one of our lads got his picture taken with Lucy and Michelle. As they took it one of the lads behind him pulled his trousers down leaving him a little embarrassed and I think the girls too.

Patrols were on the ground as I returned to the tents. They had been out for over a week in the area of Musa Qaleh. I pestered the Ops officer to find out if any re-supplies were going in. There was, and in less than 30 hours I was sitting on a Chinook with a box full of goodies flying into the Musa Qaleh area.

Chapter 11

The Wedding Crashers

The Chinook touched down and I ran off into the Afghan desert. The Patrols were all spread out over the desert box coving the heli's movements in and out. Hosting the gun line, 7 RHA sat off to the rear. Three or four 105mm artillery guns made up this mobile gun team, supporting any Patrol recces and also Musa Qaleh platoon house itself that was under constant attack.

Our harbour position here was around 15ks north-west from the town of Musa Qaleh: a mixture of wadis, small features and folds of the bedrock desert.

'Fucking hell, what you doing back here?' I was greeted with.

'Well I couldn't leave you boys out here on your Jack Jones could I?' I replied. They knew I was inbound on the flight as I had sent a secure message over the HF radio from The Joke the day before.

'Fuck me you look ill', Tommo said.

'Ha, yeah, I've been on a Stella Artois diet for the last few weeks.' I quickly got around the blokes seeing how they were then it was down to business. The teams were constantly changing now, due to blokes going on leave and finishing the tour. Lee C. had gone back to the UK for compassionate reasons; Ray had lost a lot of hearing due to the Garmsir ambush and too had gone back. Our boss, Tom, had got on the CH47 that had brought me out as he was due to go on leave and Dave was still in Bastion just having returned from leave. All in all we were down on the command side. Steve had stepped up into the boss's role and then I and Bernie had the other two Patrols. We would just have to manage with what we had.

The re-supply had been mainly 105mm shells for the gun line, scoff and obviously water. The blokes updated me on what had been going on. It seemed most of the jobs for us were around the Musa Qaleh area now, supporting the gun line. Patrol had also been engaged a few more times while I had been away in the Gauntlet area.

For the next few days we sat in the desert and conducted small recces, when the lads in Musa Qaleh asked for close support the 105mm would fire as air assets were limited for that area. Musa Qaleh had become worse and worse since I had been here last. The Danish were now supported by British troops but they still wanted out.

Another Op was in the pipeline for a RIP with the Danish. Easy Company was established: a mix of troops from different companies and attachments. CSM Scrivener (Scriv) was assigned the running of this Easy Company. Unlike most CSM Scriv was a different breed of man. He didn't need to scream and shout like most of the other Head Shed because he had the blokes' respect. He had spent most of his time in Patrols and Recce before returning to D company as the CSM. He was definitely in my eyes the best man for the job.

Patrols made our way back to Bastion after a further week in the desert. A quick turnaround and some decent scoff down our necks and we were ready to go again.

The camp was full of cabbage heads (Marines) beginning their takeover. All dressed in their smart desert combats fresh from the packaging and there was us, we probably looked a right state in their eyes. Patrols in particular wore nearly anything we wanted. Most of us wore standard desert combat trousers or shorts, either a combat shirt or a mix of T-shirts. For me it was normally an old maroon Para T-shirt with about ten holes in it, something that I began adopting from early in the tour and had become my trademark while out on patrol. As the cold nights began coming in then we wore anything from the issued softy jackets to North Face and Berghaus cold weather gear. Nearly all of us had personally bought drop legs for our 9mm pistols and a wide variation of assault and chest rigs as well as boots. On top of all that we wore our Oakley or Wiley X sunglasses, bush or baseball caps, shemaghs or just our large bouffant hairdos.

We sat and waited on the WMIKs ready for the green light to get going. We passed the time stitching up our Marine friends who were walking past. As a few passed our killing zone in front of the vehicles we would shout 'Oh mate, you have something on the bottom of your shoe' and they would normal check, taken unawares. 'Nah the other one' we'd shout. Normally no matter what size and build you are you tend to keep your toes on the ground and lift your heel while looking over your shoulder, it's a near automatic reaction. Try it, it looks very gay no matter if you're the biggest, hardest bloke on the planet. Once they were in position we would finish with an 'Ooohh sailor' in the campest voice we could. The chosen marine would realise his mistake and we would fall about laughing.

Due to all the changes we had to re-arrange our ORBAT before our next mission. My team now was completely different: I gained Chalkie as my driver, which I was chuffed with, I had always done well on the driver side. Sticks was my gunner on the .50 Cal, another lad I had known a long time. Dale was my 2i/c, Luke his driver and Mike his gunner. Again I was happy with the team I had, everyone had at some stage worked for other commanders but our SOP were nearly all the same and we all knew what was expected.

We drove off into the desert bound once more for Musa Qaleh. Our convoy was quite a size now: six Patrol WMIKs, a 7 RHA team of two WMIKs, four 105mm artillery guns towed by four Pinzgauer vehicles, two Pinzgauers with stores and medics, and LEWT lads, an attachment of guys with UAV spy planes and a few vehicles of Fusiliers who had now come in. All in all it was a big old column of vehicles.

As Tom was away Steve had taken over, so I stepped up into the platoon Sgt role although I still operated at the front as Patrols was only three teams now. Steve was at the centre with the Pinzgauers and guns behind; 7 RHA and the Fusiliers held the rear and flanks and then mine and Dave's team the front two recce and fighting vehicles. We operated in the same manner. Mine and Dave's team would navigate, clear and prove the route before the convoy moved through. At night we always tried to find an area where we could hide the gun line. Small folds and wadis were ideal for us and we also had the advantage of UAV now to fly forward and clear obstacles and VP areas.

It took well over 16 hours to get into the Musa Qaleh area this time cutting off most of the Gauntlet; it was becoming more difficult not to set patterns here. We raced through the area towards the few large wadis south-east of Musa Qaleh. Dave was leading with Bennie behind, then myself and Dale. Averaging around 100kph hour across the flat desert floor with the wind in your face it's often not possible to hear things, but a faint pop sound caught my ear. I thought maybe it was a mortar but what with our speed I though I was hearing things. It was a distinctive pop. I waited to hear an impact but there was nothing, and I slagged myself thinking it was something else. Later, once we got to our FRV and harbour, one of the 7 RHA lads told us of a mortar bouncing right in front of his vehicle without detonating.

The RIP was going to happen in the next 48 hours. Patrols would leave the gun line to fend for itself so we could get amongst our job. What we needed to do was find more crossing points to the north that could take us onto the ridge that overlooked the HLS. Early the next morning we packed up and moved out towards the north, probing towards the east (Musa Qaleh) looking for any sort of Taliban activity, crossing points, re-supply routes and access routes into the town. Our last job was to have a look at the small ridge which would be our fire support line for the advancing troops and the security of the HLS as the Op went in. This I wasn't too keen on doing during the day but it still needed to be proved. If we left it for the actual day things could go wrong. We had a number of entry points in which to move our call sign but us being in the area could break the element of surprise for the mission ahead.

We decided to dismount and move in on foot trying not to let the locals know of us being in the area. Steve was kneeling down overwatching the HLS.

'Scotty, over here!' he called. I got alongside and we discussed where to come in and where to be on the day. The HLS couldn't really change; there just wasn't anywhere else to put them. We decided we had to get out of there before we raised any more attention. The ridge was a problem in itself, only 2ks in width at the southern tip that overlooked the HLS and town, it was very channelled. Plus we knew the Russians would have covered all these overwatch areas with mines: something else to worry about while on foot and in a vehicle.

The following day we did more recces to the north keeping away from the HLS area so as not to draw any more attention to it. The afternoon was a chance to relax in the desert: battle prep and some sunbathing before the Op went in. A lot of the time between missions was quite boring. Before first light we would pack away our kit; once light we would change from night routine to day, changing optics and stags and weapon cleaning. From here it was breakfast, a brief for the commanders in case anything had occurred during the night then sunbathing and some press-ups and sit-ups till early evening and scoff again: anything to pass the time and we often wished the days by. As a soldier we often find ourselves bored out of our minds. It's the way it is. You go from jumping out of planes and tactical patrolling in the J (jungle) to here, sitting round the desert or block (accommodation) waiting for our commanders to stand us down for the day or weekend. There are always a lot of boring moments where we needed to keep entertained whether it's here or in camp. A standard SOP in Patrols was to watch for lads coming in through the main door and then get them with water balloons and buckets of water from our ambush location on our floor; this even changed to piss on a few occasions and obviously depending on who was coming in. Normally battalion life was a good laugh when things like this happened until the fun police (provost staff) turned up. On days like that you had to be more alert than when patrolling Northern Ireland: there was definitely more of a threat and everyone was a target.

We played a game called upside-down room. Leave your room unattended for more than a few minutes and everything you own would be placed upside-down, and I mean everything: from posters and chairs to your TV and your bed; stupid stuff to keep the laughs and jokes up while we waited to be let out down town on the piss.

This was when things slowed down for us all. The days dragged and were very frustrating, and we were all glad to have another mission to get on with.

We received the orders over the radio that Patrols needed to be in location before first light. The helis would come in on first light. The Estonians were also taking part coming in from the south. They were to use their armoured vehicle to hold and support the wadi while the RIP took place. As it turned to night we slowly crept the gun line forward around 3ks, giving the guns more range. In position, I decided to get some head down before we moved in the next few hours. My hammock set out, I rolled in and began to doze. This was abruptly broken by the sound of large diesel engines and one of the lads shouting. Everyone was awake now and I couldn't believe what I was confronted with. The Estonians were driving round the Cud's all lights blazing like Billy Smart's circus. Steve had obviously given then a RV of our position and they had come to liaise with us before the Op.

'You have got to be taking the piss!' we all gobbed off to one another.

'Correct me if I'm wrong lads but isn't this supposed to be a tactical mission?' I snapped. We just couldn't believe it. As they got close I sent Dale and another to grip them, getting them to push further in towards Steve and the command area, and to kill their lights and engines. They still couldn't see us till they were almost on top of us.

After a few hours of restless sleep we got up to get ready for our Op. The static from my hammock gave me an electric shock when I released it from the WMIK, making me curse the WMIK much to the laughs of the blokes. This had become a standard joke and blokes would hang around waiting to watch me get out of my hammock and get a bolt of lightning through my bastard fingers.

'Scotty, you ready?' Steve called over the radio.

'Dale, you good?'

'Yeah mate, we are ready.'

'OK, yeah Steve we are good to go.' Dave did the same.

'OK Dave, Scotty, push.

'Roger Chalkie, let's move' I said. Patrolling at night was always hard. This was made even more difficult by the threat area we were entering: navigating and driving especially. Navigating due to not being able to see your surroundings and keeping the pinprick of light to see your map invisible to anyone in the area, which is easier said than done while on the move. Driving was also hard but being lead driver was even harder. He choose the route for others to follow and had nothing to see to aim the vehicle on to apart from the 10m of green glowing desert in front of him and me whispering 'Slightly left, slightly right.' All that and also looking out for Taliban lurking in the darkness.

The first obstacle was a large wadi. It was more than 200m in depth and very steep. Having recced this during daylight hours it came across as a lot easier to navigate but in the darkness it seemed harder and due to visibility it was. My two WMIKs overwatched the wadi.

'Scotty in position, Dale in position', we called over the radio.

OK I'm moving through', Dave said. I scanned the area with my Viper sight: an amazing piece of TI equipment. The wadi floor was over 300m in width but miles and miles in length running both ways out of view. Our break point from the wadi was almost straight ahead, a track that ran out and up the steep feature. Just as the track broke out of the wadi there was a small group of buildings over on the right, slightly hidden by a group of trees. This route I hadn't been too keen on using. I had talked it over with Steve and Dave and I was more in favour of heading a little north to keep away from it. Being close to the small group of buildings we had already brought attention to ourselves over the last few days while on our recces.

Dave's two vehicles slowly disappeared down out of sight along the bank of the wadi. Something caught my eye through the TI. It was set to white hot, meaning everything normal would show a black colour and anything with a heat signature would show white. With the extreme heat over here the ground would still be a light grey colour even after the sun had disappeared several hours previously. I focused in; people were leaving the set of buildings and heading along the bank of the wadi away from us to the south.

'Sticks you see that?'

'Yeah I got them, about 10–12 pax mate', he answered.

'Scotty I have eyes on', Dale said.

'I don't like this' I muttered. Somebody must have been watching. Our route was compromised and if that had been me up ahead I would have changed my route there and then. I continued to watch Dave push through and had a horrible feeling that I was about to watch him be blown apart.

'Dave be aware you have over 10 pax heading away to your right.'

'Roger', he replied. Dave was on foot; through the TI sight I watched his white sillhouette patrol up onto the track slightly left of the trees with his team on the two vehicles creeping behind. I was relieved to see him clear the choke point and gain the high ground. Steve and the rest pushed through followed by us.

We slowly moved into position and killed the engines; we remained out of view to the town until the last safe moment and concentrated on watching and protecting the HLS and waited for daylight and the helis. Reports from Musa Qaleh were that they were still experiencing attacks at irregular intervals. Since our presence in their area and the calling in of the 7 RHA 105mm guns, by either ourselves or the lads and MFC in the platoon house, it had calmed them slightly and kept them at bay. That was something, I suppose but unfortunately to the cost of Jonathan Peter Hetherington who was killed on 27 August and Anare Draiva, a large Fijian also killed on 1 September during Taliban attacks on the platoon house.

The first rays of light came over the horizon as we whispered to one another and scanned the areas around the HLS and platoon house. We were already sweating buckets and it was only going to get worse. Like clockwork the helis moved in with the sun. Apaches moved in overhead watching the area where we now sat and the platoon house 1k east of us; there was the sound of the CH47s hugging the ground no more than 100m as they approached from the south-west up the wadi. B and C Company were in four Chinooks; the first two hit the HLS and unloaded the guys. The mortars were some of the first out and they moved off to set up the barrels on a mortar line, snipers too peeled off and gained some high ground, some of them a couple of hundred metres from our call sign. The rest being Rifle Company (bayonets) pushed forward and held the ground north-east of the HLS looking into the green belt. This time we would not be going in with them, a lesson learned on the last Op. Taking vehicles in with the advancing troops was a non-starter. We had been lucky not to have lost any WMIKs and blokes before, so this time we were to give fire support from the high ground using the range of our GPMGs and .50 Cals, and also the four 105mm guns sitting 10ks behind us hidden in the desert.

The second wave came in and dropped the rest of the cargo: 80 Paras with only one thing on their minds: getting into the green belt and smashing anything in their way. It's a weird thing. The Paras have always had a reputation for fighting and being generally complete twats on the piss. In camp the blokes are constantly governed and controlled, and frustration builds up. You could say that trained killers who then get a slap on the wrist for the slightest thing, like back chatting an incident down town, or are completely stitched involving anything major like filling in some gobby civvy who takes the piss. We are trained to be aggressive but 90 per cent of the time are kept on the leash. However now they needed that aggression and the leash was totally released. Unlike most so-called hard men down the pub, there was no time to whack back 10 pints of Stella and a few tequilas before confronting his enemy at the other end of the bar. Plus the worse he will get in return is filled in. We had to deal with being shot, blown up and even killed and this had become more of a 'when' than an 'if' as this tour went on.

The Bayonets were in position; all was quiet as we changed to day optics ready for the push. The twilight sky brought with it an uneasy atmosphere. The mortars began popping, throwing a few 81mm HE into the green belt. We got the message that the green light was on. The bayonets from B and C Company were up and advancing.

There was a call from the platoon house, Taliban were seen around the area, and they called in the 105mm and the Apaches to destroy them. A few explosions erupted to my forward right out of sight to my WMIK. By the sound of it, there were L109 British issued grenades, they were obviously clearing the compounds. This in itself took a few hours for the boys to do: there was a maze of compounds between the lads and the green zone that had to be cleared with caution. Bennie dismounted with his L96 sniper rifle to get a better position while we manoeuvred the WMIKs to give maximum coverage for the blokes down in the low ground. So far so good. Patrols had been here for around six hours already, B and C Company a few hours but I expected to be in this area most of the day.

Whoosh, something flew past between our Land Rovers by a few metres: bang! We looked round to see smoke and the aftermath of an explosion 75m to our rear.

'What the fuck was that?' the blokes shouted.

'A 107mm', Bennie shouted from his position on the rocks.

'Got eyes on their position, reference smoke signature, 900m in the green zone 9 o'clock of the platoon house', he continued to shout. Like always we laid the guns on in a split second and unloaded our weapons at the firing point in case they were about to send more in on top of us. Seeing us static on the ridge they thought they could take a few pot shots at us. I don't think they expected our response. We kept up our rate of fire for a good while, the GPMGs rattling fast and smooth and the .50 Cal banging away at its slow steady pace.

Another puff of smoke caught our eyes 100m right of the original firing point.

'Shit, incoming!' we shouted. There was nothing we could do apart from sink into our seats and wait for the rocket to pass us or worse still, hit us. It's a weird feeling to just sit and wait for it to come in. The smoke was the first thing we would notice, then the explosion around us. The noise we would hear later due to the distance the sound had to travel. Bang, it exploded to our front on the ridge.

'That was close', Dale shouted, 'I'm pulling back.' Dale's wagon had been really lucky and he thought it wise to move his position while we hammered the area with more fire. We all pushed back slightly making our vehicles a smaller target for them. Dale pushed to our rear to give rear protection. Our firing had stopped and I gave the order to watch and shoot while Steve kept his eyes on the advance of our bayonets.

Whoosh, another rocket screamed overhead this time from the south. It went straight through our vehicles once again and landed 50m from Dale's team, again.

'What's going on here?' Dale voiced over the radio.

'Looks like they have your number plate marked and recorded', I joked back. Everyone started laughing. At times like this there was very little we could do but laugh and shoot back. We lay on once more and batted the fresh area, 12 guns on rapid fire.

The troops on the ground were making progress but communication between ourselves and the bayonets was becoming lost. Trying to find out exactly where their furthest northern edge (men) were was difficult, there were big chances of blue on blue as they pushed into the green foliage and blended in with the surroundings.

The Apaches came back overhead and we called more 105mm guns in on the previous 107mm firing points they had used against us and positions around the advancing troops and platoon house. From our position on the rocks it's an amazing sight. Mayhem at our fingertips we unleashed everything we had at the Taliban to ease the pressure for the RIP while we dodged the 107mm rockets that they threw at us.

The lads in Musa Qaleh had it hard, under constant attack that had become that close that the Taliban were nearly breaching the walls on a few occasions. Once in, a RIP like this was a Battle Group operation. The amount of manpower for one RIP was outrageous but also necessary to reduce our losses and keep the Taliban on the back foot. When we would leave, our Patrols heading onto another Op and the ground troops flying off back to Bastion, this place got beasted. They knew damn well that there would be very little support in the area and took full advantage.

It had now become clear that Patrols and the gun line would have to stay out longer to support the Musa Qaleh area making the Taliban believe we had left. This seemed to work, hiding in the desert and when the attacks happened the lads of Easy Company would call in the guns which would take seconds. It had caught the Taliban out as they thought we had gone and also that any sort of air power would take 20–30mins. Sangin and Now Zad could hold their own; Sangin had the 105mm from Fort Robinson south-east of the town and Now Zad had decent air cover and wasn't as bombarded by attacks as Musa Qaleh. That wasn't to say they didn't get it hard, but compared to Musa Qaleh it was a bit easier to sleep at night.

I didn't really hear much of what was going on in the platoon house of Musa Qaleh till after the tour had ended. We would just get little bits of information which was mainly about the casualties they were getting from our desert harbour position.

Moving from the Op at Musa Qaleh with little problems we disappeared back into the desert out of sight to everything. Two days would be the maximum number of days that we would occupy a desert harbour in one area before moving. We were that far out normally that any threat during the day was minimal but still lower at night due to the visibility allowing us to strip down and chill.

Before moving to our next harbour I told Steve that we needed a re-supply, he agreed and it would be wise to get it done here than compromise our next location, which the helis would do easily due to them landing. Water and food were low (including the previous mission we had been here just under three weeks) and also the 7 RHA's 105mm shells as they were calling in at least 5 fire missions per day. With 3 guns one (standard) fire mission after all the alterations and adjustments could be around 25 105mm rounds being fired at the target.

A message was passed to The Joke to get a Chinook in to re-supply our lads. Surprisingly this took less than 12 hours. The next morning we pushed the Patrol teams out in all round defence away from the gun line giving the CH47 some room to land. The LEWT team called me up to tell me they were inbound.

'Roger that, tell the pilot that I'm popping green smoke.'

'OK I'll let them know', he replied. I caught sight of the Chinooks overhead and popped the green smoke grenade. Because of the wind I positioned myself so the CH47 would land into the wind. As the smoke cleared the Chinook came in on my hand signal, its massive downdraft covering me with sand and dust. It made a hover and dropped its underslung load which was mainly the 105mm HE, then it hovered left to touch down. Once any helicopter has its wheels down then the throttle can be lowered making the downdraft and dust around it ease considerably. The blokes in the work party got the goods off asap so the heli didn't sit around too long. The main kit on board was, like I mentioned, water, scoff and ammunition but other things like batteries to operate all night view aids and GPS systems, radios including more secure FILs (secure FILs were changed regularly to stop anyone hacking in and listening to our conversations), fuel for the vehicles, weapon parts, extra mapping, spare tyres, extra aircraft bodies for the UAV as the lads operating them could never seem to land them intact. It had become something to look forward to sometimes, the UAV would get sent up before we mounted and went on our recces and also to do first and last light perimeter checks around our positions. As the little high pitched plane would come in we would all watch and take bets on if we thought it would cream in or not: 8 out of 10 it would, much to our amusement and cheers.

Our Patrols packed up and moved off in search for another suitable harbour location, even in the massive desert we had seemed to use up all our best areas; you would think that you can place yourselves anywhere but it's not that simple. You have to think about the distance for the guns, the direction, surrounding areas like tracks, wadis and minefields (minefields in Afghan don't come marked with big signs like the movies they are just on your map). The last thing we needed was to have some locals driving by us on some desert road or us sitting in a minefield.

We pushed on to a position further north and with a call from higher (The Joke) we were to look out for suspicious activity in the wadis running north–south into Musa Qaleh. Patrols and some of the LEWT pushed up onto some high features to set up an OP that overlooked the wadi leaving the large guns in dead ground. For the remainder of the day we watched from the rocks for any Taliban. Unfortunately we didn't pick anything up but the lads of Easy Company had said that there seemed to be more combat indicators building in the town, so a decision was made to push forward of the rocks to enable the guns to get a better range on any targets moving in on the platoon house. Moving from the rocks we were exposing ourselves more than usual, plus we had closed the gap between us and the town; also the wadis were only a few hundred metres from our new position. As it turned out the platoon house came under attack from the Taliban once again, the 105mm began firing, the lads inside were fighting from the walls trying to keep the attackers at bay. It was like in most platoon houses but

Patrols had only been in the Sangin and Now Zad ones, we never got the pleasure of getting in there.

The firing died as we moved into night routine. Once again me and Dale set our WMIKs up on the forward left edge of the desert box and I stuck my hammock up for some quality head down. Dave was on the right side around 300–400m doing exactly the same.

'Scotty, Scotty', Mike whispered. I came round like a lion after being tranquillized. 'What's up?' I whispered back.

'We got movement to our front in the wadi, MSTAR has just picked it up', Mike said leaning over from the gun (stag) position. MSTAR was a new bit of kit that we had only just got to bring with us on patrols; the platoon houses had already got it and it had made a big difference. MSTAR picks up movement, so when night falls then any movement of human size in the immediate vicinity can be detected. The lads were already up and moving, I jumped out of my hammock and placed it away, getting a bolt of lightning through my finger to go with it and chuckles from the lads around me. In seconds our kit was on. I raised Dave on the net to get some more int as Chalkie started the WMIK.

'Dave it's Scotty' what's going on mate?'

'Got possibly 10 pax moving in the wadi, 300m to our front?'

'Roger that mate, get to my position and we'll move as a oner', I replied.

'Yeah Roger', Dave said.

'Scotty it's Steve' do you need illum?' (By illum he meant illumination from the 105mm which could light up 400–500m square area.)

'Negative mate, don't want to give the game away if it is Terry out there', I answered.

'OK then you and Dave check it out, I'll follow if you see anything and have the guns on stand by.'

Dave brought his two WMIKs in to me and Dale and then we slowly patrolled off towards the wadi, all four vehicles in a line. Therefore if it was an ambush we could bring all weapons to bear in an instant.

I gripped the butt of the GPMG, my finger on the trigger as I tried to scan the ground. We moved slowly, around 5mph, we weren't going to run into something we couldn't get out of and surprise was our key. The adrenalin was kicking as we drove into the darkness knowing that the Taliban were out there approaching us.

'Scotty, Dave, it's Steve. MSTAR says it's 15 targets in there now and the interpreter has picked up Taliban voices.'

'Roger', we both replied, our minds now focused to the job ahead.

We reached the wadi ridge line without any firing, which I was quite surprised with, but I felt a lot more in control from here as we held the high ground that looked into the wadi. We set the WMIK off to the flanks and across the ridge so as to get the best use from the guns on board. I used the Viper TI sight to look for any heat signatures as did the .50 Cal gunners.

'Anybody see anything?' me and Dave said over the radio. There was no reply.

'Have they got this right?' Chalkie said.

'Well they had better have not turfed me out of my bed for nowt', I answered. We all seemed to relax thinking there might have been some sort of problem on the MSTAR which gave a mixed reading.

We sat for a another 10mins and scanned the wadi. I was thinking of knocking this on the head when Dale said John (Hobbit) had seen something.

'Target interaction?' I asked.

'Wait Scotty', Dale replied. The next thing I heard was the Hobbit shouting out 'Enemy in the wadi, watch my strike.' His .50 Cal opened up deafening us all and smashing into the rocks below. I quickly put the TI sight to my eye and there they were, running around the rocks like ants on the move.

'Sticks?' I shouted.

'Already on, Scotty' he screamed back as he unleashed the .50 Cal' punishing rounds. Near all the guns had got onto the targets now and I joined in. On night Ops I would always put a belt of 100 rounds 1 in 1 (1 bit), meaning one tracer followed by one ball then again one tracer unlike the normal 1 in 4 (4 bit), excellent for night firing giving an almost steady line of red light from the weapon. We wasted no time and hosed the area with fire. We had caught them in the bottom of the wadi with little place to go; there was some amount of incoming in return but once we caught sight of their muzzle flashes we suppressed them that much that there was hardly any chance of them returning heavy accurate fire on us. Steve on hearing the contact ahead drove up to get 'eyes on' from our rear. He brought with him the Fusiliers that were also attached to the gun line. Our drivers disembarked and were also firing down on the Taliban, every weapon system we had was engaging the enemy below.

After a long period of rapid fire our firing slowed and stopped and we again scanned the area. Nothing moved but I knew this wasn't over just yet, they were obviously taking cover and waiting a chance to break out or to engage us.

After a quick chat with Dave we pulled the WMIKs off the ridge out of sight. We now waited for the Taliban to make their move. We called up a fire mission, a mix of illum and HE but didn't give the order to fire till we knew they were moving. A few of the lads pushed forward and scanned the ground.

'We have movement again', a voice said over the radio.

'Reference fire mission 10 round fire for effect, over' was called onto the gun line.

'Roger shot over', came the reply. We pushed forward with the WMIKs at a snail's pace just as the 105mm fired from behind us. We could see the Taliban clearly now, sorting themselves out and helping each other out of the rocks.

'Rapid fire!', Dave shouted. Again our weapons sprang into life smashing the target area, illum exploded above us lighting both us and the Taliban in the wadi. They made an attempt to return fire and take cover but most were cut down in the process. The 105mm exploded in the wadi floor; a quick flash of light and sparks from metal and rock flew all over the Taliban position. I eased up and let the boys finish the cleaning up, there wouldn't be much left.

After it fell silent once more, we again pulled back believing this was finished. We had been on the ridge nearly two hours; any survivors would be insane to go back in and well on their way home, getting chased by the 105mm rounds we kept adding a little distance to.

'Scotty, Dave, hold your position', Steve said over the radio, 'MSTAR are picking up more movement.' We were all quite amazed and shocked that they would dare to come back to confront us. 'Another 10 targets are pushing back into the wadi.'

Our teams pushed back up and another fire mission to the gun line was sent. Sure enough there were Taliban creeping down the side of the wadi. Whether they believed we would all go back to the harbour, high-five each other and all get some proper sleep, thinking they wouldn't dare come back, I don't know. The fire mission went in and our gun started for the last time that night. We agreed we wouldn't stop till the MSTAR reported that either they were well on the move back to Musa Qaleh or the movement on their screen had totally stopped, and that's exactly what happened.

There were no cries or shouts of happiness, we returned to the harbour in silence and back in to night routine; nothing much was said.

The next day all the lads on and around the gun line were intrigued about what had happened last night; they had seen some of the fire fight from a distance and caught some of the show on camera. Months later I saw some of the footage and it was weird to see the blackened shapes of our WMIKs against the 105mm illum out in the distance, tracer fire from both ourselves and the Taliban whizzing between our vehicles and lighting the night sky.

We didn't really go into detail about the previous night. In our eyes it was our job, and our job was done. It turned out, after gathering the information from the interpreter, that it was a Taliban ambush coming to hit our harbour from the wadi. The LEWT and interpreter had picked up their conversation before they hit the wadi. Realising that every time they hit the platoon house they were coming under indirect fire from our gun line, this they had to stop. They had kept hitting the platoon house to draw us in, making us believe that the Taliban would not come out into the Cud's to take us on. Like British forces the Taliban used codewords. This was picked up and at first the LEWT had difficultly working out what exactly what they were talking about. They talked about going to the wedding just up the road and having a big old party. I understood them using codewords like ourselves but going to a wedding after 02:00hrs in the morning in the middle of the desert seemed hard to believe. Obviously the lads picking up the radio waves narrowed it down to a rough area but once the MSTAR had pinged the exact location of this wedding party they put two and two together. The only information we received was the news of the group of Taliban moving in. They didn't realise we had this capability and to be honest it could have been a different story if we didn't have MSTAR.

Long story short, we had ambushed the Taliban ambush heading to the wedding. Patrols had gained a new name that night, 'The Wedding Crashers'.

My team with a US and Afghan team at Garmsir, July 2006.

Patrols having mixed baths in the Helmand River. A day later, only 4ks
downstream, Patrols was caught in a major ambush on the river.

Me playing the part of Lawrence of Arabia. Shemaghs were used to
keep off the burning sun and shelter us from dust storms.

The damage by passing shrapnel from incoming on Tom's vehicle
suffered during the ambush at Garmsir, July 2006.

Me (left) and lads from the Patrols feeling lucky but calm in the ERV after the ambush at Garmsir. Note the lads checking and fixing the damage to our vehicles behind.

The standard way Patrols move. A patrol of two WMIKs moves through and clears a wadi system in Taliban country.

Blokes under contact taken by the combat camera crew, firing
the GPMG from the shoulder due to the long grass.

Major Blair (left) and CSM Bolton (right) sit with village elders.
They were ambushed as they left. Gereshk, June 2006.

The aftermath and damage done by an IED ambush on the Household Cavalry Regiment south of Musa Qaleh, which resulted in Alex Eida, Ralph Johnson and Ross Nicholls being killed.

Chalkie, myself, Dale, Luke, Mike and Sticks. This is my team around the 'wedding crashers' time, somewhere in Taliban country, August 2006.

Jack, Mike and Sticks chilling in an open harbour position. Life was often boring in the open desert. Note all essential kit is packed away, and weapons are at the ready.

The typical layout of my Patrol whilst resting. A desert harbour in the Musa Qaleh area. I'm in my hammock. August 2006.

Dave, myself and Dale during a recce north of Musa Qaleh, August 2006.

The author firing a 105mm gun on a live fire mission into Musa Qaleh.
We normally called in and adjusted the fire. This fire mission destroyed
five Taliban vehicles leaving a number dead and injuried.

My 2ic's WMIK during a recce north of Musa Qaleh. Dale, Luke and Mike.

Bry Budd in Afghanistan before he was killed in a firefight with Taliban forces and awarded the VC. (©DPL)

Chapter 12

Bloody Days

Leavening Musa Qaleh for Bastion again didn't go without incident: a mine strike taking one of our WMIKs erupted just west of the Musa Qaleh area. We knew the mine threat in and around here but it was just unlucky. It injured the three lads on board, the gunner losing his leg but our medics saved his life by applying tourniquets.

Throughout our tour we had been lucky, considering, but to see a guy we worked alongside lose a limb wasn't a good thing. During our time in Afghanistan we were involved in a few mine strikes, mostly involving serious injury. This could have been any of our WMIKs, it was what we call Brecon Bingo (especially on the CP front in Iraq where roads were lined with IED). You just never knew who had the unlucky number. Sometimes we would laugh by joking 'Who's got the golden ticket on this patrol?' as almost every patrol had some sort of incident whether mine, IED or firefight. It was again a way our sick humour controlled our fear as the risk was getting larger by the day. We were all keen on keeping our limbs attached yet it was the reality of war.

On another patrol, again heading from the Musa Qaleh area to Bastion, Patrols were involved in yet another mine strike. This time I believe it was deliberate. We had a convoy of logistic vehicles to escort home, this like I mentioned affected our route massively. Dave led the convoy and got us to a crossing point over a major wadi. We had used this crossing point previously, some weeks before, and there were few choices to choose from. Dave's team pushed down the channelled route, over the wadi to the other side, and my team followed. Once in place like always the convoy began to push, one of the large HGVs triggered a land mine, knocking the huge tyre off and into the sky: it took the impact and minimized our casualties. I guessed it was triggered on the weight of the vehicle or maybe the Taliban had dug it in too deep. Either way our teams that had pushed through had been lucky.

After this on any main obstacles that we had to go through we used the 9 Squadron engineers to clear first; it was one of their many jobs. We also got friendly with some of the locals who lived close by, one elder in particular and his sons would sit out on a night and watch over their small area including the track that ran into the wadi past their house. We used his track on a few occasions and got quite friendly with them, we got by hand signals and small amounts of English and Pashtu. They could talk about as much English as a Glaswegian on the piss but we manged. They were strong anti-Taliban people but I always kept that little barrier up and even when he said it was clear of danger and Taliban we would keep them entertained with food and drink and Bradder's amazing impressions as the lads checked it out. You just never know. But it was always clear.

On return to Bastion the camp was littered with Marines ready for the takeover. The end of the tunnel was in sight but we knew it wasn't over just yet. Patrols would have the job of getting the Marines up into the areas of Sangin and Musa Qaleh for the RIP to take place. As the boys got some down time I briefed some of the Marine reece teams on what to expect on the ground and how we operated and adapted to it, the situation in the platoon houses and the kit and equipment we carried, as this could be of benefit. Maybe it was me or the news coverage and intelligence reports that they had read stated otherwise, but they looked at me like I was talking bollocks, especially when it came to the platoon houses. They had also minimized the kit they had brought into theatre which included no .50 Cals. This I told them was going to be a problem but again they were all, Yeah, yeah, we'll manage. Unfortunately they were going to learn the hard way.

Speaking recently to an ex-Sgt in the Marines who came to relieve us, he agreed on what I had said. They believed we had proper bigged this tour up: exaggerating on everything that had happened. In his own words he said 'It wasn't till we got into Sangin that we realised it really was like the Wild West.'

On 6 September news bounced round that an incident was developing in Kajaki Dam. Stu Hale, a friend from the snipers, had been hit by a land mine while he had tried to get to a position of observation to watch for Taliban. A rescue team had already gone out to help him from the dam complex. This was mainly commanded by Stu Pearson and Mark Wright, two full screws in Support Company. The information that came next shocked us all. The rescue party had got to Stu Hale; carrying him back would have meant certain death due to the loss of blood so the lads carried out further mine drills and prodded their bayonets and knives into the ground making a clear route out to a piece of ground that they believed to be safe, and would use as a medical HLS. Mark Wright called in the METHINE report (CAS-E-VAC report) and insisted that a Chinook should not be used; first it was far too big, second its downdraft could set off more mines and thirdly it would have to touch down as it had no winch capability. The lads cleared the route, prodding the desert bedrock with knives and boxing round the mines they found. This in itself must have took some balls after seeing what had happened to Stu Hale Unfortunately Stu Pearson had caught another one near their new HLS. Both Stu Hale and Pearson now had lower limb injuries. With serious wounds to the leg especially the femoral artery and thigh this could result in bleeding out in under a minute.

The medical helicopter came in as Mark and the rest of the blokes conducted first aid on the two Stus; to the horror of the lads on the ground it was a Chinook, something they had said they didn't want. The pilot tried to touch down; Mark Wright tried to signal for them not to land and to fly off. Due to the downdraft and Mark crouching down to avoid dust and debris another mine exploded. Mark Wright was now injured and the pilot realised his presence was not helping matters. A medic attached in Kajaki, called Tug, managed to get to the casualties, Andy Barlow was also with them and stepped away to make room for Tug and set off another mine, this also injured Dave Prosser close by as the shrapnel flew everywhere. For the lads this had turned into a nightmare: five men were now lying in the desert seriously injured, bleeding to death. Both the Stus and Andy had lower leg injuries, their limbs completely shredded. Mark had hand, arm, chest, face and neck injuries but seemed the most laid back and controlled. Dave received chest injuries from the flying debris. A Blackhawk was requested to get the lads out although why this wasn't sent immediately after Mark's request was beyond me. The lads had to conduct self aid with the help of the medic Tug, they dripped each other with morphine, patched themselves as best they could using FFD, bandages and tourniquets then just had to sit it out and wait for the heli. Considering what had gone on they were in high sprits, trying not to let the situation get on top of them. They lay and took the piss out of one another about not doing any more tabbing and in Mark's case any more wanking, he joked. This was typical Paras. Anyone else would have been in pieces, the average Civvy hysterical. Not these brave lads, they just held together, joked and reassured each other, proper blood clot style. Mark had even gone on about his girl and family back home and the wedding plans they were sorting, as they waited. After a pain waiting few hours in the baking sun they got the CAS-E-VAC but unfortunately Mark Wright died during the flight.

I had known Mark many years, his soldiering skills were brilliant and his ability to call in the mortars while under attack which was his job in Afghanistan was outstanding. He had saved the lives of many ground troops in that department and had also on this day ran to the aid of his friends here with no fear for his own safety, all that mattered was saving his mates and getting them out, he even co-ordinated with the pilot while lying injured. Mark was presented with the George Cross for his brave actions that day. Nearly two years later Stu Pearson, having lost his leg, began training as hard as ever, trying to get back to his normal standard of fitness and wellbeing rather than just sitting around, making the best out of his bad situation. He received news that he would have his disability badge removed because he was able to get around better, because he had grafted to get back on his feet, than some 25st person who decided to fill their fat faces. He was shocked. Again, another insult to the lads who gave up their lives for this country and receive nothing in return. It was the same in many scenarios, the poor standards of military medical welfare back in the UK and now this. I'm sure if it had been an illegal immigrant then they would have received much more.

Unfortunately this wasn't the only bad news of the day. Sangin and Musa Qaleh had been under attack yet again. C Company was now in Sangin platoon house, they had taken over from B Company and with it the fighting. A mortar landed in the orchard where there were two sangars, Luke McCulloch had been hit by shrapnel in the head and was in need of immediate CAS-E-VAC or he would certainly die. In Musa Qaleh a further two soldiers had been injured. Panapassa Matanasinga and Dominic Whitehouse from the Royal Irish had taken shrapnel wounds, a mate from snipers Hugh Kier had also been hit earlier whilst under attack but could carry on.

With limited Chinooks for CAS-E-VAC this had become a major issue, something we had all addressed very early on in the tour. We had always complained about the lack of support, whether .50 Cal rounds, kit and equipment or the lack of helicopters. Three different areas needed the support of the CH47s yet this was impossible to do with the lack of helicopters in theatre. This had never happened before but that was no excuse, we had all be in situations where we had been extremely lucky and this could have been a repeat many times over but it had never happened, till now. There were seven major casualties in three areas with approx 80ks between each incident. The US Blackhawks had come to the aid of the British in Kajaki, for the others our Chinooks were already taking off, heading for Sangin then Musa Qaleh. Some of us went down to see the lads from Kajaki coming in, again like other incidents during our time in Afghanistan, Iraq and other theatres of war we felt an unbelievable feeling of not being able to help.

The CAS teams were already there waiting to take the casualties to the RAP as the Blackhawks approached. Some of the boys tried to lend a hand but we were just in the way to be honest. Personally if I were in their shoes I would have wanted to see my mates at the other end and not the Head Shed who didn't even know your name. On arrival we heard the news of Mark Wright, it was a massive blow. The rest had been lucky and had lost a lot of blood but would be OK. For the two Stus and Andy they would lose a lower limb.

For the lads in Sangin and Musa Qaleh their CAS-E-VAC had failed, both areas were swarming with Taliban and every attempt in both areas were called off after the Chinooks were constantly engaged on approach. They waited till nightfall before going again this time with success although the CH47 had taken enemy rounds a few clipping the rotors as it left the Musa Qaleh camp and was lucky to have not been knocked out of the sky.

Luke McCulloch was pronounced dead on arrival, another big blow to the lads. This was completely topped off with the death of Paul Muirhead on the same day; he had been critically injured after an attack in Musa Qaleh on 1 September but unfortunately died of his wounds on the 6th. It had been a 'Lick' of a day; all in all we had lost three men and another a few days before, and over eight casualties.

The loss had an impact on us all; for me I needed to be back on the ground. Sitting in camp just made things worse. In a day or two we got such an order, it was back to Musa Qaleh. Once we made our way up the long and dangerous journey north rumour had it that the Taliban were offering a ceasefire. I laughed; you got to be joking, I said

'Nah they want to put a ceasefire on Musa Qaleh', Steve replied. This I thought was an absolute joke. We had obviously smashed them to the point where they hadn't the capability to carry on with their attacks. Even the interpreters and LEWT team had picked up Pakistan accents over the radios, giving a strong indication, and even mentioned that all the Afghan leaders were dead. So now because it suited them, as they were now 'in rag' they needed a ceasefire. Our lads never got a break in the platoon houses of Sangin, Musa Qaleh, Now Zad, Kajaki or Gereshk. In the first two of these they had been under constant attack for weeks at a time with no let up. I knew the US and British forces' Head Shed would agree and this made my piss boil. Not because I wanted to fight more, I understood the lads in the platoon houses were taking the brunt of it, but they needed the ceasefire so they could gather more men. The Taliban in Musa Qaleh had been smashed like Sangin. They needed time to rest, bring in and train more Taliban, change and practice different tactics, gather more weapons and ammunition and be able to gain more close intelligence, and what better way to do that but during a ceasefire when they could get as close as they wanted? Patrols sat in the desert, we snapped about this possible ceasefire. We all agreed that this was for their benefit only, were we the only ones to see this? Are the Head Shed up in Kandahar blind, we shouted? The crack den had obviously moved location but was definitely in full party mode.

In days the Taliban came back out for the second ever time into the desert to meet us. The first time had been the night of the wedding crashes and they would never do that again. I couldn't even bear to watch this happen. The Battle group Head Shed had flown in to meet them and Patrols gave them the protection they needed in the desert. Tribal leaders and Taliban closed in on our desert harbour. It was agreed that the ceasefire was going ahead.

This lasted some several weeks in Musa Qaleh but the Battle group had made one elephant-sized shit of a fuck-up. With the impression that the ceasefire would hold indefinitely, the Marines decided not to send in troops to that area. However the Head Shed had decided not to remove our forces while the ceasefire was going on either. Later 3 Para Battle group left and handed over to the Marines of 3 Commando Brigade who, because of the ceasefire, would not take over in Musa Qaleh; because of this our troops were left in the platoon house. A month later we had all left theatre, down town on the piss and seeing loved ones and families, apart from the lads of Easy Company still trapped in the Musa Qaleh platoon house. They even relied on the tribes to bring in food and water for them. This was never explained or mentioned in the papers or press. Instead the media interviewed some of the members of C Company, a lot of young lads who had only spent a little time in Sangin; one lad in particular commented on sitting around and reading magazines and that it wasn't too bad. He obviously wasn't there when all the proper firing was happening. Nobody had asked A Company what it was like for them or all the other troops who had been in the big hotspots in the other outstations that were constantly attacked. But the worse was that nobody outside of the Battle group knew about the lads still in Musa Qaleh.

Again even in the UK we felt helpless. Hugh, my mate and neighbour from snipers, told me how they eventually got out. A *shura* happened with the Taliban; British forces were to leave the area if a ceasefire would be maintained while they left. The Taliban agreed and law and order would be handed over to the local tribes who were against the Taliban. An old Afghan jingle truck was sent into the camp. With most of Easy Company on board and their own vehicles they patrolled out and through Musa Qaleh to the open desert under the eye of the Taliban

I was amazed; they had got out and the Taliban tribes had stuck by their word. But what if they hadn't, what if they just attacked the convoy killing all on board knowing little support was in the area? It was a big bluff, as a RIP couldn't be organised due to manning. I couldn't believe that in this day and age this had been allowed to happen. I was fucking disgusted. It could easily have gone wrong big time, and to be escorted out by the Taliban, too. I saw the same in 2007 when the British pulled out of the Basra Palace, they told the insurgents (Jam) that they would leave so as not to attack them, the Jam lined the roads as the Brits pulled out. They weren't attacked but only because it benefited them. If there is one thing I do know it is not to trust any Taliban or Jam member.

In 2007–8 British forces had to fight their way back into Musa Qaleh in order to gain control of the town. Once the Taliban (like we knew they would) gained the manpower, weaponry and ammunition they took control of the Musa Qaleh town, killing all the tribal members and anyone who helped the British troops when they were there. Our Battle group had moved in holding the ground for many months before being told to pull out as no troops would be replacing them. Now it had happened all over again, British forces fighting their way into Musa Qaleh. What a waste, I thought: a waste of resources, a waste of time and a waste of life.

Chapter 13

The Battle for Cyprus and Colchester

Patrols made a few more missions to various areas in Helmand before our tour ended: most without major incident. The next big job, however, would be the RIP on Sangin to get the Marines in and our boys out. This would be another major Op. To bring out all our troops and equipment and replace it with a fresh Battle group was going to take some effort.

Patrols' task was to recce and clear the route to the west of Sangin and the river and to escort the Marine call sign that would then move in. Once we got within range Patrols would move off independently and provide the fire support from the ridge that looks over the river and District centre while the RIP takes place. HCR who were still in Sangin at this stage would come out, down over the river and hold it so then the Marines would move onto the District where C Company would have pushed out into the areas around the building to provide security.

The last time a RIP happened in Sangin, Patrols again held the high ground while C Company moved in and took over A Company. As this took place the Taliban moved in and ambushed elements of B Company who were also sent in to help C Company. Then 5 Platoon pushed into the 'Chinese restaurant' which was a codename for a building constantly occupied by Taliban for attacks and ambushes on the platoon house and patrols in the town. The Chinese restaurant was north of the platoon house; it would have to be secured to stop an attack happening while the RIP took place. JDAMs were sent in to destroy anything that was already sitting in there. The Taliban had different plans.

Paddy Caldwell was 5 Platoon's Sgt, he moved up and took a few lads onto the roof of a ruin, it was from here that they saw a Taliban patrol skirmishing through the bombed out buildings and sparse trees. The lads wanted to open fire but Paddy made them wait, he wanted the 81mm mortar to drop on them first causing maximum damage and confusion and then take them on with small arms in the contact (ambush) point. Paddy called in the fire mission of mortars and then the firing began. Immediately there was a reply of fire from two different groups of Taliban. Paddy went flying back: he had taken a round to the neck and shoulder. Karl Jackson was a section commander in 5 Platoon and ran to Paddy's aid, returning fire and dragging Paddy out of the contact area and into the relative safety of the low ground, and then carrying him to a drainage ditch for a CAS-E-VAC. Karl had again showed the bravery of the lads on the ground. When Paddy had gone down Karl had moved under fire to his platoon Sgt, his mate without hesitation knowing fine well he could be next, and again when your instinct tells you not to go forward Karl had done just that because if he hadn't Paddy would have certainly died that day. As it turned out Paddy received major injuries.

Patrols escorted the Marines 10ks away from the ridge; we would harbour up in the wadi fold for the night and then move in during the day. As always once night had fallen I moved from my vehicle and into the boss's position further in the wadi for a brief and to go through exactly what was going to happen that day. We had decided to use more of the ridge this time and spread our teams as much as possible to cover the area.

In the early morning while still dark our Patrol WMIKs pushed in. Using the natural folds of the ground we came up on the ridge; my call sign held the furthest left or southern position. I could then liaise with the HCR who would venture across once the Marine convoy had pushed through and were safely in the platoon house. Our gunners fired into possible Taliban areas before the CH47 came in carrying a mix of paratroopers and Marines. Sangin platoon house had a hesco wall around its building and the nearby the fields that we used as the HLS. The hesco wall was a metal wire frame which, once opened up, could be filled with sand making a large sandbag box of chest height and about a metre squared. The engineers had spent many weeks constructing these and other defences while the Taliban constantly attacked them and our lads held them back. It definitely gave the platoon house a little more security and provided the helis with a little more cover as they sat and unloaded.

We got the call that the RIP was beginning in the platoon house. Our lads from the district centre moved out as daylight opened and cleared some of the buildings to the north and east. Our Patrols concentrated on watching the north and southern green zones for Taliban movement.

What we all had to be very clear of was the ID of troops before we opened fire. With the amount of troops now pushing in and around the platoon house it is very easy to mistake a section for a group of Taliban. We had to be certain, and the reliability of information passed as to where the ground troops were and moving to precisely. The first HCR team came up on my right side approx 200m away. Their 30mm cannon began firing at a compound to my front over the river, they had obviously seen something but from their angle being further south their arc of fire ran in the north-east direction which could easily continue and hit the platoon house and certainly the area to the south where I knew a few sections were operating.

Bennie went down to get them to check fire, just as Sticks caught sight of movement in and around the compound.

'Scotty we got movement, is there any of our lads in that area?' he shouted down, his eye still looking through the SUSA .50 Cal sight.

'Nah nothing mate', I scanned the compound with my binos. Sticks stared firing.

'There's fucking Taliban in there', he called over the noise of the gun.

'Yeah got them', I said taking hold of the GPMG and squeezing off a few bursts. The lads who arrived by Chinooks had started the RIP while the sound of explosions could be heard over to our left as the lads of B and C Company cleared the compounds. We moved into a watch and shoot and called in an air strike. There was definitely Taliban down in the compound and surrounding areas and it had looked like we had kept their heads down for a while. Once the Apaches fired a few rockets it looked like their heads would remain permanently down. They hadn't even attempted to fire back. With all of Patrols dominating the ridge, Apaches on top cover, HCR now moving into the wadi and ground troops to their north, it looked like it was now the Taliban who were surrounded.

News came back that two lads in the northern compounds had been injured, later it was deemed as RPG frag but I was informed of a different story: I still don't know the full details. Two officers had been caught by frag while throwing grenades into the compounds. What officers were doing throwing grenades when they have toms (private soldiers) to do that was beyond me, plus two offices metres apart was just basics. As any soldier will tell you your command element should never be that close to the front and also to another commander, in this case both commanders were now out of the game. It was a good job the section and Patrol commanders could just get on with it anyway.

The remainer of the RIP went without incident. The Marines were now firmly in place as our troops waved goodbye to Sangin town. Pulling back from the ridge our job was done. It was strange to think that this would be our last job.

Back in Bastion we went through the process of stripping kit, cleaning weapons and getting ready for the move back to the UK. A rumour of us staying in Cyprus for a piss-up on the way back caught our ears but I took this as a wind-up. As it turned out it did happen; it was called decompression. The last thing they wanted was the Battle group returning home to smash all the pubs up. This way, kept in house, we could all let out some frustrations before getting home.

A Company and Patrols would be the first to leave theatre, we had arrived first and therefore were first out. This I was happy about, we had worked alongside in the early days of the tour and also had more to do with them than we did with B and C Company. Getting up to Kabul gave us a chance to chill. It was like another world up here. All the fighting with the Taliban had been down in the south in Helmand province. Kabul was quiet, yet there were soldiers from all countries here. French, Belgians, Hungarians, Swedes, Germans, Spanish, Czechs and a lot more: swanning about in their clean uniforms and filling their fat faces with mountains of scoff and cold cans of coke. We couldn't believe it. There was us eating rations for weeks at a time, hot water that made you want to vomit and fighting the Taliban on a daily basis and here were all these troops whose governments had refused to send their soldiers down south as it was deemed too dangerous. I believe that countries that did that should have been kicked out of NATO, end of chat. The only other nations I had seen down here fighting alongside us was the Canadians, the US, Estonians and the Danish. The last two only had small parts to play but still played them all the same..

There was going to be one more thing that was going to snap us before the day was over. Heading down to the Air Force 1 bar Patrols sank a couple of coronas. That was till all the A Company Head Shed came in and tried to put a stop to the drinking. I was livid and so too were the rest of the lads. Me and Dave got some of Patrol together; a plan was arranged, one final mission. A few of us pushed on a recce for another bar, once in and recce'd and cleared a runner would be sent back for the remainder who would leave in drips and drabs as not to cause suspicion. In a few minutes we found one, a Belgian bar hidden away amongst old buildings and bunkers. Again we made a best use of our time till it shut around 1 a.m.

With the taste of beer on our lips we couldn't leave it there. The mission for more booze was on. We caught up with some Danish who pointed us in the direction of a watering hole. Mega, we all joked, let's go. On getting there we were hugely disappointed much to the amusement of the Danish lads who knew it was closed.

'On the other side of this is the bar, beer within arm's reach', a Danish soldier said in his broken English.

'Problem is there is a tent wall in the way', he laughed. This joke had gone too far, they had beer on tap here. We hadn't. But instead of despatching these with a few lefts and rights one of our lads, who again shall be anonymous, said 'That's no problem' and flicked out his greber knife. The Danish lads' faces dropped thinking it was all going to get nasty. Our lad then made a huge door with his knife. Hey presto! We had all the beer we wanted. The lads still around made our way to the flight line and cracked open a few drinks, by the time it came to getting ready to leave Kabul we were well shit faced.

Me and big Dan Jarvie were offered to sit up front with the pilots as they flew into Cyprus.

'Me and Scotty are just off to land the plane', Dan joked as we made our way to the front. We sat and watch the pilots bring in the Tristar over the golden coast.

'Beats a heavy Chinook flight into Sangin getting shot at', we joked.

The aim of Cyprus was decompression, as it was described from one of the staff, 'fun'. The first night was just a major piss-up and the next day some water sports (not involving pissing on each other this time) on the beach.

The location was a small training camp: a mess hall, lecture room and accommodation made up this set-up in the middle of nowhere in the hills of Cyprus. In a small courtyard was a line of tables set up for the night. After a few dos and don'ts which were mainly do whatever you want, we were briefed on post traumatic stress and other such things. From there we went to the tables for a BBQ and a few beers. There was more cached at the rear and soon the beer was flowing. With it there was bound to be dramas. A few hours in, leftover food began getting thrown around, nothing special, then empty cans. A couple of fun fights erupted further up then as it always does it all got out of control. All hell broke loose all at the same time and all over the place, tables, chairs and anything else we could get hold of. It turned into a full on riot, everyone went nuts.

Tables and chairs got used as weapons; full cans got thrown at anyone in range. The first few minutes were proper hairy, we might as well have been back in Afghan. Me and the rest of Patrols managed to get a flank and began targeting anybody that wasn't with our group. There was even a full cake thrown straight into someone's face, I could hardly stand with laughing like it was some sort of Carry On film. A few boys just sat in the middle of this riot and drank beer getting pelted with objects. As the tempo slackened and groups of lads charged others, things got nasty. Full cans were thrown at people's heads at point blank range starting fights, table and chairs too. I personally have a scar on my arm after a quick raid, on my way out something caught my eye. I turned to see the metal frame of a three or four foot table in mid air heading straight for me. It nearly took my arm off.

This must have lasted a good few hours and in all my time with being in Northern Ireland in riots and suchlike it was probably the worse riot I had been in. All in all some 15 or 20 lads had to go to hospital. Others like me just patched ourselves up.

The next day, still pissed, we boarded a bus for the beach; this was named the fun bus. It was like a school outing with the worst bunch of lunatics you have come across. Hitting the beach we just chilled and used their equipment. It was definitely time to relax now. Speaking to others as we chilled we hadn't realised some of the medical Head Shed were there and the padre, they were watching last night's activities. The main army doctor was trained in post traumatic stress and counselling. Many believed that we would need this after our bloody tour and some did. I think it was him who needed it most though. He came out to see what all the shouting was. In earshot of some of our own Head Shed he said it was the worse thing he had ever seen in his life. He was watching 80–90 blokes, who had just come back from the worst fighting since the Korean War, kicking the living shit out of one another using anything that could be picked up. He witnessed a lad just in front of him get a metal bin lid smashed into his head taking him off his feet as someone had used it as a frisbee.

Our time in Cyprus finished and we headed back to Brize Norton and the UK.

Returning to the UK it seemed that nothing had changed. There was no welcome home party for us, not that we were bothered; we just got into camp, raided our boxes that were left behind, necked some Jack Daniels and got straight down town on the piss. Waiting for the rest of the Battle Group to return I headed back to the north-east for a few days on my GSX-R only to hit an oil patch a mile and a half from my gaff. Fucking typical, I thought while lying in the Sunderland General Hospital. I went all the way through that shit without a scratch only to get a massive gash on my arm off a riot in Cyprus and to spend a few nights in hospital after crashing my pride and joy. Fucking mega, welcome home, I laughed. I hadn't even been back in the UK 48hrs.

Before getting back we heard more news of the incident with the bouncers in town. This time I felt better, 2 Para and some of 3 Para who had got back earlier had conducted an operation that would have made Wellington proud of us. The lads involved got some of the blokes into the club. Another group then kicked off at another bar up the road, a place that the bouncers from the Gipperdrome helped out with. The fight was massive and the bouncers were called up to help, leaving a minimum number of bouncers on the club. The lads in the club were notified it was time for the main assault. A small group started a fight in the club, drawing in the bouncers and leaving the exits clear. One of the lads smashed open the emergency exit, waiting in the alleyway were more Paratroopers. Let's just leave it at that. The bouncers got what they asked for that night and the one who started it with all the comments went into hiding which to be honest was a good move because the blokes wanted to tear him apart and still do.

A number of awards were given out on return to the UK once everyone was back. This was expected; a lot had gone on some of which I wasn't even aware of due to being elsewhere, like some incidents in Sangin, Musa Qaleh. I knew exactly what was going happen so I didn't even bother going to the Scale A parade. Amongst all of the awards there was one VC for Bryan Budd, one GC for Mark Wright and eleven MCs. I was chuffed for the lads, they deserved it, but pissed off about all the MIDs that were 80 per cent officers and SNCO. Nothing was mentioned about the toms on the ground, the lads who went forward and cleared the targets or the L/Cpl and screws that led the patrols in the streets and attacks. I know from experience that a few of them had been written for each other. Some of them were well deserved, don't get me wrong, but some lads did much more on more than one occasion, and received fuck all.

My mate Lee C. was an example. After going to the aid of Bash while we were fighting in Now Zad, nothing. Again the Head Shed had looked after their own. This wasn't the only thing that got our goat. A lot of jobsworths (mostly SNCO) had managed to get over for the last part of the tour, so they could get an Afghan medal yet had done fuck all. They know who they are, the lads who were at the sharp end can look at theirs knowing damn well they deserved it, I doubt they can. The very last thing was the statement given to the press about our fallen comrades. Normally the CO, RSM or other officer gave their remarks. In my opinion this was bollocks. It wound me up to the fact they didn't ask us, the blokes they fought alongside with, lived with, eat and grafted with, had a beer with. They asked the CO and RSM who didn't really know the lads; they got reports about their soldiering but that was it, they didn't know them at a one-on-one basis like we did. If they want the real insight they should ask their mates not commanders who barely knew them.

A month later on Remembrance Sunday I went down to the Sunderland cenotaph, one of the biggest remembrance parades outside of London. If I'm in the country I always go down and pay my respects for the people who laid down their lives for us. I wasn't expecting anything major to be said about the Afghanistan troubles that had hit the headlines. I did expect something, though. I along with all the others respected our fallen comrades from all conflicts and wars throughout history. Maybe I expected after such a degree of fighting that Afghanistan would be mentioned as this was the start of something big. Not only that but a few of lads who had fought over in Helmand had attended this parade in uniform, although not showing off in our desert kit which was absolutely ruined, nobody would have known. But the final nail in the coffin for me was that a friend, Sunderland born and bred Damian Jackson (Jacko) wasn't even given a mention, not a thing, being one of the last soldiers to be killed in action, in an environment that was fresh on everyone's lips, 19 years of age and this was his home town. I walked off in disgust.

In the summer of 2006 the 3 Para Battle group were sent into Helmand province south Afghanistan, what we called the 'break in'. Back to basics living in often shit holes or out in the desert our role soon changed to all out fighting. Around 500 contacts with the Taliban had been recorded since our arrival in April, most of it at close quarters, something not seen to this degree at a large scale since Korea. The Taliban gave us everything they had and in return it was estimated that we killed more than a thousand Taliban fighters. Unfortunately it wasn't all one way, we returned home having lost 18 members of the Battle group and around 50 others receiving serious injuries. They had paid the ultimate price for their country and mates in a land far away from home. Many question why we went in and still hold and operate this ground still. At the end of the day it is our job, it's what we do and strange how it may seem we all wanted a chance to test ourselves. All I will say to people who constantly question the above is don't, just support and be proud of our troops.

For the Battle Group and 3 Para it was the end of Afghanistan, for now. Everyone knew there would be a quick turnaround before the Paras saw themselves back here. In April 2008 this happened, they are still in Helmand although with the break in, Bastion, outstations and troops already in place it was going to be that little bit easier.

For me I moved on into the Close Protection world, working in a few different locations before finding myself back in the desert of Iraq. This time rather than looking for trouble and taking the fight to the enemy I find myself trying to avoid the IED and insurgents that are always on the look out for us as we escort our clients from one site to the next.

Although CP is good money many of us actually enjoy our job, it's my opinion there are very little job prospects for ex-soldiers out there. I think it's important to inform people that around 85 per cent or more of CP operators are ex-soldiers. Some of the men are mentioned in this book and others go as far back as the Falklands, some like myself actually liberated this country back in 2003. The lads have the opportunity to better themselves and their families. Again we find ourselves in a very difficult and dangerous environment where we have to deal with the loss of other operators and friends on a monthly basis, sometimes more.

This unfortunately is the nature of the beast in the CP world and in today's army. More and more men will die and suffer before this is all resolved but the Paras have proved their worth once more. They had taken the fight directly to them and never gave up or were defeated. In the words of Winston Churchill 'Every man an Emperor'.

We constantly raise a glass of beer or shot of port to our fallen comrades and look at the plaque that sits on the wall of the Cpl Mess. It reads 'Paratroopers don't die – They go to hell and Re-group. Airborne!'

Utrinque Paratus – Ready for anything.

The Blood Clot.

Related titles published by Helion & Company

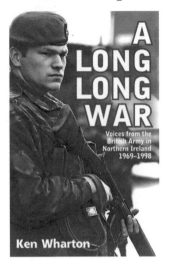

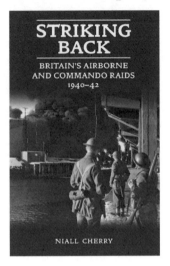

A Long Long War: Voices from the British Army in Northern Ireland 1969-98
Ken Wharton
544pp, c 150 photos, maps   Hardback
ISBN 978-1-906033-18-7

Striking Back: Britain's Airborne and Commando Raids 1940-42
Niall Cherry
496pp, c 100 photos, 20 maps, 40 diagrams, charts, docs   Hardback
ISBN 978-1-906033-25-5

A selection of forthcoming titles

A Journey to Hell and Back. A Photographic Record of 3 Para in Afghanistan 2006
J. Scott & D. Edwards   ISBN 978-1-906033-35-4

*Bombs, Bullets and Cups of Tea.
Further Voices of the British Army in Northern Ireland 1969-98*
K. Wharton   ISBN 978-1-906033-34-7

Diary of a Red Devil: by Glider to Arnhem with the 7th King's Own Scottish Borderers
A. Blockwell   ISBN 978-1-906033-20-0

Bloody Streets: the Soviet Assault on Berlin 1945
S.A. Hamilton   ISBN 978-1-906033-12-5

HELION & COMPANY
26 Willow Road, Solihull, West Midlands B91 1UE, England
Telephone 0121 705 3393   Fax 0121 711 4075
Website: http://www.helion.co.uk